DK COLLECTOR'S GUIDES

COSTUME JEWELLERY

Miriam Haskell pendant necklace and earrings
of amber glass stones and beads. *1940s*
N: 45cm (17½in) circ; E: 5cm (2in) long **£80–120 RITZ**

DK COLLECTOR'S GUIDES

COSTUME JEWELLERY

JUDITH MILLER

with John Wainwright

Photography by Graham Rae

A Dorling Kindersley Book

LONDON, NEW YORK,
MELBOURNE, MUNICH AND DELHI

A joint production from **DK** and
THE PRICE GUIDE COMPANY

Dorling Kindersley Limited
Project Editor Paula Regan
Project Art Editor Kelly Meyer
Assistant Designer Anna Plucinska
Senior Editors Caroline Hunt,
Angela Wilkes, Amber Tokeley
Senior Art Editor Mandy Earey
Managing Editor Julie Oughton
Managing Art Editor Heather McCarry
Art Director Carole Ash
Category Publisher Jackie Douglas
Production Joanna Bull, Rita Sinha
DTP Designer Mike Grigoletti

The Price Guide Company Limited
Publishing Manager Julie Brooke
Digital Image Co-ordinator Cara Miller
Editorial Assistants Megan Watson,
Sara Sturgess

First published in Great Britain in 2003 by
Dorling Kindersley Limited
80 Strand, London WC2R 0RL

Penguin Group

The Price Guide Company (UK) Ltd
Studio 21, Waterside
44–48 Wharf Road
London N1 7UX
info@thepriceguidecompany.com

2 4 6 8 10 9 7 5 3 1

Colour reproduction by Colourscan, Singapore
Printed and bound by L.E.G.O., Italy

Discover more at
www.dk.com

Contents

Art Nouveau p.42

Designer profiles 54

Fahrner p.73

A-Z of designers and makers 134

Bakelite p.159

Gallery of
unsigned pieces 214

Appendices
and index 236

Unsigned necklace p.217

Maison Gripoix p.91

How to use this book

DK Collector's Guides: Costume Jewellery is divided into four main sections: the story of costume jewellery, detailing the changing styles of costume jewellery from ancient times to the present day; designer profiles, focusing on the life and career of 20 major costume jewellery designers; an A-Z of designers and makers, with information and representative sample pieces; and a gallery of unsigned pieces, divided into necklaces, bracelets, bangles, pins, and earrings.

Designer Information
Gives a fascinating insight into the life and career of the costume jewellery designer. Also highlights the particular characteristics of his or her jewellery and offers advice on what styles, motifs, or limited editions are best to collect.

Biography
Provides an at-a-glance history of the designer's career. Significant events are listed, such as birth and death dates, the creation and closure of costume jewellery companies, when key design staff were hired, and the year popular lines were brought out.

Feature Box
Details a particular person or event that influenced the profiled designer, or a material or style central to his or her costume jewellery designs.

Further Features Bar
Indicates the influences and inspirations behind the costume jewellery. It may also highlight important commissions – often from famous clients – that had a positive effect on the designer's career.

ABBREVIATIONS:
The following abbreviations are used in the captions:

B = bracelet or bangle
E = earrings
N = necklace
P = pin
Pd = pendant

circ = circumference
NPA = no price available

The Caption
Describes the piece of jewellery, including the materials used, the date it was made, and its length, width, or circumference (*see abbreviations above*).

Pendant tassel necklace and earrings by Mitchell Maer for Dior of faux gold with round-cut haematite stones. *Early 1950s*
Largest Pd: 10cm (4in) long; E: 5cm (2in) long
£750–850   **WAIN**

The Price Guide
All prices are shown in ranges to give you a ball-park figure of what you should expect to pay for a similar piece.

The Source Code
With the exception of museum pieces, every item in the book was specially photographed at an auction house, dealer, antiques market, or private collection. Each source is credited here by code and can be checked against the Key to Dealer Codes on pp.246-247.

Mini Feature Box
Highlights a particular motif, style, material, or technique used by the designer. It explains why that piece or type of jewellery is so collectable and includes advice on how much you can expect to pay.

Good, Better, Best
This feature compares three specially selected pieces of jewellery - all of the same type and by the same designer. It explains why certain characteristics make each piece more or less desirable to costume jewellery collectors.

6

Foreword

Costume jewellery appeals to me on so many levels: it is undeniably beautiful to look at, it reflects the fashions of the era it was produced in, and the quality of workmanship and materials used are often as good as or better than those used in "real" or precious jewellery. What is even more exciting to those of us who are dazzled by all that diamanté is that costume jewellery was meant to be affordable, and was therefore often produced in large quantities, so there are plenty of examples out there just waiting for a collector to find. And, perhaps even more importantly, it's a collection you can wear and which will always attract compliments and admiring glances!

In the last few years the market for costume jewellery has started to grow and so I believe the time is right for a comprehensive full-colour guide that tells collectors more than simply who made a piece and when, what it is made of, and how much it costs. So, in addition to all this vital information, *DK Collector's Guides: Costume Jewellery* also explains what makes one piece more collectable than another and provides tips on what to look for when buying. Plus, we have researched the history of the designers and manufacturers – not just the major ones but many smaller and lesser-known names whose pieces are only now starting to become collectable. We also look at how costume jewellery developed over the years to take in new technologies and materials.

Costume jewellery collections take many different themes. Some people are faithful to a particular designer or era, others tailor their collections to include only flowers, figures or fruit, birds, beasts, or bugs. We have reflected this by including many unsigned pieces, which are collectable simply because they are wonderful to look at – not because they have a famous name stamped on the back.

If you already collect costume jewellery, I hope this book will add to the joy this brings you. And to new collectors all I can say is beware – all that glitters may not be gold but it certainly can be addictive!

Judith Miller.

Robert Goossens
p.199

Introduction

Costume jewellery is essentially a 20th-century term for jewellery made from non-precious materials, such as imitation gemstones and faux pearls, set in silver or inexpensive base metals. In fact, however, early costume jewellery dates back thousands of years and many pieces incorporate semi-precious stones. Costume jewellery was often produced in large quantities, with pieces designed to go with each new season's outfits. Much of it was unsigned and was never intended to last for a long time, or represent a financial investment, like fine jewellery. However, despite the inexpensive materials used, much costume jewellery is just as beautiful and as highly crafted as its precious counterpart, and it is now considered highly collectable.

Suffragette jewellery p.38

WHY COLLECT COSTUME JEWELLERY?

Not only is costume jewellery beautiful in its own right, it is often more innovative in design than precious jewellery, which in many case relies on the intrinsic value of the materials used for desirability. In fact, the best reason for collecting costume jewellery is so that you can wear the pieces yourself. Since new jewellery designs were produced every season, it is also a fascinating reflection of changing fashions and social history, from the early 19th century through every decade to the present. Although most pieces are affordable, some are now highly sought after and difficult to find, all of which adds to the excitement and pleasure of collecting. As designers are constantly creating new pieces, costume jewellery is a collecting field with a future, and its popularity is reflected in the fact that more and more pieces are commanding high prices.

HOW TO GET STARTED

The best way to find out more about costume jewellery is to do some thorough background research before buying. Books, decorative arts museums, and exhibition catalogues are a good starting point, as are costume jewellery websites. Visiting specialist dealers will give you an opportunity to see a wide variety of pieces at first hand. Pick them up so that you can have a closer look and feel how much they weigh. Dealers are always happy to talk to enthusiasts, so ask questions about the background and history of the pieces you like. All of this will help you to become familiar with different periods and styles of jewellery and to recognize the characteristics of particular designers and makers.

WHERE AND WHAT TO BUY

When buying pieces to collect, good condition is of paramount importance. Specialist dealers and auction houses are the most reliable source of good-quality costume jewellery and will provide a receipt and information about the age of each piece and its maker, if known. For less expensive pieces and bargains, it is fun to rummage through old jewellery at car boot sales, antique markets, and vintage clothes shops. There is also a vast selection of costume jewellery available on the Internet.

You can build up a jewellery collection that simply complements your own wardrobe. Alternatively, you can collect pieces from a particular period or designer, collect just one type of jewellery such as pins, or go for a subject-themed collection. Examine each piece carefully with a magnifying glass before buying, to check for defects and make sure that any clasps and other fastenings work properly.

FAKES AND FORGERIES

As costume jewellery has risen in value, forgeries have become more common, particularly at the upper end of the market. Some pieces, such as Trifari's Jelly Belly pins and Eisenberg Originals, have been widely forged and often have a fake maker's mark. Until your eye is sufficiently well trained, it is wise to buy pieces in the mid and lower price ranges and to avoid buying expensive pieces from non-specialists. Building up a relationship with a reputable specialist dealer is the best way to avoid expensive mistakes.

CARE AND REPAIR

Costume jewellery is fragile and should be looked after with care if you want it to last. Do not let it come into contact with soap, face creams, scent, or hairspray and store pieces flat in individual boxes, wrapped in acid-free paper. Clean your jewellery with cotton buds or a soft toothbrush and a little distilled water, making sure it doesn't sink into the settings. Pat each piece dry and use a jeweller's cloth to clean metal settings.

The best way to repair costume jewellery is to take it to a specialist, but it's expensive. You can replace lost stones in less valuable pieces by buying replacements from gem wholesalers and art and craft shops, then using jeweller's cement to glue them back in place.

Chanel p.56

The story of costume jewellery

From ancient cultures to the present day

Although the term "costume jewellery" wasn't actually coined until the 1920s, the concept is in fact as old as our most ancient civilizations. From as far back as pre-Christian Mesopotamia, via Ancient Egypt to the Roman Empire, and from the Middle Ages and the Renaissance right up to today, people have always derived great pleasure from adorning themselves with decorative artefacts. Such artefacts, although undoubtedly beautiful, are not, however, in themselves necessarily valuable, unlike precious jewellery.

The story of costume jewellery is a fascinating reflection of social history. It lies partly in the constant quest for the new: for amazing new materials and the most modern methods of manufacture. Above all, however, it is the story of the never-ending and tantalizing search for the new in both fashion and style.

An ancient art form

As trade routes began to link up different parts of the world, so various cultures started to influence and build upon each other's jewellery styles. New materials were discovered and exploited and jewellery design became increasingly complex and sophisticated.

A PRIMITIVE DESIRE

The desire for self-embellishment stretches back to our most ancient cultures, when people first began transforming the natural objects around them into decorative pieces to wear. Gradually, numerous styles and forms of ornament were established that not only inspired later civilizations, but which also still resonate today. By around 3,000 BC, trade routes had already linked up North Africa, Europe, and the Near and Middle East, and the transmission of jewellery styles, forms, and manufacturing techniques began in earnest.

The Sumerians in Mesopotamia, now Iraq, were widely admired as jewellers, and had mastered many techniques still in use today. In particular, they discovered and exploited the potential of gold, which became prized not only for its rarity and aesthetic qualities, but also for its malleability. Silver, lapis lazuli, and red cornelian were other typical components of Sumerian jewellery.

The Egyptians absorbed the Sumerians' skills, and went on to develop their own distinctive style, which has enjoyed numerous revivals over the centuries, most notably in the 1920s. The Egyptians concentrated on graphic designs that

mirrored their hieroglyphics and were also heavily influenced by African styles. They also used precious metals, especially gold, as well as precious and semi-precious gemstones, faience, and pearls from the River Nile.

Egyptian style was later absorbed by the Phoenicians, who also helped to cross-pollinate jewellery styles through their huge trading empire, which stretched across the Mediterranean to Spain. By around 500 BC, these styles had filtered through to the Etruscans in Tuscany and Umbria. Expanding on the skills of the Egyptians and Phoenicians, their jewellery already displayed tremendous technical expertise: in particular, they refined the technique of granulation – the soldering of tiny grains of metal on to a metal surface.

CLASSICAL STYLES

By 350 BC, when ancient Greek culture dominated the Middle and Near East, jewellery design had become remarkably uniform. Gold was in relatively plentiful supply and the Greeks exploited it to produce fine, intricate filigree work fashioned, for example, into sprays of flowers often inlaid with colourful enamels. Emeralds and pearls also became increasingly popular and new motifs were introduced, such as the reef knot, crescent shapes, and gods such as Eros. However, it was the introduction of different colours through the inlay of stones and coloured glass that made Greek jewellery particularly distinctive.

Greek style later gave way to Roman, although the latter retained certain aspects including the Greek preference for emeralds, pearls, and sapphires. Filigree work, however, was abandoned in favour of smooth, stark, bold pieces, and Christian motifs began to appear as Christianity spread. Other popular Roman jewellery motifs were scrolling acanthus leaves and key patterns, some of which were inspired by Greek prototypes.

A WEALTH OF RESOURCES

By the time the Roman empire was declining in around the 4th century AD, jewellers had access to a wealth of natural resources. Gold was being mined throughout Europe and Africa; ivory was imported from India and Africa; pearls had been discovered in the Red Sea and off the Indian coast; and a variety of gemstones including emeralds, amber, lapis lazuli, garnets, and onyx had all been added to the design palette.

By the 6th century AD, the jewellers of the Byzantine Empire, and particularly Constantinople, were fully exploiting this wealth of materials. The most innovative technique of this early Byzantine period was *opus interrasile* metalwork, in which gold sheet was pierced using tiny chisels. Earlier styles were also reworked, notably those emanating from Persia

and India. Precious stones were used with increasing frequency and jewellery design generally became more complex. Other new techniques included damascening, in which a soft metal such as silver or gold is inlaid into a hard base metal, and gold cloisonné enamel.

Byzantine and Medieval European jewellery styles overlapped, with the Crusaders bringing back a host of influences and earlier styles from North Africa and the Middle East. Generally, Medieval jewellery featured precious stones set in gold or silver and inscriptions were popular. Above all, Christian iconography really came to the fore and numerous Christian motifs, most notably the cross, were employed.

OLD WORLD, NEW WORLD

While Byzantine and Christian styles and motifs continued to be produced throughout the Renaissance, which spread across Europe from the 14th to the early 17th century, this period was essentially characterized by the rediscovery of classicism and, in particular, Greek and Roman styles of jewellery. At the same time, Spain's activities in the New World in the 15th century resulted in a treasure trove of gold, silver, and precious gemstones flooding into Europe. Consequently, fashionable jewellery became increasingly ostentatious, desirable and, most significantly, the preserve of the super-affluent. With a growing and increasingly fashion-conscious European population, the need to find convincing and cheaper substitutes for precious materials was now pressing.

Egyptian scarab pectoral of gold, lapis lazuli, amber, and semi-precious stone. *1361–52 BC*
The Egyptian Museum, Cairo, Egypt

Egyptian scarab anklet of gold, lapis lazuli, and cornelian. *1070–945 BC*
The Egyptian Museum, Cairo, Egypt

Egyptian bird-scarab pectoral of gold, paste, and semi-precious stones. *c.1370–52 BC*
The Egyptian Museum, Cairo, Egypt

Egyptian necklace with blue and turquoise faience beads and amulets. *c.500 BC*
35.5cm (14in) long **£1,000–1,300 ANA**

Egyptian necklace with gold and blue faience beads and turquoise amulets. *c.500 BC*
45.75cm (18in) long **£1,000–1,500 ANA**

Phoenician earrings cut from sheet gold in the form of an ankh. *600–500 BC*
The British Museum, London

Mesopotamian necklace, bracelet, and earrings from ancient Assyria. *c.2200–350 BC*
The British Museum, London

Mesopotamian child's diadem of gold, lapis lazuli, and cornelian. *c.2500–2300 BC*
The British Museum, London

Egyptian necklace with gold and tubular brown faience beads. *c.1800 BC*
40cm (15½in) long **£600–800 ANA**

The beauty of natural forms...

From the earliest times, people have adorned themselves to enhance looks, signal status, ward off evil, and to celebrate the beauty of the natural forms around them. The first jewellery was fashioned from bone, shell, and feathers. Later, clay, natural glass, precious metals, and gemstones were used. Meanwhile, various civilizations from the Sumerians to the Etruscans gradually built on each other's manufacturing methods and style influences. Traders, particularly the Phoenicians, transported both the raw materials and jewellery around their extensive routes, which helped to spread these techniques and styles. The most enduring of these came from the ancient Egyptians.

Mesopotamian hoop earrings of solid gold and gold wire. *c.1000 BC*
1.25cm (½in) wide **£200–250 ANA**

15

Greek ring made of gold and set with a precious or semi-precious stone. *330–27 BC* *The British Museum, London*

Creations for gods and mortals...

Ancient Greek jewellery was worn to enhance a woman's beauty and to demonstrate wealth. It was given as a gift at births and weddings, and precious pieces were often buried with their owner. Although few such pieces have survived, lists of treasures unearthed from the Parthenon and the sanctuary of Apollo at Delos, reveal that the ancient Greeks also dedicated jewellery to their gods. The Greek style was delicate: intricate filigree work was made into flowers, spirals, and waves, often infilled with enamel and set with garnets, emeralds, and pearls. Before long, however, a starker, bolder Roman taste was in the ascendant.

Greek necklace made of gold. *c.200 BC* *The British Museum, London*

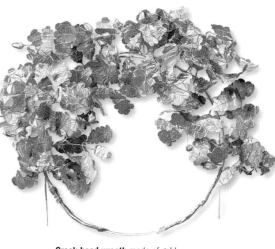

Greek head-wreath made of gold. From the Dardanelles. *400–300 BC* *The British Museum, London*

Roman bronze wheel pin with remnants of inlaid polychrome enamels. *AD c.200. 7cm (2¾in) wide* **£450–500 ANA**

Reflections of Empire...

The Roman Empire produced a style of ornamentation that was bold, striking, and in some respects utilitarian. Filigree work was abandoned in favour of starker, burnished gold pieces, although certain aspects of Greek style were absorbed, including a liking for precious stones. As Christianity started to spread through the Empire, Christian motifs such as the cross and lotus flower appeared. Byzantine jewellery represents a continuation of the Greco-Roman tradition, but it evolved its own unique style as it swiftly adapted to new tastes: solid gold jewellery fell out of fashion, to be replaced by delicate gold leaf work.

Roman solid gold cloak pin in the shape of the Christian cross. *AD c.100–200 6.25cm (2½in) long* **£20,000–26,500 LNXG**

Late Roman–Byzantine gold earrings with sapphires and low-grade pearls. *AD c.400–500 5.75cm (2¼in) long* **£1,335–1,665 LNXG**

Byzantine bronze cross with incised figure of Jesus. *AD c.900 10cm (4in) long* **£450–500 ANA**

Byzantine filigree gold wire pendant with coloured glass stone centre. *AD c.500–600 4cm (1½in) long* **£3,335–4,000 LNXG**

Roman solid gold ring with a carved blue agate cameo of a female bust. *AD c.100–200 1.25cm (½in) wide* **£3,335–4,000 LNXG**

English ring pin of punched ornament inlaid with bands of niello. *1200s*
The British Museum, London

Emblems of wealth...

Medieval royalty, noblemen, and even rich merchants invariably kept a store of precious and semi-precious stones, and it was they who supplied the costly raw materials to the goldsmith when jewellery was commissioned. There was no gender distinction in the wearing of jewellery, although women's pieces tended to be more complex and varied. Brooches were especially popular, although girdles and cloak clasps, chains and collars, circlets and chaplets were also worn by both sexes. Cloisonné – enamel with a gold ground – was popular and favoured motifs included stylized dragon heads.

Medallion collar of gold set with pearls and jewels with filigree and enamel. *1100s*
The Kremlin Museum, Moscow, Russia

Jewelled disc pin of gold with garnets and pieces of shell. AD *400–900*
The Ashmolean Museum, Oxford

Kingston pin AD *500–600*
City of Liverpool Museum, Merseyside

Renaissance splendour...

Spain's activities in the New World in the 15th century led to vast hoards of gold, silver, and gemstones flooding into Europe. Medieval austerity gave way to ostentation as the royal courts found themselves awash with flamboyant jewellery. A new fashion was set for jewels of incredible size and profusion. Greco-Roman styles were rediscovered, and miniatures came into vogue in the 17th century after French goldsmiths led by Jean Toutin developed a way of painting them in enamel on gold.

Renaissance cat pendant with natural baroque pearl. *1450–1600*
S.J. Philips Antique Dealers, London

Italian Renaissance earrings of gold with flower and cherub motifs. *1450–1600*
Location unknown

Enamelled pendant of gold with rubies, emeralds, and diamonds. *Late 1500s*
The British Museum, London

Early imitations

As the 18th century got underway, a thriving costume jewellery trade began to develop in Europe. Pastes and metals were improving steadily, along with production techniques, and faux jewellery was becoming increasingly desirable.

A FASHION FOR FAKES

Eighteenth century Europe witnessed the emergence of an increasingly well-off middle class for whom this was a new and exciting period of affluence. Clothes and jewellery became more extravagant, and gemstones decorated everything from sword hilts to hair ornaments. There was a passion for large set jewels, especially diamonds, and good fakes inevitably became increasingly sought after.

Gablonz in Bohemia, now the Czech Republic, started producing high-quality paste stones and a thriving costume jewellery business began to develop in Europe. The advent of machine cutting allowed the production of large numbers of glass stones of regular size and quality, and jewellery became more affordable. Other techniques also improved. Like precious gems of the time, glass and paste were foil-backed to increase brilliance and lustre. Ironically, the craftsmanship was sometimes finer on the paste settings than on precious stones, and they were also more innovatively cut and faceted. All these factors made costume jewellery ever more desirable.

As daytime and evening fashions became more defined so did jewellery, with daytime jewellery becoming significantly more restrained. Diamonds remained the gem of choice for after dark, but convincing substitutes remained elusive: Bohemian stones were not hard enough to withstand the required cutting process. One alternative was rock crystal, a naturally occurring colourless quartz. A seam near Bristol, England, provided a plentiful supply, sometimes known as Bristows or Bristol stones; others came from France, Spain, and Portugal. Then, a Frenchman, Georges Frédéric Stras, began exploring the potential of a glass developed by Englishman, George Ravenscroft. It proved hard enough to use as a diamond substitute and Stras went on to produce such spectacular paste jewellery that he established it as a remarkable creation in its own right.

A BOOM INDUSTRY

In London, top quality paste was often sold alongside precious jewels while in France, working with paste became such a boom industry that by the 1760s, over 300 jewellers and designers belonged to the guild of faux jewellers. For the first time, jewellers could chose from a vast range of precious and non-precious materials to work with, and design started to become significant.

Despite the 18th-century passion for diamonds and diamond look-alikes, gold remained highly valued. The first convincing gold substitute was pinchbeck, named after its creator, Christopher Pinchbeck. It combined well with paste, and ladies often had their favourite gold pieces reproduced in pinchbeck to take with them on their travels. It was later used as an affordable alternative to gold during Queen Victoria's reign (1837–1901), especially for pins. Gold and pinchbeck chains were worn by both sexes. The châtelaine also came back into style: this was an arrangement of chains and clasps to which various useful items, from thimbles to perfume bottles, were attached by a clip and worn around the waist.

THEMES FROM NATURE

Many 18th-century pieces of costume jewellery typically incorporated both large and small stones and often reflected a theme from nature, such as flowers or insects. Parures – matching sets of four or more pieces – became fashionable, and there was also a craze for wearing bow brooches. These mimicked dress trends in which costumes were covered with large silk bows, and jewellers worked hard to imitate in paste jewellery the fall of fabric. Men were equally keen on jewellery, and cravat pins and shoe buckles were particularly popular: apparently you could tell a man's social standing by the quality of his buckles.

From about 1760 onwards, mechanized cutting techniques gave rise to a fashion for jewellery made from cut steel – a hard, durable alloy of iron and carbon, which had previously been used for swords. Steel was also used as a setting for cameos, and ornate shoe buckles of steel, tin, and paste became an essential part of fashionable dress. Another popular innovation of this period was *en tremblant* jewellery, in which paste stones set on steel springs trembled and shimmered when the wearer moved.

MYRIAD INFLUENCES

The second half of the 18th century was the era of the Grand Tour when people flocked to see the great archaeological discoveries at Pompeii and Herculaneum. This gave rise to a neoclassical movement in which jewellery forms and decorative imagery were inspired by Etruscan, Greek, and Roman prototypes.

At the same time a backlash began against the extravagant indulgences that had so dominated the courts of Europe. In the past, jewellery had been a clear indicator of social standing, but the success of the paste trade resulted in these markers becoming blurred.

The desire for social equality really exploded at the end of the 1780s with the French Revolution. French jewellers soon found themselves out of work, since flashy jewels were considered suspect and people were encouraged to give up their wealth and jewels for the cause.

However, such austerity was relatively short-lived. Ostentatious fashions re-emerged with the advent of the Napoleonic era and the regency of the extravagant George IV in England.

Floral motif pin in gilt metal set with
rings of faux diamond pastes. *c.1780*
4.5cm (1¾in) wide **£550–650 CSAY**

22

Floral motif earrings with gold wire and round- and pear-cut French jet glass stones. *c.1720. 4cm (1½in) wide* **£600–800 CSAY**

Floral cross pin with round- and navette-cut emerald pastes in gold metal. *c.1820 4cm (1½in) wide* **£450–550 CSAY**

All the sparkle of a real jewel...

A plentiful supply of "gemstones" made from high-quality paste and glass sparked a frenzy of creativity among jewellery designers in the 18th and early 19th centuries. For the first time, they could experiment in a way that would have been too risky with precious gems. Exciting new designs developed, as well as new cutting and setting techniques. It was the beginning of an era in which jewellery was appreciated for its design and craftsmanship rather than the intrinsic value of the materials used. Ever growing numbers of people could now afford to wear eye-catching "aristocratic" jewellery, and it was becoming increasingly difficult to tell the real from the fake.

Sprig of flowers pin in gilt metal with faux diamond pastes. *c.1830 6.25cm (2½in) long* **£550–650 CSAY**

Sapphire blue paste earrings with four round-cut clear pastes. *c.1780 2.5cm (1in) long* **£600–700 CSAY**

Pendant necklace and earrings with ruby paste cabochons. *c.1714. Pd: 6.25cm (2½in) long; E: 2cm (¾in) wide* **£2,500–3,000 LB**

23

All that glitters is not gold...

Highway robbery was a significant problem in the 18th century. So, wealthy people took the precaution of having their favourite pieces of jewellery copied in paste and pinchbeck, for use when travelling. Pinchbeck was the first really successful gold substitute. True pinchbeck was only made by Christopher Pinchbeck and his son until the 1830s, when the term passed into general usage to describe any quality gilt metal. Made from an alloy of zinc and copper, it was highly malleable and had a warm, burnished appearance. Unlike real gold, however, it was relatively lightweight.

Feather motif pin in pinchbeck with emerald green paste cabochons. *c.1830* *5cm (2¼in) long* **£200–300 MARA**

Butterfly pin in pinchbeck with a body and head of French jet. *c.1860* *7.5cm (3in) wide* **£500–600 CSAY**

Shield pin in pinchbeck with floral motifs, tassels, and green paste cabochons. *c.1830* *6cm (2⅜in) long* **£200–300 MARA**

If used in minute quantities, real gold was reasonably affordable. Jewellery inlaid with tiny flakes of the precious metal, known as piqué, was particularly popular.

Multiple-pendant necklace and earrings
with inlaid gold and silver piqué. *c.1850*
N: 37cm (14½in) circ; E: 1cm (⅜in) long
£4,000–5,000 CSAY

Pendant earrings in pinchbeck with
prong-set emerald green pastes. *c.1830*
4cm (1½in) long **£200–300 MARA**

Drop chain brooch in pinchbeck with
clear and emerald green pastes. *c.1830*
4.5cm (1¾in) long **£100–200 MARA**

Oval link bracelet in genuine pinchbeck
with barrel clasp. *c.1770. 18cm (7in) long*
£350–400 RBRG

Oval link necklace in genuine pinchbeck
with barrel clasp. *c.1770. 96cm (37½in) long*
£1,200–1,400 RBRG

Floral, fruit, and foliate motif pin of cut steel. *c.1840. 4.5cm (1¾in) wide*
£300-350 CSAY

Pendant hoop earrings of cut steel. *c.1780 5cm (2in) long* **£500-600 CSAY**

Steely style...

Although cut steel jewellery made an appearance in the 17th century, it provided new inspiration in the 18th century when it became a fashionable alternative to diamonds. The blue-grey steel was either pierced or carved into faceted studs that were attached to a steel backplate. It was used in a wide range of jewellery, but most notably buckles, buttons, necklaces, bracelets, tiaras, and châtelaines. The wearing of cut steel jewellery was certainly not confined to those unable to afford precious alternatives: the Empress Josephine in France had cut steel jewellery in her collection. Fashionable for most of the 19th century, it enjoyed a small but notable revival in the 1940s.

Cut steel provided a less expensive alternative to the more traditional gold or silver settings for cameos.

Wedgwood brooch with a white on blue carved cameo in a cut steel frame. *c.1770 7cm (2¾in) long* **£900-1,000 RBRG**

Pearl drop necklace of cut steel with a red velvet tie. *c.1830 44cm (17in) circ* **£600-700 CSAY**

Pendant necklace of cut steel with mother-of-pearl cabochons, by Munsy & Co. of Cambridge. *c.1785. Pd: 7.5cm (3in) long* **£1,100–1,300 CSAY**

Cut steel tiara with a four-prong tortoiseshell hairgrip. *c.1800 14cm (6¼in) wide* **£550–650 CSAY**

Floral motif bracelet of cut steel riveted to brass. *c.1825. 17cm (6¾in) long* **£200–300 MARA**

Georgian-style earrings of cut steel with Venetian glass cabochon centres. *c.1910 3cm (1⅛in) wide* **£50–100 MARA**

Butterfly pin of cut steel riveted to brass. *c.1825. 4cm (1½in) wide* **£100–160 MARA**

A time of change

The 19th century saw the Machine Age grind into high gear and its impact on costume jewellery was profound. Mass production ensured that ordinary people could now afford to buy jewellery and a constant desire for novelty led to a proliferation of styles.

A FASHION FOR MOURNING

When the young Victoria ascended the throne in 1837, jewellery styles were romantic and patriotic. The new queen adored jewellery and was to become something of a style setter. Victorian paste and glass were steadily improving and colours were becoming ever more realistic. Industrialization, better production techniques, and social change all contributed to the rising popularity of faux jewellery.

Two developments characterize the costume jewellery of this era: quantity and variety. Mass production lowered costs and made it available to all, while constantly changing fashions led to an extraordinary profusion of styles.

Ancient European and Asian influences continued to feed through and, in the 1830s, the discovery of ancient Etruscan jewellery in Italy inspired a craze for an archaeological style. This often featured Etruscan-type filigree work and granulation. Arm bracelets, amulets, and Roman coin jewellery were all popular by the mid 19th century – as was mosaic jewellery, and enamel pieces featuring scenes from classical antiquity.

For the first time since the Renaissance, religious jewellery became widely popular. Christian motifs, notably crosses, were common, many made in Berlin ironwork. Other fashionable motifs echoed medieval Gothic designs such as trefoils or quatrefoils, and were often used in large belt buckles that drew attention to fashionably tiny waists.

Mourning jewellery, a peculiarly Victorian phenomenon, also made its appearance. Known as *memento mori*, or "reminder of death", pieces were often engraved with macabre symbols such as a skull and crossbones and worn alongside grander paste jewels. After the death of Victoria's consort, Prince Albert, the fashion for mourning jewellery really took off. Black mourning jewels were made from materials such as jet, onyx, enamel, and vulcanite. Hairwork jewellery comprising bracelets or necklaces of woven hair (sometimes human, but more often horse) was also popular in this context.

AN AGE OF SENTIMENT

Sentimental jewellery was very much a signature theme of the Victorian era. A lock of hair or a loved one's portrait was often incorporated into a locket or brooch, inscriptions were etched on to the back of settings, and motifs were used that symbolized love or affection. Some dated back to ancient Rome, such as clasped hands denoting friendship or faith. Often the choice of stones held a secret message of love or affection. For example, rubies, emeralds, garnets, amethysts, rubies again, and diamonds, or their paste equivalents, spelt out the word "R-E-G-A-R-D". Men's jewellery, however, became increasingly discreet although rings, and the newly invented cravat pins, showed great originality and were often highly personalized.

Oriental themes began influencing jewellery design in the 1850s and 60s when, after centuries of isolation, Japanese wares were displayed at the Great Exhibition of 1851 in London. Flora and fauna themes were also typical of the time, reflecting the Victorians' interest in nature. Organic materials became fashionable, and there were also bizarre curiosities such as stuffed hummingbirds mounted on pins, and bracelets or necklaces hung with real, brightly coloured insects.

Gold continued to be imitated and in the latter half of the century an alloy called Abyssinian gold became particularly popular. In the United States, where diamonds were not imported until the 1850s, costume jewellery was genuinely appreciated for its decorative qualities rather than its monetary value. Much of it was inexpensively produced by plating base metals with a thin layer of gold or silver.

A BACKLASH AGAINST INDUSTRIALIZATION

As the 19th century progressed, mass production resulted in a lowering of costume jewellery standards. In Europe, there was a backlash against industrialization, which gave rise to the birth of the Arts and Crafts movement. Led in England by William Morris and John Ruskin, it favoured simple handmade designs based on indigenous floral, ancient Celtic, and Medieval designs. These were created using traditional handmade methods of craftsmanship, rather than machine-made and mass produced. Silver was the metal of choice, together with uncut and cabochon-cut stones.

Interestingly, in Britain and the United States, many Arts and Crafts jewellers were women – a development echoed in the late 19th and early 20th centuries in the appearance of suffragette jewellery. Incorporating green, white, and violet coloured stones, the jewellery spelt out the aspiration: "Give Women the Vote".

END-OF-CENTURY TRENDS

Other notable end-of-century trends include fashions for Italian art jewellery, and a revival of *en tremblant* jewellery in which spring-loaded floral or figural motifs – especially insects – acquired an additional lively presence through the movement of the wearer. Newly discovered gemstones also made their appearance, notably vivid green garnets from Siberia, golden tiger's eyes from Africa, black opals from Australia, and sapphires from Kashmir. Inevitably, all were soon copied in paste.

As the 19th-century drew to a close, society had undergone extraordinary change, largely due to industrialization and a growing, moneyed middle class. However, the emergence of Art Nouveau – a new art for a new century – the exploitation of plastics, and the advent of *couture* design were set to change things even further.

Eagle belt buckle with faux diamond pastes set in a brass casting. *c.1865 14.5cm (5¾in) wide* **£150–250 RITZ**

Rococo-Revival pin of gilt metal with a black and red paste cabochon. *c.1860s 5.5cm (2⅛in) long* **£100–120 MARA**

Rococo-Revival pin of gilt metal with a large citrine paste centre. *c.1860 6.25cm (2½in) long* **£50–100 MARA**

Steel shield-shape pin set with oval-cut ruby and round-cut clear pastes. *1850s 7cm (2¾in) long* **£150–180 PC**

Continental pin of white metal with crystal diamanté and an aquamarine paste. *c.1905. 4cm (1½in) long* **£300–400 MARA**

Vauxhall glass bee pin and earrings with ruby and turquoise glass and gilt metal. *1870s. P: 4cm (1½in) long; E: 3cm (1⅛in) long* **£350–550 LYNH**

Romance and realism

The Victorian era saw a steady improvement in the quality of paste and glass, with costume jewellery design and techniques getting better and better. By 1830, open settings were being used for both precious and faux stones. These allowed more light to pass through the stones, enhancing their sparkle. "Gemstone" colours were becoming more realistic and, at the same time, fantasy colours were being introduced. In keeping with Victorian sentiment, different gemstones became associated with particular birthdates and superstition held that wearing the appropriate birthstone brought good luck.

Vauxhall glass flower pin with clear navette petals. *1850s. Flower: 5cm (2in) long* **£100–130 LYNH**

Vauxhall glass was popular for much of the 19th century. Its name comes from a mirror glassworks in Vauxhall, London, owned by the Duke of Buckingham. Vauxhall glass was easy to cut, foil, and set and it was often a burgundy-red colour. Early Vauxhall glass is rare and valuable.

Early Vauxhall glass crown pin with ruby and dark amethyst glass stones and gold pin. *c.1890. 4cm (1½in) long* **£180–220 CSAY**

Berlin ironwork ring of gilt metal with inscribed band of iron. *c.1914* 0.75cm (¼in) wide **£400–500 CSAY**

Berlin ironwork floral motif earrings with gilt highlights. *c.1820s* 6cm (2¼in) long **£1,000–1,200 CSAY**

Berlin ironwork necklace with alternating "S" scroll and cross motifs. *c.1810* 95cm (37in) long **£1,750–2,000 RBRG**

A Gothic austerity...

Berlin ironwork came about after a drop in demand for Prussian cast-iron products inspired armourers to experiment in the production of decorative wares. The trade was boosted around 1813 when Prussians who donated their gold jewellery to the Napoleonic campaign funds were given a gift of ironwork. Fashioned from linked cast iron panels, and often featuring delicate fretwork, Berlin ironwork was frequently used for the Gothic Revival jewellery styles popular from the 1820s. It symbolized constancy and durability and its black austerity also made it suitable for mourning jewellery.

Berlin ironwork bracelets with floral motifs and V-spring clasps. *c.1880* 19cm (7½in) long **£100–120 PC**

Whitby jet carved bead necklace
with Maltese Cross pendant. *c.1860*
Pd: 5cm (2in) long **£200–300 MARA**

That old black magic...

The fashion for jewellery made of black jet – a fossilized pine similar to coal – began

in the 1850s when Queen Victoria wore it while mourning a cousin. There were

large, natural jet deposits at Whitby, Yorkshire, which soon became a busy industrial

centre for jet jewellery. Mourning jewellery really took off after the death of Prince

Albert in 1861, and both jet and Berlin cast iron made ideal materials for this type

of jewellery. By the end of the 19th century, jet imitations were being produced

from hardened rubber or "vulcanite", and a shiny black glass called French jet.

Whitby jet pendant with carved Egyptian
pharaoh motif. *c.1900. 6.5cm (2½in) long*
£100–200 MARA

Unsigned earrings with jet cabochons
in filigree gold-plated metal. *c.1880*
3.5cm (1⅜in) long **£80–100 PC**

Whitby jet pin and pendant earrings
with angel coral cameos. *c.1900*
P & E: 5cm (2in) long **£300–400 MARA**

Twin-hearts and bow pin in gilt metal
with diamond and emerald pastes. *c.1880*
2cm (¾in) wide **£150–200 LYNH**

The language of love...

Love and sentimentalism are both hallmarks of Victorian jewellery. Hearts, cupids, and love-birds were common romantic motifs, while anchors symbolized hope, and serpents, especially those with their tails in their mouths, represented eternal love. A romantic "language of flowers" developed and was mirrored in jewellery with the use of appropriately coloured gemstones that became coded tokens of love and affection. Jewellery was often inscribed with loving messages, and another popular device was to spell out a loved one's name using the names of the stones used in the setting.

Cuffed hand and anchor pin cast in silver
and bronze. *c.1880s. 4cm (1½in) wide*
£100–200 LYNH

Cuffed hand and rose pin in
tinted mother-of-pearl. *c.1880*
5cm (2in) long **£100–200 LYNH**

"Regard" pin with faux rubies, emerald,
garnet, amethyst, and diamond. *c.1860*
4.5cm (1¾in) wide **£250–350 CSAY**

Back of pin

Commemorative pin with gold frame, black enamel, and hair over chalcedony. *c.1850* 5.75cm (2¼in) wide **£150–200 MARA**

A lost art...

Around the 1840s, jewellery made from human hair became incredibly popular. Called "hairwork", it is now virtually a lost art. Tightly woven lengths were arranged into a pattern, glued into place, and mounted in pinchbeck or other metals. Miniature paintings were also made into pieces such as pins, using ground hair as the colouring agent for the paint. The leading makers were Forrer in London and Lemonier and Charleux in Paris. Hairwork also became a popular hobby among Victorian ladies who made jewellery or framed hair pictures as a token of love or friendship, or for mourning.

Early commemorative pin with paste border and "J.W." initials in woven hair. *c.1800* 4.5cm (1¾in) long **£500–600 CSAY**

Woven horsehair bracelet with gilt metal clasp engraved with a floral motif. *c.1840* 17.5cm (6¾in) circ **£100–200 MARA**

Gold pin with a lock of hair and enamel flowers over chalcedony. *c.1850* 5.5cm (2⅛in) long **£150–200 MARA**

Pendant hoop earrings of black and red
tortoiseshell with bands of gold inlay. *c.1880*
4.5cm (1¾in) long **£750–1,000 LYNH**

Crescent moon tortoiseshell pin with
inlaid gold and silver floral motifs. *1880s*
3.75cm (1½in) long **£400–450 LYNH**

Hand and flower love token pin in mother-of-pearl. *c.1900. 5cm (2in) long*
£100–200 LYNH

Kingfisher pin of carved horn with a pearlized finish. *c.1900. 7.5cm (3in) long*
£75–150 LYNH

Culled from nature...

The Victorians had an insatiable thirst for novelty and this era witnessed a proliferation of costume jewellery styles. Organic materials such as tortoiseshell, bone, ivory, coral, and the teeth and claws of tigers became highly fashionable, although their roots can be traced back to ethnic jewellery. Building on the Victorians' interest in nature, flora and fauna were also popular decorative themes. Other influences came from the discoveries of 19th century explorers, early tourists, and the British Empire.

Winged insect pin carved from horn. *c.1900 9.5cm (3¾in) wide* **£80–200 LYNH**

Jewellery made from nuts was fashionable in the 19th century. Often carved by sailors on long sea voyages, such pieces are generally referred to as "Mariner's Art".

Pendant hoop tortoiseshell earrings with inlaid gold floral and foliate motifs. *1880s 4.5cm (1¾in) long* **£750–1,000 LYNH**

Mariner's Art nut necklace carved with floral and foliate motifs and lacquered. *c.1840. 44cm (17in) long*
£1,500–1,800 CSAY

37

Silver pendant necklace with green,
white, and violet pastes. *c.1900*
Pd: 3.5cm (1⅜in) long **£250–300 LYNH**

Votes for women...

Suffragette jewellery was the Victorian equivalent of a modern-day political badge or T-shirt. Pins and pendants were especially popular and featured green, white, and violet stones. These were the suffragette colours, with their initials standing for "Give Women the Vote". Pieces of suffragette jewellery could be worn as a quiet, understated way of showing support for the movement. Suffragette jewellery is sometimes confused with royal memorablia, as green, white, and violet were also the royal colours. Violet was Queen Alexandra's favourite colour, while the green echoed the Prince of Wales's preferred stone, peridot.

Pendant necklace with green, white, and
violet pastes and faux pearls. *c.1900*
Pd: 5.5cm (2⅛in) long **£250–350 LYNH**

Basket of flowers pendant necklace with
green, white, and violet pastes. *c.1900*
Pd: 3.5cm (1⅜in) long **£250–350 LYNH**

Gold chain necklace with multiple
fluorescent green moth pendants. *c.1900*
Pds: 2cm (¾in) long **£250–450 LYNH**

Gold twin-pendant necklace, with two
quartets of fluorescent blue beetles. *c.1900*
Pds: 4cm (1½in) long **£750–1,200 LYNH**

Necklace detail

The beauty of bugs...

The Victorian craze for insect jewellery was sparked off by a love of the bizarre
and an ongoing fascination with natural history, heightened no doubt by the
theories of Charles Darwin. Jewellery was fashioned using real insects, which
were often imported as curiosities from far-flung corners of the British Empire.
Often extraordinarily vibrant in colour and comparatively large, these lacquered
and mounted insects still have the power to amaze and even shock today. Given
their fragility, few examples have survived, and even those in pristine condition
are almost impossible to value with any degree of certainty.

A coming of age

During the first half of the 20th century, costume jewellery finally came into its own. Thanks to couturiers such as Coco Chanel, it became fashion-led, selling at every price range. At times, it was even regarded as more desirable than precious jewellery.

TWO DISTINCT STYLES

In the early years of the 20th century, costume jewellery was caught between two distinct styles, a desire to keep things as they were, and a yearning for the new, sensual lines of Art Nouveau and plique-à-jour jewellery.

The flowing curves of Art Nouveau supposedly echoed the desire for female emancipation, and role models such as actress Sarah Bernhardt (1844-1923) had a tremendous influence on jewellery design; cut-price copies of her pieces flew off the shelves.

More conventional motifs included floral baskets and bows. Light colours became popular, which revived an interest in diamonds and pearls, along with platinum in fine jewellery. Costume jewellery jumped on the bandwagon, using silver as an obvious substitute for platinum, along with imitation and cultured pearls.

The rarity value and extraordinarily high prices commanded by real pearls, (an American skyscraper exchanged hands for the price of a pearl necklace), increased the need to find convincing substitutes. These came in the form of cultured pearls from Mikimoto Pearls in Japan, who began production in the 1890s.

Genuine diamonds were often combined with synthetic stones and the best ones, especially faux emeralds, were hard to distinguish from the real thing.

During the 1920s and 30s, Czechoslovakia produced its own distinctive costume jewellery made from crystal stones and beads. Daniel Swarovski (*see p.203*) made the finest paste stones and his firm is still in production today.

Other popular styles in the 1920s and 30s included an Egyptian Revival, and the Indian-inspired "fruit salad" jewellery, but this period is probably most strongly identified with Art Deco. The geometric forms drew their inspiration from Cubism, and although pre-war figural subjects such as flower baskets still appeared, these were highly stylized rather than natualistic.

ART DECO TECHNIQUES

Square stones were sometimes "calibre-cut" to follow the exact outline of an irregularly shaped design. These cuts were used for invisible settings, where gems were drilled from the back and mounted edge to edge on invisible rods to create a seamless surface. Careful stone matching and setting techniques became vital. Bracelets were a key Art Deco accessory and several were often worn on each arm. Dress clips were also in vogue.

One of the most popular synthetic materials for jewellery between 1920 and 1940 was Bakelite, favoured for its malleable qualities and bright colours. It could be worked on a lathe and lent itself to Art Deco styling.

By the mid 1930s, costume jewellery really came into its own, and its new-found confidence was reflected in bigger and chunkier designs. Instead of simply imitating precious jewellery, it was evolving its own fashion-led, mass-market identity and it sold at every price range.

Fashion designers such as Schiaparelli (*see pp.108–111*) and Chanel (*see pp.56–59*) had a great impact during this era and Coco Chanel was the first to use costume jewellery to create the finishing touch to her overall look. Faux jewellery was now more stylish than its precious equivalent.

THE AMERICAN INFLUENCE

French couturiers opened the doors to costume jewellery, but Americans produced and wore more of it than anyone else. After World War I, the United States became fully industrialized and by 1930 it was ready to produce costume jewellery on a scale impossible in war-ravaged Europe. For the first time, women had a huge choice of constantly changing fashions that offered both style and quality, and costume jewellery was an ideal way to accessorize and personalize a mass-produced outfit.

Hollywood also had a huge influence on fashion at this time and whenever a star's jewellery made an impact on the silver screen, factories rushed to reproduce it in costume copies. Trifari's success was based on the firm's ability to reproduce brilliant copies of precious contemporary pieces, and by the mid 30s they were producing cocktail jewellery inspired by Hollywood (*see pp.118–129*).

A welter of historical "costume" movies gave rise to an American "antique" style of jewellery. Antique motifs such as bows and lockets were revived along with châtelaines, which now took the form of paired pins attached to either side of a jacket or cardigan by a chain.

Around the late 1930s, there was a vogue for enamel flower brooches in pastel colours. Also, the Art Deco style was reworked into a dramatic retro style popularized by actresses such as Joan Crawford. Large and solid, it combined free-form swirls with geometric shapes. Retro costume jewellery was usually set in gold-plated metal dominated by a single, large, plainly cut stone or cabochon – a contrast to the small, fancy cut stone designs of Art Deco. It could also be worn day-into-evening – a boon to the new breed of working women.

A SUBSTITUTION FOR SILVER

Due to restrictions on raw materials during World War II, manufacturers had to improvise and they did so with tremendous success. Materials such as Bakelite and Lucite came into their own, but the most significant change was the substitution of sterling silver for the various base metals. By 1942, silver was the only metal that was allowed for costume jewellery. By then, most American costume jewellery metal was made of vermeil (gold-plated) sterling silver. Coro's 1940 vermeil pieces are particularly collectable (*see pp.68–71*).

Cocktail costume jewellery became a useful way of cheering up the austere, wartime look and it became so popular that Stateside sales had tripled by 1945. The industry was now well placed to take advantage of the coming postwar boom.

An illuminating style...

Meaning "window of light", the plique-à-jour enamelling technique came into fashion in the late 19th century and is closely associated with Art Nouveau style. Translucent enamels are fused to span across a network of open-backed metal cells, allowing the light to shine through and illuminate it. The effect is similar to stained glass. More technically complex and fragile than other enamelwork, plique-à-jour jewellery is highly prized by today's collectors. Masters of the art include Fernand Thesmar, Gustave Gaudernack, and Rene Lalique, although many pieces are of unknown origin.

Silver pendant with red and green plique-à-jour and diamond and ruby pastes. *c.1915*
3.75cm (1½in) wide
£320–350 RBRG

Gilt metal floral earrings with red, green, and yellow plique-à-jour and pearls. *c.1910.*
3.75cm (1½in) long **£650–700 RBRG**

Gilt metal pendant necklace with plique-à-jour and a baroque pearl drop. *c.1910*
Pd: 3.75cm (1½in) wide **£650–700 RBRG**

French silver hanging basket pin with "fruit salads" and crystal diamanté. *Early 1920s 3.75cm (1½in) wide* **£125–150 CRIS**

Inspired by the Tree of Life...

The exotic designs and colours of the Indian Moghul "Tree of Life" jewels inspired the hugely popular Cartier-designed precious pieces of the 1920s and 30s. Instead of the stones being faceted, they were carved to resemble flowers, fruit, and leaves. They were then inlaid into swathes of tiny, faceted diamonds to form stylized Art Deco designs, notably baskets and vases, in platinum settings. Cartier began the trend, but other companies, including Van Cleef and Arpels and Trifari, followed suit and produced similar designs – precious and faux – dubbed "Fruit Salads" or "Tutti-Frutti".

French silver pot of flowers pin with "fruit salads" and crystal diamanté. *Early 1920s 4.5cm (1¾in) long* **£125–150 CRIS**

Trifari vermeil sterling silver pin with "fruit salads" and crystal rhinestones. *1940s 5.75cm (2¼in) long* **£275–325 CRIS**

Trifari sterling silver pin and earrings with faux "fruit salads" and pavé-set crystal rhinestones. *1940s. P: 8.25cm (3¼in) long; E: 2cm (¾in) wide* **£900–1,000 CRIS**

Fluid and sculptural...

Emerging in the 1880s and fashionable among the avant-garde until World War II, Art Nouveau jewellery turned its back on the rigidly symmetrical forms of 19th-century classical designs and embraced a more fluid, sculptural style of ornament. Inspired by the curvaceous forms inherent in nature and the underlying assymetry of Japanese art, typical motifs include sinuous, elongated roots, stems, blooms, and foliage; winged insects such as dragonflies and butterflies; and *femmes-fleur* – sensuous young women with flowing hair, often entwined with flowers and tendrils that came to symbolize the emancipation of women from the restraints of the Victorian era.

Silver shirt buttons with red glass cabochons and blue and green enamelling. *c.1900* *1cm (⅜in) wide* **£200–250 LYNH**

Dragonfly pin with turquoise cabochons, enamelling, and diamanté. *c.1900* *7cm (2¾in) wide* **£250–450 LYNH**

Silver belt buckle with foliate motifs and turquoise and green enamelling. *c.1900* *8.25cm (3¼in) wide* **£250–300 LYNH**

Silver scarab pin with turquoise, purple, green, blue, and red enamel. *1920s* *4cm (1½in) wide* **£160–120 MARA**

Pharoah heads bracelet in gold-tone metal with turquoise glass stones. *1920s* *18cm (7in) circ* **£60-100 MARA**

Egypt revisited...

The discovery of Tutankhamen's tomb in 1922 provoked a craze for Ancient Egyptian styles of ornament that endured well into the 1930s. There had been earlier Egyptian revivals, in the late 18th and mid 19th centuries, but this one had far greater popular appeal – a phenomenon fuelled by newsreel footage of archaeological digs and numerous Hollywood biblical epics. Typical motifs employed in Egyptian Revival jewellery include scarabs, snakes, pyramids, palm trees, hieroglyphs, and sphinxes – the latter with the body of a lion and the head of a pharoah, ram, hawk, or falcon.

Pyramids pendant necklace, bracelet, and earrings of gilt metal with enamel. *c.1930* *Pds: 5cm (2in) long; B: 16cm (6¼in) long; E: 4.5cm (1¾in) long* **£150–200 CRIS**

English glass necklace with triangular and shield-shape blue faceted glass stones. *Late 1920s* 40cm (15½in) long
£60–100 ECLEC

French shield-shape pendant of blue enamel with clear crystal rhinestones. *1930s* 5.75cm (2¼in) long **£535–600 TR**

Fahrner silver bar pin with an aquamarine glass stone. *1930s. 5cm (2in) wide* **£435–465 TR**

English silver pin with a ruby red paste and clear crystal rhinestones. *1930s* 5cm (2in) wide **£150–200 RG**

French engraved silver bracelet with a large emerald green paste. *1930s* 4.5cm (1¾in) wide **£665–735 TR**

American sterling silver bracelet with engraved floral motifs. *Late 1920s* 19cm (7½in) long **£135–200 JJ**

A bold new age...

Fashionable during the 1920s and 30s, the Art Deco style reflected the new feeling of optimism and excitement that gradually emerged after the privations of World War I. Its abstract and geometric shapes and often bold colour combinations were inspired by the early 20th century art movements of Cubism and Futurism. Recently discovered Egyptian and Aztec styles also had an influence, along with the streamlined forms of Machine Age products such as the motor car. All of these marked a radical departure from the organic forms and sinuous sensuality of pre-war Art Nouveau imagery.

English bracelet of red Bakelite and chromed steel. *Late 1920s* 19cm (7½in) circ **£120–130 RITZ**

English sterling silver necklace with clear crystal rhinestones. *1930s* Pd: 3.75cm (1½in) long **£350–400 RG**

English geometric form necklace with alternating silver and Bakelite. *Late 1920s* 38cm (14¾in) circ **£140–160 RITZ**

English necklace with silver chain and yellow and black Bakelite pendant. *Late 1920s* Pd: 5cm (2in) wide **£140–160 RITZ**

A brave new world

Since World War II, costume jewellery has grown steadily more popular and it is now part of mainstream fashion. Quality varies, but a host of new materials, styles, and techniques have evolved to take us forward in the 21st century.

FROM NEW LOOK TO HOLLYWOOD

The post-war period in the United States was a boom time of prosperity and optimism. Dior's New Look in France offered a welcome return to feminism and luxury after the streamlined austerity of the war, and costume jewellery was well made, feminine, and showy. The removal of wartime restrictions on Czech and Austrian pastes resulted in a trend for huge, vividly coloured stones that were unashamedly fake.

Meanwhile, a parallel trend had started for more subdued, realistic pieces, largely due to the post-war resurrection of the Paris fine jewellery trade. Hollywood continued to be a major trend setter, and a vogue for cocktail parties inspired a craze for quirky "conversation piece" jewellery. Figural pins also became popular, especially those made in plastic, since it lent itself to more complex shapes.

CHEAPER TECHNIQUES

By the end of the 1940s, base metals were becoming available again and new electroplating techniques were developed, including Trifari's "trifanium", a matte gold known as Russian gold plating (*see pp.118–129*). Soon, the growing demand for costume jewellery prompted a search for new production methods and this led to machine stamping. Also, the prong-setting of stones by hand was often replaced by the faster, cheaper method of glue setting. However, these techniques adversely affected quality, and pieces by designers such as Miriam Haskell, who retained handmade techniques and produced limited editions, remain the most collectable.

ANYTHING GOES

During the 1950s and 60s, Op and Pop Art were influential, with artists such as Andy Warhol fuelling the inspirational fire. The 1960s "anything goes" youth culture resulted in jewellery that was larger and more over-the-top than ever. This was the time when the twin cults of image and celebrity really started to take root, so visual impact became increasingly important. Styles were fun and young, with a bold use of plastics and strong, unsaturated colours.

Acrylic jewellery came of age in the 1960s, when it was used either on its own for the bold, chunky rings and bangles that were a hallmark of the period, or as decorative features on necklaces and earrings. Substantial yet light-weight, acrylic could be coloured and textured or left smooth, so it was ideal for the designs of the time.

The fantasy pastes of the previous decade were now given an extra psychedelic edge. Black metal became a new and popular foil for the resulting acid colours, and white and green metals were also used, along with colourful enamel pieces. A hugely experimental era, the 1960s churned out a bewildering diversity of "looks", from flower power, ethnic, and gypsy to various retro revivals. The first moon missions also inspired a Space Age look, with costume jewellery producing plain metal, plastic, or metal and enamel in geometric shapes.

The American designer, Kenneth J. Lane (*see pp.84–85*), was one of the few who managed to harness the many diverse strands of 1960s influences into an integrated and original style. His love of bold, photogenic jewellery perfectly mirrored the times. He also produced a successful "Jackie O" line based on Jackie Onassis's celebrated sense of style.

However, the vast majority of jewellery from the 1960s was designed to be "throwaway". As a result, it quickly fell out of fashion and only the big, signed pieces with a strong period flavour have stood the test of time.

BACK TO NATURE

The pendulum swung yet again in the 1970s with a return to handmade values and ethnic jewellery. Natural materials such as wood and feathers, as well as Native American silver and turquoise, were widely worn, although the popularity of brightly coloured enamel, used for flower brooches, bangles, and necklaces, continued from the 1960s.

Glitz and glamour burst back on to the scene in the 1980s, creating another boom for costume jewellery. This was the "Dynasty" era when even the gaudiest glitter was flaunted in daytime. In line with the 1980s devotion to designer labels, the Chanel "CC" logo was stamped on everything from belt buckles to earrings. In response to consumer demand, costume jewellers started making reproduction Victorian, Edwardian, and Art Deco pieces. These designers combined the best from the past with a clutch of exciting new ideas and materials. Imaginative combinations of papier-mâché, glass, mirrors, wood, and rhinestones resulted in a new genre of craft costume jewellery.

MILLENNIUM STYLE

By the mid 1990s, the approach of the new millennium inspired another nostalgic craze for retro and vintage, and numerous costume jewellery companies such as Ciro and Fior started producing a range of traditional styles. Beads came back in, especially those made in Murano glass. Recently, in contrast to this harking back o the past, new styles and materials have also filtered through. Designers such as Dinny Hall (*see p.155*) in Britain have produced ultra-modern, sculptural shapes in innovative materials; America's Robert Lee Morris has created organic forms which have been described as "jewellery without gems".

The potential of costume jewellery as a collectable continues to increase steadily. Although some modern and contemporary pieces are cheaply made, the better pieces should rise in price over the coming decades and are likely to be good investments.

Murano glass necklace with alternating oval
clear and opaque blue glass beads. *c.1920s*
85cm (33in) long **£220-240 RBRG**

The glory of glass...

In the 20th and early 21st centuries, most costume jewellery has been created from
various combinations of metals, alloys, faux pearls, enamels, plastics and, above all,
faceted rhinestones. However, pieces made from coloured glass beads have been a
popular alternative, especially since the 1920s. Strung into necklaces and bracelets,
the finest beads have come from Murano in Venice, and the Czech Republic.
Produced in diverse colours, textures, and degrees of opacity and translucency,
the beads lend themselves particularly well to popular fruit and foliate designs.

Multicoloured glass necklace with
pale green and blue, red, black, lilac,
and coffee glass beads. *c.1930s*
39cm (15¼in) long **£40-60 ECLEC**

Wheat motif necklace with green, red,
turquoise, black, and beige glass beads.
c.1930s. 44cm (17in) long **£40-60 ECLEC**

Fruit garland necklace with poured glass
leaves and glass bead fruits. *c.1930s*
42cm (16¼in) long **£40-60 ECLEC**

Zulu earplugs made from wood
and Perspex with chrome studs.
1960s. 6.25cm (2½in) wide
£100–125 (per pair) EL

All things ethnic...

A backlash against much of the cheap, throwaway costume jewellery of the 1960s
created a desire for purer designs and traditional standards of craftsmanship. As a
result, consumers started turning to ethnic jewellery. Authentic tribal necklaces,
bangles, and earrings imported from Africa and Asia, and Western-made copies, became
particularly fashionable, while in the United States Native American jewellery also
came into vogue. Made from materials such as beaten metal, stones, earthenware beads,
bone, wood, and feathers, these pieces were the height of fashion throughout the 1970s.

Bead necklace with alternating smooth
black and carved red composite beads.
c.1970s. 37cm (14½in) long **£30–40 PC**

Leaf motif earrings in hand-beaten
white metal with wire wraps. *c.1960s
6.5cm (2½in) long* **£60–80 PC**

Austrian lariat necklace with woven ropes
of jet and white glass beads. *c.1950s
110cm (44in) long* **£240–270 CRIS**

*Some African necklaces
made in the 20th century
were made with reclaimed
stones first used in tribal
jewellery hundreds or
thousands of years ago.*

Amazonite necklace made with
c.1000–200 year-old polished stones
from Mauritania and Niger. *c.1900
51cm (20in) circ* **£1,200–1,400 PC**

Anoush Waddington "Autumn" necklace in blue and red nylon with silver fastening. *c.2002. 9cm (3½in) wide* **£700–800 LCG**

Kathie Murphy pendant earrings in resin set with blue threads. *c.2002 5.75cm (2¼in) long* **£80–100 LCG**

Jane Adam bangle in abstract pattern of anodized polychrome aluminium. *c.2001 7.5cm (3in) wide* **£160–180 LCG**

Gail Klevan bangle in semi-translucent yellow acrylic with coloured inclusions. *c.2002. 10cm (4in) wide* **£90–100 LCG**

Carla Edwards bangle of pinkish-red resin with layered wire inclusions. *c.2001 10.75cm (4¼in) wide* **£140–160 LCG**

Anoush Waddington "Autumn" ring in silver and blue and red nylon. *c.2002 9cm (3½in) long* **£210–240 LCG**

On the cutting edge...

While the forms and imagery employed by late 20th- and early 21st-century jewellery designers have rarely been new, their presentation and the materials they are made from have often pushed creative boundaries. Significant trends have included the use of coloured, rather than plain, aluminium, and the fashioning of abstract or naturalistic patterns from materials such as cotton and wire set in semi-translucent resins. More unusual and even startling examples have been the multiple-medium pieces in which expensive precious metals such as gold or silver have been combined with inexpensive colourful plastics such as polypropylene.

Andrew Last pin in "twist on" rotor blade form of purple aluminium. *c.2000 5cm (2in) wide* **£110–130 LCG**

Kate Wilkinson "Purple Passion" necklace in feathers, glass beads, and steel wire. *c.2002 15.25cm (6in) wide* **£620–670 LCG**

Anna Sandford "architectural" ring in translucent yellow and opaque red acrylic. *c.2001. 22.25cm (8¾in) long* **£70–80 LCG**

Designer profiles

Major 20th- and 21st-century costume jewellery designers

Everyone who collects costume jewellery, or who is simply interested in it, has their own favourite designers and makers, so describing some designers as "better" than others will always be subject to debate. Nevertheless, there are some outstanding 20th- and early 21st-century designers and makers who have figured more prominently than others, and who have acquired a standing beyond personal preference.

Of the 20 leading designers featured over the following pages, some are most admired for their innovative style or influential design, others for their high standards of craftsmanship, and some for the sheer diversity of their output. In most cases, the beautiful and highly collectable jewellery created by these designers displays all of these desirable qualities.

Chanel

One of the legendary stars of French *couture*, Coco Chanel was the first designer to incorporate costume jewellery into her fashion philosophy.

A RENOWNED TRENDSETTER

Credited by Christian Dior for revolutionizing fashion "with a black pullover and ten rows of pearls", Gabrielle "Coco" Chanel was a renowned trendsetter. She created the little black dress, sportswear, the cardigan suit, beach pyjamas, costume jewellery, and even perfumes. Her staggering success ensured that her designs were copied worldwide.

Inspired by a desire for practical, comfortable clothes in easy-fitting fabrics, such as wool jersey – a complete departure from the corseted restraints of the past – Chanel's innovative style was hugely influential in the 1920s and 30s.

Her first shop opened in Paris in 1914, with the financial backing of her wealthy lover, Boy Capel. Concealing her age and humble origins, Chanel reinvented herself, launching into a world of high fashion and big business. By the 1920s, she was one of the leading Parisian designers.

Chanel then cleverly opened a boutique in her Paris salon dedicated to accessories and jewellery. Instead of copying fine jewellery trends, her designs complemented the simple lines and colours of her clothes, adding a personal "finishing touch". This novel approach catapulted costume jewellery into a fashion-led market.

Above: "Bijoux de Fleurs" orchid pin in shades of pink and red enamelled pot metal with smokey brown crystal rhinestones. *1940s. 7.5cm (3in) wide* **£600–700 CRIS**

ORIGINAL BOXES

Chanel jewellery was, and still is, sold packaged in a box bearing the company name. The individual pieces of parures and demi-parures are all boxed separately. When early Chanel jewellery comes back on to the market, it usually does so without its original box. If a piece still has its box, the value of the jewellery can be increased by up to 30 per cent.

Floral necklace and earrings by Maison Gripoix for Chanel with gold-plated links and poured glass petals. *c.1930. N: 38cm (15in) wide; E: 2cm (¾in) wide* **£950–1,100 CRIS**

Floral motif necklace and earrings shown left in their original brown paper-covered cardboard Chanel boxes, lined with the original tissue paper.

SIMPLY PEARLS

Chanel wore pearls by the metre, starting a trend that became a model of elegance for Parisian women. Indeed, multiple strands of pearls have now become a traditional Chanel accessory. Showy baroque pearls also featured in many of her historically inspired pieces, such as her Byzantine and Renaissance style crosses and earrings.

Single-strand faux pearl necklace with gilt metal links and a shield clasp with the interlaced "CC" Coco Chanel logo. *1980s* 66cm (26in) long **£80–120 RG**

INFLUENCES

Chanel's wealthy lovers are credited with influencing her taste in jewellery. However, she drew inspiration from many things: historical jewellery, stained glass windows, Russian icons, Byzantine mosaics, animals, and even the Venetian Republic.

BYZANTINE

The Byzantine jewels in the Treasury of St. Marks, Venice, influenced Chanel's jewellery. She substituted *pâte-de-verre* and gilt for the cabochon stones and antique gold settings, as in these floral earrings of gold-plated metal with green poured glass, pavé-set clear rhinestone petals, and red glass cabochon centres. *1980s* 4cm (1½in) wide **£275–300 SUM**

EXOTIC

Much of Chanel's jewellery is reminiscent of the cultures of India, Persia, and Egypt. She used carved glass beads in Moghul-style designs, such as this necklace with carved ruby glass beads and emerald glass stones encased in filigree metal with ruby glass cabochon highlights. *1950s. 42cm (16½in) long* **£1,800–2,000 WAIN**

Simplicity and understated elegance were the hallmarks of Chanel's design style, and she often mixed faux with fine jewellery. She was known for her ropes of faux pearls and gold-tone chains, "poured glass" jewellery by Maison Gripoix, and Maltese Cross cuffs designed by Verdura.

"If you want to start a collection, start with a brooch because you will find most use for it. It can be pinned on a suit lapel, collar or pocket, on a hat, belt, or evening gown."
Coco Chanel

POST-WAR COMEBACK

After the war, Chanel worked with Parisian designer Robert Goossens (*see p.199*) and throughout the 1960s they produced dramatic rosary-style necklaces with long chains decorated with pearls and beads; *pâte-de-verre* eagles copied from Anglo Saxon belt buckles; and huge Maltese Cross brooches decorated with glass cabochons of green and red, Chanel's signature colour combination.

Chanel continued building her vast empire until her death in 1971. Seven years later, Christie's auctioned her costume jewellery, fetching prices comparable to those of precious

gems and gold. The company continued to produce Chanel collections that were faithful reissues of her style until 1983, when Karl Lagerfeld took over as director, with a brief to reinterpret and modernize. Like that of his legendary predecessor, Lagerfeld's jewellery became an essential part of a distinctive new Chanel look.

Multiple pendant necklace with faux pearls, blue, red, and green poured glass beads (some carved) and clear crystal rhinestones. *c.1970*

Longest Pd: 10.5cm (4in) long

| £1,800–2,200 | | SUM |

Symmetrical pendant-pin with green and blue glass stones and faux pearls in gold-plated settings. *1950s*

8.25cm (3¼in) long

| £250–300 | RITZ |

Oval pendant-pin with red and green glass stones, faux pearls, and clear crystal rhinestones in gilt metal settings. *1930s*

9.5cm (3¾in) long

| £280–320 | RITZ |

Rare Mr Punch pin with trembler head, in white, red, and black enamelled lead, and with pavé-set rhinestones. *1920s*

6cm (2⅜in) high

| £1,500–1,800 | BY |

Exotic oval pin with red, green, and blue glass cabochons, faux pearls, and round and baguette clear crystal rhinestones. *c.1970*

7cm (2¾in) wide

| £400–500 | SUM |

Fiery dragon pin by Maison Gripoix for Chanel, with a gold-plated wire frame set with green, red, and black poured glass. *1940s*

10.5cm (4in) wide

| £250–300 | RITZ |

Good, Better, Best

The prices of these three Chanel pins diverge widely because of their ages, subject matter, and varying complexities of design and craftsmanship.

£80-100

This **Maltese Cross pin** features green, red, and pink poured glass cabochons set in gilt metal. Although one of Chanel's signature motifs, crosses in general are not popular with contemporary collectors. 1990s. 6.5cm (2½in) long **PC**

£265-400

This **floral bow pin** has green, blue, and red poured glass, pink and amethyst glass beads, crystal rhinestones, and faux pearls set in gilt metal. It is rarer and more complex than the Maltese Cross pin. 1930s. 6.5cm (2½in) long **BY**

£930-1,065

This **stylized floral pin** features green, red, blue, and black poured glass beads and stones, faux baroque pearls, and pavé-set clear crystal rhinestones. Older and rarer than the floral bow pin, it is the most striking and complex in design of all three. 1920s. 10.5cm (4in) high **BY**

Rare peacock pin with turquoise, aquamarine, and red poured glass feathers and pavé-set clear crystal rhinestones. *1930s*
14cm (5½in) long

£1,665-2,335   **BY**

Unsigned heart pin and earrings of poured glass with red and clear crystal rhinestones and faux pearls. *1920s*
P: 8.25cm (3¼in) long; E: 2.5cm (1in) long

£200-250   **CRIS**

Chunky pendant earrings of antiqued, stamped gilt metal with faux pearls and green glass cabochons and drops. *1970s*
9.5cm (3¾in) long

£250-300   **SUM**

ENAMELLED LEAD

In the late 1920s and early 30s, Chanel retailed a series of pins made from enamelled cast lead with crystal rhinestone highlights. The majority were creature pins, notably frogs and cats, although some were "novelty" subjects. It is generally assumed that they were made in France, but many were actually of American manufacture. The enamelling and the rhinestones (often pavé-set) are invariably of high quality. All too rare nowadays, these pins change hands for considerable sums of money.

Rare frog pin with green, black, and red enamel on a lead casting, and with pavé-set clear crystal rhinestone webbed feet and eyes. *1927*
6cm (2⅜in) long **£1,500-2,000 CRIS**

Christian Dior

The great dictator of European and American style, Christian Dior's glamorous and striking designs dominated the world of fashion during the late 1940s and 50s.

CHRISTIAN DIOR
1905–57

1905 Born in Normandy, France

1938–41 Works for Parisian couturiers Robert Piguet and Lucien Lelong

1946 Opens Maison Dior in Avenue Montaigne, Paris

1947 Introduces glamorous post-war "New Look" in first collection

1947–57 Twice-yearly collections of clothing and jewellery plus licensing establishes Dior as a global brand

1957 Dior dies suddenly and protégé Yves Saint Laurent becomes head designer

1960 Mark Bohan becomes head designer

1987 Maison Dior bought by Louis-Vuitton-Moët-Hennessy Group

1989 Gianfranco Ferré becomes head designer

1996 John Galliano becomes head designer

Indian-style pendant necklace of gilt metal with faux pearls, lapis beads, teardrop cabochons, and clear rhinestones. *1970. N: 40.5cm (16in) circ; Pd: 9cm (3½in) drop* **£250–300 RG**

60

POSTWAR GLAMOUR

Born in Normandy in 1905, Christian Dior began his career in fashion in the mid 1930s selling sketches of hats and dresses to Parisian couturiers. Following wartime service in the south of France, he returned to Paris in 1941 and gained considerable experience working for leading designer Lucien Lelong. In 1946 he established Maison Dior with the financial backing of textile manufacturer Marcel Boussac. A year later, his first *haute couture* collection – the "New Look" (*see below*) – marked a sensational departure from the austerity of the war-torn 1940s. Not only did it help to re-establish Paris as the centre of world fashion, it also set the tone for the more prosperous decades that followed.

Unlike many of his contemporaries, who accessorized their clothing with unobtrusive, "off-the-peg" jewellery for fear of it detracting from their costume, Dior designed jewellery as an integral part of his collections. Although early designs were almost exclusively *couture* pieces made for particular outfits or individual clients – notably the Hollywood actresses Marilyn Monroe and Bette Davis – his later pieces were produced under licence in far greater numbers for sale through exclusive retail outlets. These included pieces conceived in his spirit by the House of Dior over the decades following his sudden

Above: Textured gilt metal earrings with irregular-shaped faux jade cabochons and clear rhinestone highlights. *1967 2.5cm (1in) wide* **£50–65 ROX**

THE "NEW LOOK"

Introduced in February 1947, Christian Dior's "New Look" was characterized by an extravagant use of fabric, dropped hemlines, exaggerated and softened curves, and a sense of formality enhanced by high heels, stockings, hats, gloves, and costume jewellery. In a post-war Europe where food, fabrics, and other essentials were still in short supply – and in some cases still rationed – such an extravagant use of materials was highly controversial. However, despite some initial and vehement protests, this glamorous and overtly feminine look took root and set the style for women's fashions well into the 1960s.

A 1955 black crepe cocktail dress by Dior is accessorized with an Ottoman bonnet and an opulent faux pearl necklace and earrings.

MITCHELL MAER

Having moved to London in the late 1930s, American-born Mitchell Maer established a metal castings and costume jewellery company known initially as "Metalplastics", and later as "Mitchell Maer". In 1952 Christian Dior licensed Maer to make jewellery for the Dior collections, and for the next four years he produced some of Dior's most innovative and distinctive designs. His floral and unicorn pins in particular (*see below and right*) are much sought after by current collectors.

Stylized floral pin by Mitchell Maer for Dior of rhodium-plated metal with clear rhinestones and a central faux pearl. *Mid 1950s. 7cm (2¾in) wide* **£80–120 RG**

Unicorn pin by Mitchell Maer for Dior of rhodium-plated metal with pavé-set clear rhinestones. *Mid 1950s 6.25cm (2½in) long* **£70–100 RG**

death in 1957. It is these pieces that collectors are most likely to encounter today.

Maison Dior's concern that costume jewellery sold under the Dior brand should mirror the quality of its clothing design is reflected in the reputation of the companies and individual designers commissioned to produce the pieces. They include Henry Schreiner (*see p.165*) and Kramer (*see p.178*) in the United States; Mitchell Maer in England (*see above*); Henkel & Grosse in Germany (from 1955); Josette Gripoix in France (*see pp.90–93*) and, most recently, Robert Goossens (*see p.199*). The list of innovative designers who headed the company after Christian Dior's death is equally impressive: from Yves Saint Laurent, via Mark Bohan and Gianfranco Ferré, to *enfant terrible* John Galliano.

CLASSICAL AND MODERN

Stylistically, Dior jewellery draws inspiration from a wide range of historical styles. Yet pieces are never simply reproduced. Characteristically, they are given a modern twist by the incorporation of unusual pastes and stones – the colour and figuring of which is often deliberately artificial and invariably visually striking. Chief among these are the iridescent, polychromatic *aurora borealis* rhinestones that Dior developed with Swarovski (*see p.203*) in 1955.

Apart from unusual components and a diverse range of historical forms, Dior jewellery is also characterized by an extensive use of floral motifs – a reflection of Christian Dior's personal love of gardens and the French countryside. Wild flowers, roses, and, especially, lily of the valley are recurring designs – the latter having virtually aquired the status of signature motif for Dior. In addition, some equally sought-after figural pieces – including fish, circus animals, and unicorn pins – have been produced. Collectors should note that most Dior pieces are signed and dated.

Rare *en tremblant* flower pin designed by Mitchell Maer for Dior of gilt metal with aquamarine and clear rhinestones. *1951. 10cm (4in) long* **£900–1100 WAIN**

GLAMOUR

The opulence of the ground-breaking "New Look" collection of 1947 was sustained by Maison Dior during the late 1950s and 60s. Presented as an essential component of costume, rather than simply an accessory, Dior jewellery continued to push fashion beyond the privations of World War II into a more affluent and optimistic age.

ORIENTAL

Oriental influence is clearly evident in this sumptuous Dior outfit originally shown in *Vogue* in November 1961. The velvet jacket is embellished with sable cuffs and iridescent and gilt beads. Characteristically, the outfit is further elaborated with stunning costume jewellery – faux pearl earrings and an extravagant multi-chain necklace of gilt and faux pearls.

MIDDLE-EASTERN

Ancient Middle-Eastern styles provide much of the inspiration for this elaborate Dior pendant necklace from the late 1950s. Designed to be worn with a strapless evening gown, it comprises a shower of gilt chains encrusted with fine-quality rhinestones that extend across the shoulders and down the back of the wearer.

Floral necklace, gold-plated with faux pearls, prong-set yellow cabochons, and topaz and emerald green rhinestones. *1958*

37cm (14½in) circ

£400–500 **CRIS**

Pendant tassel necklace and earrings by Mitchell Maer for Dior of faux gold with round-cut haematite stones. *Early 1950s*

Largest Pd: 10cm (4in) long; E: 5cm (2in) long

£750–850 **WAIN**

Floral necklace and earrings, rhodium-plated with round- and navette-cut faux rubies and clear rhinestones. *1959*

N: 40cm (16in) circ; E: 4cm (1½in) long

£320–450 **ROX**

Necklace, bracelet, and earrings by Mitchell Maer for Dior, rhodium-plated with prong-set, rectangular-cut faux sapphires and round-cut aquamarine rhinestones. *Early 1950s*

N: 42cm (16½in) circ; B: 20cm (8in) circ; E: 3cm (1⅛in) wide

£1,100–1,300 **WAIN**

Empire-style necklace, pin, and earrings, by Mitchell Maer for Dior with festooned and flattened gilt and enamel chains, and diamanté. *1951*

N: 46cm (18in) circ; P: 9cm (3½in) wide; E: 3cm (1⅛in) long

£1,500–1,800 **WAIN**

Floral motif necklace and earrings with lapis lazuli glass beads and cabochons, and clear rhinestones. *1959*

N: 35.5cm (14in) circ; E: 4.5cm (1¾in) long

£900–1,100 **FM**

MUSICAL LOCKETS

Some of the most unusual and distinctive pieces of Dior jewellery were made by Mitchell Maer during the early 1950s (see p.61). The rare Maer locket below is of chased, gold-plated metal embellished with faux pearls and a large, plum-coloured glass cabochon. Its form and decoration, particularly the flying cherubs, recall Renaissance and 18th-century imagery. However, in function it has a decidedly more modern twist: the locket conceals a music box mechanism that plays a romantic tune.

Flying cherubs locket, gold-plated with plum glass cabochon and prong-set faux pearls. *Early 1950s*
6cm (2⅜in) long **£NPA LB**

Floral pin by Mitchell Maer for Dior with *en-tremblant* flower-head, of white metal with clear rhinestones and small faux pearls. *1951*
10cm (4in) long

£800–1,000   **WAIN**

Pendant cross pin, rhodium-plated with prong-set royal blue glass stones and *aurora borealis* rhinestones. *1958*
7.5cm (3in) long

£100–140   **RG**

Floral motif pendant pin, rhodium-plated with clear rhinestones and eight faux baroque pearls. *1963*
10cm (4in) long

£115–180   **ROX**

Rhodium-plated flower pin by Kramer for Dior with pavé-set rhinestones and a large clear rhinestone in the centre. *1960s*
3.75cm (1½in) long

£140–160   **FM**

Stylized fruit pin with faux sapphires, rubies, diamonds, and pearls. *1962*
6.25cm (2½in) long

£250–300   **RG**

Good, Better, Best

Dior necklaces were designed in numerous styles that were fashionable after World War II. While desirability is a matter of personal aesthetics, price is largely determined by sophistications of craftsmanship and extravagance of materials and design.

£350–400

This late 1950s **interlinked hoop necklace** is of gilt-finish metal set with topaz rhinestones. Its desirability resides in the simplicity and clarity of the design. If sold with matching bracelet and earrings it would be worth £550–650. 37cm (14½in) circ **FM**

£600–700

This 1970 **gold-plated necklace** with paste cabochons and faux pearls commands a high price owing to its exotic design and intricacies of craftsmanship. *56cm (22in) circ* **WAIN**

£1,300–1,400

This 1963 **gilt-metal pendant** with jonquil pastes, enamel cabochons, faux pearls, and clear rhinestones is the most expensive piece because it encapsulates the essential characteristics of Dior: unashamed opulence and style. 37cm (14½in) circ **FM**

Necklace and earrings
of rhodium-plated metal
with prong-set faux moonstones,
ruby pastes, and clear rhinestones. *1959*

N: 35.5cm (14in) circ; E: 3cm (1⅛in) long

£900–1,000 FM

Necklace and earrings in
rhodium-plated metal with large
emerald green pastes and clear
rhinestone clusters. *1967*

N: 35.5cm (14in) circ;
E: 3cm (1⅛in) long

£300–350 RG

Floral necklace and earrings of
rhodium-plated metal with faux
pearls, iridescent topaz, and
haematite paste stones. *1959*

35.5cm (14in) circ

£1,500–2,000 WAIN

Stylized floral necklace
with textured gilt squares
and triangles, and
black and fluorescent
blue pastes. *c.1966*

43cm (17in) circ

£900–1,000 FM

Necklace and earrings
by Mitchell Maer, rhodium-
plated with rhinestones and
green cabochons. *Mid 1950s*

N: 38cm (15in) circ;
E: 3.75cm (1½in) long

£350–420 RG

KRAMER

Together with Mitchell Maer and
Henkel and Grosse, the best-known
manufacturer of Dior's jewellery
designs is Kramer of New York, which
as well as producing under its own
brand (*see p.178*), made numerous
pieces for Dior in the 1950s and
60s. These are marked "Christian
Dior by Kramer".

Sapphire blue earrings with round black
and round and navette-cut blue pastes.
1959

3.75cm (1½in) long

£75–90 PC

Pin and earrings by Kramer, rhodium-
plated with blue glass and clear
rhinestones. *Late 1950s. P: 5cm (2in) long;*
E: 3.75cm (1½in) long **£420–480 CRIS**

Gilt bow earrings with prong-set round
and navette ruby red and emerald green
rhinestones. *1959*

3.75cm (1½in) long

£45–60 PC

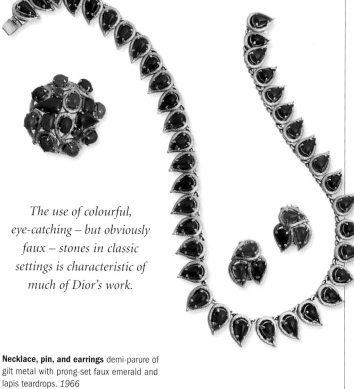

The use of colourful,
eye-catching – but obviously
faux – stones in classic
settings is characteristic of
much of Dior's work.

Necklace, pin, and earrings demi-parure of
gilt metal with prong-set faux emerald and
lapis teardrops. *1966*

N: 43cm (17in) circ; P: 4.5cm (1¾in) wide; E: 2.5cm (1in) long

£300–350 RG

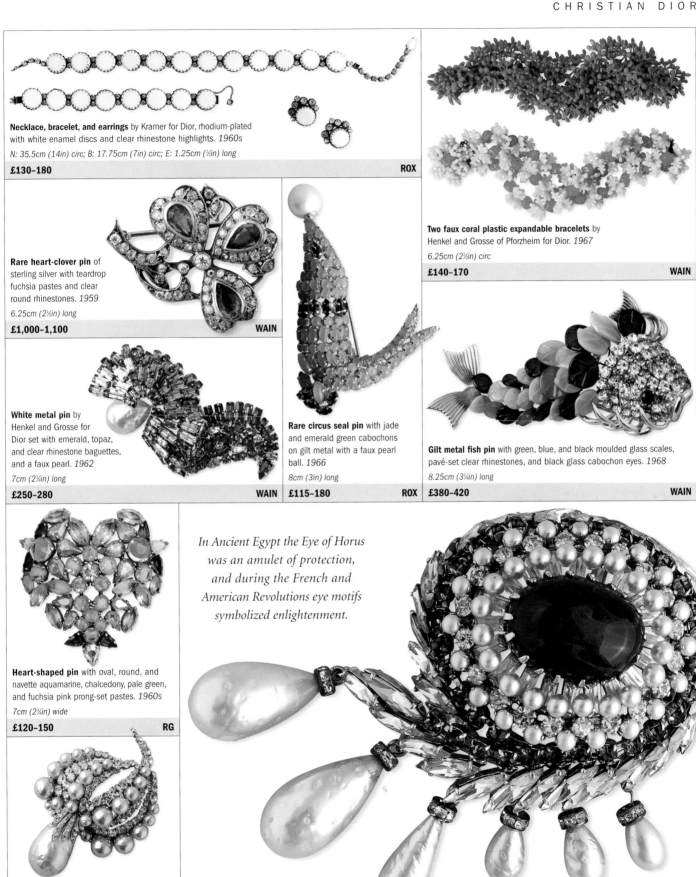

Necklace, bracelet, and earrings by Kramer for Dior, rhodium-plated with white enamel discs and clear rhinestone highlights. *1960s*

N: 35.5cm (14in) circ; B: 17.75cm (7in) circ; E: 1.25cm (½in) long

£130–180 ROX

Two faux coral plastic expandable bracelets by Henkel and Grosse of Pforzheim for Dior. *1967*

6.25cm (2½in) circ

£140–170 WAIN

Rare heart-clover pin of sterling silver with teardrop fuchsia pastes and clear round rhinestones. *1959*

6.25cm (2½in) long

£1,000–1,100 WAIN

White metal pin by Henkel and Grosse for Dior set with emerald, topaz, and clear rhinestone baguettes, and a faux pearl. *1962*

7cm (2¾in) long

£250–280 WAIN

Rare circus seal pin with jade and emerald green cabochons on gilt metal with a faux pearl ball. *1966*

8cm (3in) long

£115–180 ROX

Gilt metal fish pin with green, blue, and black moulded glass scales, pavé-set clear rhinestones, and black glass cabochon eyes. *1968*

8.25cm (3¼in) long

£380–420 WAIN

Heart-shaped pin with oval, round, and navette aquamarine, chalcedony, pale green, and fuchsia pink prong-set pastes. *1960s*

7cm (2¾in) wide

£120–150 RG

In Ancient Egypt the Eye of Horus was an amulet of protection, and during the French and American Revolutions eye motifs symbolized enlightenment.

White metal pin by Henkel and Grosse for Dior with faux pearls and clear rhinestones. *1960*

7.5cm (3in) long

£330–380 WAIN

"Eye"pin, rhodium-plated with a sapphire blue cabochon, rings of faux pearls, blue and clear rhinestones, and six faux pearl drops. *Late 1950s*

6cm (2⅜in) wide

£220–240 CRIS

COPPOLA E TOPPO
late 1940s–1986

Late 1940s Bruno Coppola and his sister Lyda Toppo found Coppola e Toppo in Milan. Its early pieces are marked with the name of their pet dog "Mikey"

1950s In addition to producing its own designs, marked "Made in Italy by Coppola e Toppo", it also produces jewellery for Dior, Balenciaga, and Schiaparelli

1960s The company's own designs, especially its beaded necklaces and bracelets, become increasingly sought after. Coppola e Toppo is also commissioned to produce ranges for leading Italian designers Pucci and Valentino

1972 It is absorbed by a large Italian company, which continues production of Coppola e Toppo jewellery

1986 Production ceases

Coppola e Toppo

Much of the work Coppola e Toppo did for Italian and French fashion houses may be consigned to anonymity, but the sumptuous compositions it produced in its own name brought much-deserved recognition and acclaim.

FROM BEHIND THE SCENES

Brother and sister jewellery designers Bruno Coppola and Lyda Toppo formed the Coppola e Toppo company in the late 1940s in Milan, Italy. Impressed with samples of its work, the Parisian-based fashion houses of Dior and Balenciaga utilized Coppola e Toppo's design talents behind the scenes for a number of catwalk and retail line pieces – an important, albeit sporadic arrangement it maintained for the next ten years. In contrast, the 1950s' commission it received from Elsa Schiaparelli (*see pp.108–111*) to make a line of faux coral bead jewellery, entitled "Bijoux Voyages", proved both lucrative and high profile. Further commissions from Italian couturiers such as Pucci and Valentino (*see opposite*), enabled Coppola e Toppo to substantially increase the number of pieces released under its own trademark "Made in Italy by Coppola e Toppo".

EXTRAVAGANCE AND INNOVATION

Part of the explanation for Coppola e Toppo's rise to prominence from the late 1950s to the early 70s lies in the fact that this period saw the epicentre of fashion switch from Paris to Milan, Coppola e Toppo's base. However, its success was ultimately guaranteed by its innovative multiple strands of crystal, Murano glass, and plastic beads (*see below*). This "swinging sixties" style suddenly made diamanté and faux pearl jewellery seem decidedly "old hat". Numerous collectors, prepared to pay increasingly high prices for Coppola e Toppo's pieces, would still agree.

Above: Multiple strand necklace with gilt metal clasps, baroque pearls, and clear glass beads. *1950s 35cm (13¾in) circ* **£1,600–1,800 FM**

BEAUTIFUL BEADS

Although Coppola e Toppo produced many pieces incorporating materials such as gilt metal, silver, faux pearls, and crystal rhinestones, these were usually used as accents or highlights within extravagant compositions dominated by colourful beads. Whether Venetian glass, Austrian crystal, or plastic, beads were combined by Coppola e Toppo in striking combinations that captured all the glamour and spirit of late 1950s and 60s Italian *Dolce Vita*.

Stylized floral motif necklace with dark blue, pale green, and turquoise glass beads. *Early 1960s 72.5cm (28½in) circ* **£1,400–1,500 FM**

Multiple-strand necklace with pink and cranberry red plastic beads, and a gilt metal clasp embellished with glass beads. *1960s 7.5cm (3in) circ* **£700–800 SUM**

Multiple-strand necklace with red glass beads, finished with gilt metal and red bead clasps. *1960s*

66cm (26in) circ

£535–665   **ROX**

Four-strand necklace of lava stone beads, and ornaments of gilt metal, beads, and faux pearls. *1960s*

49.5cm (19½in) circ

£700–800   **FM**

VALENTINO

Coppola e Toppo received numerous commissions from eminent fashion houses (*see opposite*), but some of the most prestigious were from the Italian couturier Valentino. The stunning gilt metal and sapphire blue and clear diamanté pendant necklace shown here was designed for a Valentino line in 1970. At this time Valentino was generally recognized as the "King of Fashion" with a celebrity client list that included Jacqueline Kennedy and Hollywood stars such as Elizabeth Taylor.

Pendant necklace and earrings, designed for Valentino, with blue and clear Swarovski crystals set in gilt metal. *1970. N: 33cm (13in) circ; E: 2.5cm (1in) wide* **£1,800–2,000 WAIN**

Bow motif necklace with five strands of turquoise, mauve, and black glass beads, with matching earrings. *1960s*

N: 33cm (13in) circ; Pd: 3.75cm (1½in) wide; E: 2.5cm (1in) wide

£1,300–1,400   **FM**

Multiple-strand necklace of faux pearls and clear glass beads, and beaded gilt metal clasps. *1950s*

5.75cm (2¼in) wide

£250–380   **ROX**

Beaded choker with blue, red, amber, and clear Bohemian crystal beads and beaded clasps. *1950s*

5cm (2in) wide

£450–500   **WAIN**

Four-strand necklace of black and clear plastic beads, and a black-beaded oval clasp. *1960s*

49.5cm (19½in) circ

£500–600   **FM**

Multiple-strand necklace of amber, topaz, and citrine coloured crystal beads. *1960s*

6.25cm (2½in) wide

£750–850   **SUM**

Gilt metal clasp necklace with strands and pendants of clear crystal, and citrine and green plastic stones. *1960s*

6.25cm (2½in) wide

£400–500   **SUM**

Coro and Corocraft

At the height of production in the 1930s and 40s, the Coro company employed nearly 3,500 staff. A prolific output meant that they covered most styles and price points, from 50-cent pieces sold at "five and dime stores" to jewellery worth hundreds of dollars.

PRODIGIOUS OUTPUT

Although not officially incorporated as Coro Inc. until 1943, Coro effectively came into existence as Cohn and Rosenberger in 1901. Founded by businessmen Emanuel Cohn and Carl Rosenberger as an accessories boutique in New York City, it outsourced much of its costume jewellery from independent designers and makers until 1929, when it opened a large factory in Providence, Rhode Island. Thereafter, under the design and sales directorships of, respectively, Adolph Katz (*see below*) and Royal Marcher, the company expanded rapidly. By the mid 1930s, with retail stores in most American cities and manufacturing plants established in Britain and Canada, it was well

on the way to becoming the largest costume jewellery manufacturer in the world.

Cohn and Rosenberger's, and subsequently Coro's, commercial success can be attributed to various factors. Not least was its employment of highly talented designers such as Katz, Gene Verecchio, Robert Geissman, Massa Raimond, François, Oscar Placco, and Albert Weiss (*see pp.132–133*). Underpinning it all, however, was the sheer volume and diversity of its output, which catered for most income brackets using a number of brands of different quality and varying price.

Above: Corocraft bunch of grapes pin with prong-set faux moonstone, and chalcedony glass stones, and sterling silver leaves. *1940s. 7.5cm (3in) long* **£180–220 CRIS**

ADOLPH KATZ

Appointed Coro Design Director in 1924, Adolph Katz made an enormous contribution to the success of the company. In addition to selecting designs, he also created numerous pieces and mechanisms himself. He is most admired for his exquisite *en tremblant* floral pins and Coro Duettes. Equally sought after, however, are his diverse static figurals, such as Jelly Bellies and animal subjects, and various other whimsical designs.

Corocraft fish pin designed by Adolph Katz. The head, tail, and fins in sterling silver with enamelling, crystal rhinestones, and cabochons; the "belly" is of semi-translucent white Lucite. *1940s. 7cm (2¾in) long* **£275–300 RG**

Coro horse's head pin and earrings of gold-tone metal with aquamarine rhinestone eyes, pink rhinestone ears, red enamelled flowers, and green enamelled leaves. *c.1960. P: 5cm (2in) long; E: 2.5cm (1in) long* **£130–150 ABIJ**

MARKS OF QUALITY

For the most part, pieces marked "Coro" are of good quality and were originally targeted at he middle and lower sections of the market. Nearly all fashionable styles were covered, employing imagery ranging from patriotic motifs, to floral and foliate, to figural. Its double-pin Coro Duettes are much sought after and have become a collecting field in their own right (*see pp.186–187*). Of their upmarket brands, Coro Craft is the best known. It embraces equally diverse subjects, but the pieces are made in more expensive materials, such as sterling silver and European crystal rhinestones. (Its equally impressive Vendome line became a subsidiary company in 1953 [*see pp.130–131*]).

Sometimes innovative, sometimes commercial imitations of other companies' popular designs, Coro and Corocraft pieces appeal to as broad a spectrum of collectors today as they did to their original consumers.

Coro floral bracelet and earrings with white plastic petals and gold-tone metal centres with pale green and blue and clear crystal rhinestones. *Mid 1950s. B: 15.25cm (6in) circ; E: 3.75cm (1½in) wide* **£30–40 MILLB**

Coro's "Diadem Jewels", promoted by a 1947 magazine advertisement, which bore their top-line "Coro Craft with Pegasus" branding. The sense of refined luxury is typical of Coro designs and advertising in the immediate aftermath of World War II.

Good, Better, Best

Materials used and current appreciation of particular styles ultimately determines the price of these Coro pins.

£15–20

Made in the late 1950s, this inexpensive **starburst pin** is a simple but well-defined radiating design made from brightly polished, lightweight gold-tone metal with a centre of clear and ruby rhinestones. *5.75cm (2¼in) wide* **MILLB**

£20–25

This is a late 1950s **Space Age motif pin**. It commands a slightly higher price than the starburst pin because the body of the pin, which radiates out from a pearlescent metallic cabochon, is cast from a heavier white metal with a more sophisticated finish. *5.75cm (2¼in) wide* **MILLB**

£35–50

Made in about 1950, this **floral pin** is a more traditional motif than the other examples (*see left and above*), which makes it more appealing to a broad range of collectors. However, its higher price is also influenced by the fact that it is cast from vermeil sterling silver, which lends it both physical substance and a pleasing antique gold-tone finish. It is also enhanced by the incorporation of good-quality, clear crystal rhinestones of Austrian or Czechoslovakian origin. *5cm (2in) wide* **MILLB**

Corocraft floral pin in vermeil sterling silver with pavé-set clear crystal rhinestones. *1940s*

7cm (2¾in) long

£200–250 RG

Coro Victorian-style love token pin of gold-tone metal casting in the form of a hand proffering a rose. *1950s*

6.25cm (2½in) long

£30–40 JJ

Badge and shield pin with matching earrings in gold-tone metal; the shields with white and red enamelling. *1940s*

P: 5cm (2in) wide; E: 2.5cm (1in) long

£30–40 ABIJ

Coro floral motif necklace and earrings of gold-tone metal with faux coral beads, clear crystal rhinestones, and white enamelling on some of the leaves. *1950s*

N: 40.5cm (16in) circ; E: 2.5cm (1in) wide

£50–65 MILLB

Many of the pieces in Coro's upmarket Corocraft line were produced in high-quality sterling and vermeil sterling silver.

Corocraft pin of scrolling forms and stylized floral motif in vermeil sterling silver set with ruby red glass cabochons and round-cut clear crystal rhinestones. *Mid 1940s*

8.25cm (3¼in) wide

£120–150 CRIS

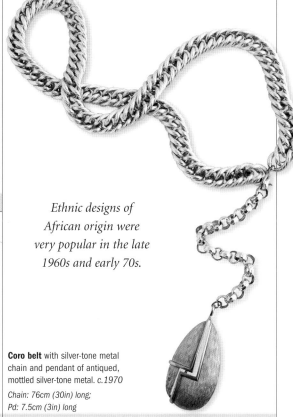

Corocraft bracelet of gold-plated metal with ruby and emerald crystal cabochons, pavé-set clear crystal rhinestones, and green enamelled leaves. *1940s*

7.5cm (3in) wide

£250–300   **CRIS**

Corocraft rose pin in sterling and vermeil sterling silver with clear crystal rhinestone highlights. *1940s*

6.25cm (2½in) long

£200–250   **RG**

COLOURED LUCITE

Together with many other costume jewellery manufacturers, Coro enthusiastically adopted the "plastic" Lucite after it was developed by the Du Pont company in 1937. Like Trifari (*see pp.118–129*), Coro employed Lucite primarily in its translucent white form for its Jelly Belly figural pins. However, available in varying degrees of opacity and a wide range of colours, it also proved a very effective substitute for various rock-forming minerals, such as moonstone and chalcedony, often used in precious jewellery.

Coro basket of fruits pin of white metal with clear crystal rhinestones and pale blue and moonglow Lucite cabochons. *c.1940.* 2.5cm (1in) long   **£30–35 JJ**

Coro bracelet with silver-tone metal links and leaves and jonquil-coloured crystal rhinestones. *1950s*

17.75cm (7in) long

£25–30   **MILLB**

Coro floral motif earrings of antiqued goldwash metal with faux baroque pearls and red crystal rhinestones. *1950s*

3.25cm (1¼in) long

£30–35   **MILLB**

Coro Native American chief earrings in pewter-tone white metal castings.
c.1960

2.5cm (1in) long

£30–35   **MILLB**

Coro floral motif earrings in gold-tone metal with pink, aquamarine, and citrine crystal navettes.
c.1945

2.5cm (1in) long

£15–25   **MILLB**

Coro floral earrings with pale pink plastic petals and *aurora borealis* crystal rhinestone centres. *c.1955*

6.25cm (2½in) long

£15–25   **MILLB**

Coro châtelaine pin with a pair of ballerinas of gold-tone metal castings linked by a a twin-strand gilt metal chain. *Late 1940s*

Ballerinas: 6.25cm (2½in) long; Chains: 15.25cm (6in) long

£75–85   **JJ**

Ethnic designs of African origin were very popular in the late 1960s and early 70s.

Coro belt with silver-tone metal chain and pendant of antiqued, mottled silver-tone metal. *c.1970*

Chain: 76cm (30in) long;
Pd: 7.5cm (3in) long

£20–30   **MILLB**

FAHRNER
1855–1979

1855 Georg Seeger and Theodor Fahrner, Sr. open a jewellery factory in Pforzheim, Germany

c.1883 Theodor Fahrner, Jr. takes over the running of the company

1900 Fahrner jewellery wins silver medal at Paris World's Fair

1901 The "TF" trademark is introduced and Fahrner begins exporting to Britain via Murrle Bennet & Co.

1910 Introduction of the "Fahrner Schmuck" trademark

1919 Theodor Fahrner, Jr. dies. The company is sold to Gustav Braendle and becomes Gustav Braendle-Theodor Fahrner Nachf

1979 Production ceases

Fahrner

A spectacularly successful blend of art and industry, Fahrner's exquisite, and often semi-precious, Art Nouveau and Art Deco jewellery commands understandably high prices – provided it bears the company stamp.

ARTISTIC DESIGNS

Founded in Pforzheim, Germany, in 1855, and run by Theodor Fahrner, Jr. from about 1883 onwards, the Fahrner company was one of the most successful European jewellery manufacturers of the late 19th and early 20th centuries. Sold in 1919 to Gustav Braendle and renamed Gustave Braendle–Theodor Fahrner Nachf, the company continued to thrive well into the 1950s and remained in production until 1979.

Prior to the mid 1920s Fahrner was known for its Art Nouveau, Arts and Crafts, and Celtic Revival jewellery. Designed by eminent German artists and industrially produced in limited runs, many pieces were exported via other companies, such as Murrle Bennet & Co. in England. Subsequently, Fahrner

was acclaimed for its striking geometric designs, which encapsulated the spirit of the Jazz Age and Art Deco movement.

MATERIALS AND MARKS

While Fahrner believed that the true worth of any piece lay in its artistic merits, rather than the value of the materials used, the company often incorporated semi-precious stones and pearls into its designs. Understandably this is reflected in the high prices Fahrner jewellery now commands. However, the absence of a Fahrner stamp detracts by anything up to 75 per cent from the value of a marked equivalent.

Above: Art Deco pin in silver and marcasite with black onyx and coral cabochons. *c.1929. 8.25cm (3¼in) long* **£1,660–2,000 TR**

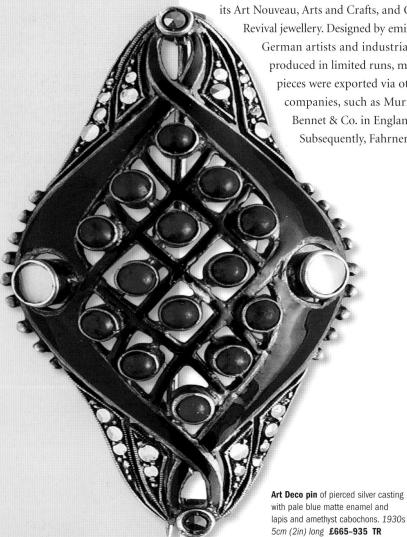

Art Deco pin of pierced silver casting with pale blue matte enamel and lapis and amethyst cabochons. *1930s 5cm (2in) long* **£665–935 TR**

Fahrner Schmuck 1929 advertisement in *Die Dame* for a range of jewellery by Gustav Braendle-Theodor Fahrner Nachf. The "Fahrner Schmuck" trademark was registered in May 1910.

Art Deco pin of gilded silver with an amazonite bar and two faceted blue glass triangles. *1927*

5.5cm (2⅛in) wide

£865–1,200   **TR**

Floral motif pin in silver and matte rock crystal with turquoise cabochons. *Late 1920s*

3.75cm (1½in) long

£1,000–1,225   **TR**

Art Deco gilt metal pendant with turquoise matte enamel and cabochons and a large pink quartz stone. *1930s*

5cm (2in) long

£1,465–1,800   **TR**

Pendant earrings in silver, marcasite, onyx, and coral. *Late 1920s*

5cm (2in) long

£1,335–1,665   **TR**

Pierced ivory pin in silver with blue enamel, pearls, and an emerald glass cabochon. *Late 1920s*

5.75cm (2¼in) long

£465–535   **TR**

Floral motif bar pin in silver with matte black enamel and an aventurine quartz cabochon. *c.1925*

7cm (2¾in) long

£500–550   **RBRG**

Art Deco pin in silver, marcasite, black matte enamel, and haematite. *Late 1920s*

4.5cm (1¾in) long

£2,335–3,000   **TR**

Art Deco pin in silver and marcasite with amazonite bars, blue glass cabochons, and a pink quartz stone. *Late 1920s*

4.5cm (1¾in) long

£735–935   **TR**

Necklace and bracelet in gold-plated metal with turquoise cabochons. *1930s*

N: 35.5cm (14in) long; B: 20.5cm (8in) long

£2,335–3,000   **TR**

Silver and marcasite pendant with green enamel and a green glass cabochon. *1920s*

5cm (2in) long

£300–335   **TR**

Stylized leaf pin in silver and marcasite with a single pearl highlight. *1920s*

4.5cm (1¾in) long

£280–320   **RBRG**

Hattie Carnegie

For almost half a century, petite Austrian-born Hattie Carnegie strode the world of American fashion like a colossus. Innovative and invariably high-quality, her costume jewellery still commands serious attention.

HATTIE CARNEGIE
1886–1956

1886 Born Henrietta Kanengesier in Vienna, Austria

c.1904 Emigrates to the United States and works as milliner's assistant and messenger at Macy's, New York

1909 Having changed her name to Hattie Carnegie, opens her first shop – Carnegie-Ladies Hatter – in partnership with seamstress Rose Booth

1918 Founds Hattie Carnegie Inc., launches first full-scale collection, and starts manufacturing high-quality costume jewellery to complement her clothing

1928 Launches Hattie Carnegie Originals ready-to-wear line and over ensuing years substantially expands retail outlets across the United States

1934 Establishes Spectator Sports to wholesale less expensive lines

1956 Hattie Carnegie dies but production of clothing and jewellery continues

1976 Hattie Carnegie Inc. is acquired by the Chromology American Corp.

ENTREPRENEURIAL SPIRIT

In 1904, aged 18, Henrietta Kanengesier emigrated to the United States from Vienna. On the ship bound for New York she purportedly asked the name of America's richest man. Her subsequent adoption of the entrepreneurial Andrew Carnegie's surname proved appropriate. From a single shop opened in 1909, Hattie Carnegie went on to found a chain of exclusive fashion boutiques across the United States. At the time of her death in 1956, the sheer size of her empire reflected not only her commercial success, but also the enormous impact she had made on American

fashions. A uniquely American reinterpretation of French *couture*, Carnegie's style was epitomized by her trademark: the "little Carnegie suit". Her jewellery, produced from 1918 onwards, attracted an elite clientele, including Tallulah Bankhead, Joan Fontaine, Norma Shearer, and Joan Crawford.

DISTINCTIVE DESIGNS

Commissioned from many designers, Carnegie jewellery was made in numerous styles. Flowers, leaves, and fruit are recurring motifs, while more unique imagery is employed in her oriental figure and stylized animal pins (*see opposite*). Favoured materials include enamel, faux pearls, rhinestones, and glass beads – often in unusual combinations. Marked "Hattie Carnegie", "Carnegie", or "HC", these fine-quality pieces are as eagerly sought-after today as when they first appeared.

Above: Mask pin of gold-plated casting with faux pearl, turquoise, coral, and diamond highlights. *1950s* 6.5cm (2½in) long **£200–250 CRIS**

Flower pin of gold-tone metal with clear crystal rhinestones. *1950s* 10cm (4in) long **£100–150 CRIS**

Carnegie silk brocade dress accessorized at the ribcage with a large Carnegie pear pin studded with rhinestones. Photograph from a 1961 issue of *Vogue*.

Merman pin with iridescent white enamelling, faux pearl drops, and faux ruby, sapphire, and gilt metal highlights. *Mid 1950s*

11cm (4⅜in) long

£250–315   **ROX**

Lion head pin with iridescent white enamelling, faux pearl drops, and banded faux ruby, emerald, sapphire, and gilt metal highlights. *Late 1950s*

10cm (4in) long

£180–250   **ROX**

Pendant leaf motif necklace and earrings of gold-washed metal with faux pearl highlights. *1960s*

N: 43cm (17in) circ; E: 4cm (1½in) long

£130–135   **JJ**

Three-strand necklace of polychrome Murano glass and Austrian crystal beads. *c.1960*

40.5cm (16in) circ

£90–105   **ABIJ**

Antiqued gold-plated earrings with aquamarine glass cabochons encircling dark faux sapphire glass centres. *1950s*

2.5cm (1in) wide

£30–35   **MILLB**

STYLIZED ANIMAL PINS

Of all Carnegie's figural pins, the most instantly recognizable are the stylized animal subjects. Mostly of African inspiration, they are made of vibrantly coloured Lucite, and include sparkling clear rhinestones, coloured beads, and gilt highlights. Diverse species include fish, goats, and – the most sought after of all – anteaters.

Fish pin of black, green, and yellow Lucite, with gilt metal and clear rhinestone highlights. *1950s*

5cm (2in) long

£150–170   **CRIS**

Stylized African anteater pin of turquoise and orange-red Lucite with gilt metal and clear rhinestones. *1950s*

8.5cm (3⅜in) long   **£200–220 CRIS**

Pansy pin with large "cabochon" centre, of base metal coated with metallic-yellow cold enamel. *1970s*

5cm (2in) wide

£40–50   **ABIJ**

Stylized goat head pin of orange-red and green Lucite with lapis glass beads and clear rhinestones. *1950s*

9.5cm (3¾in) long

CRIS

£150–180   **CRIS**

HOBÉ
1887–present

1887 The original Hobé Cie is founded in Paris by master goldsmith Jacques Hobé

Early 1920s One of Jacques's three sons, William Hobé, begins selling theatrical costume in the USA

Mid 1920s Florence Ziegfeld commissions William Hobé to create costumes and jewellery for his *Ziegfeld Follies* productions on Broadway

c.1927 William Hobé founds the American Hobé Cie jewellery company

1930s Hobé begins selling its retail lines through up-market stores

1950s Hobé designs pieces for many Hollywood stars, including Bette Davis and Ava Gardner

1960s William Hobé's sons Robert and Donald take over the running of the company

1980s William Hobé's grandson James continues production

Hobé

Worn on stage and screen, promoted by Hollywood stars, and sold through up-market retail outlets, Hobé's high-quality pieces lived up to its advertising slogan: "Jewels of Legendary Splendour".

PARISIAN ORIGINS

A son of master goldsmith Jacques Hobé, who had established Hobé Cie in Paris in the late 19th century, William Hobé set up the American Hobé Cie in about 1927 in New York.

Essentially launched on a prestigious commission to produce both costumes and jewellery for the *Ziegfeld Follies* (*see below*), Hobé Cie rapidly expanded to become, together with Joseff of Hollywood (*see pp.78–83*), the major supplier of pieces for theatre and film during the 1940s and 50s. This high-profile work, enhanced by postwar advertising campaigns with leading Hollywood actresses and top models, ensured an enthusiastic reception from the public for Hobé's retail lines.

TOP QUALITY

Always relatively expensive, Hobé jewellery was only sold by leading department stores and exclusive boutiques. Apart from the jewellery designed by Lou Vici, who worked for the company from the 1930s to the 70s, all Hobé pieces were designed by members of the Hobé family. They invariably display the same techniques and high standards of craftsmanship found in precious jewellery. The materials – vermeil, platinum, high-quality pastes, and sometimes semi-precious stones – are equally impressive. Of numerous exotic designs, which include reproductions of historical pieces owned by European royalty, Hobé's floral pins (*see opposite*) are among the most sought after.

Above: Hinged bracelet of gilt metal with crystal rhinestones and faux amethyst pastes. *1970s. 6.5cm (2½in) wide* **£115–120 MAC**

Roses and heart locket pin in sterling and vermeil sterling silver with metallic faux pearls and white metal tassels. *1940s* *14cm (5½in) long* **£335–400 BY**

ZIEGFELD FOLLIES

Hobé's first major commission in the USA came in the mid 1920s from the legendary impresario Florence Ziegfeld. In accepting an offer by William Hobé to provide costumes for his spectacular *Ziegfeld Follies* Broadway productions, Florence also asked Hobé to create inexpensive but realistic looking jewellery to complement the outfits. This successful commission had the effect of substantially enhancing Hobé's profile and similar orders from other theatre companies and Hollywood film studios soon followed.

Miss Angel Forbes of the *Ziegfeld Follies* wearing stylized Native American jewellery and costume.

Bib necklace, bracelet, pin, and earrings parure in gilt metal with strings of faceted faux topaz and red *aurora borealis* beads with overlaid spherical blue and pink Venetian glass beads. *c.1960*

N and P: 6.5cm (2½in) long; B: 16.5cm (6½in) circ; E: 3.75cm (1½in) wide

£300–335 **BY**

Heart-shaped pin and earrings of filigree gilt metal with clear crystal rhinestones and large, faceted faux sapphire pastes. *1950s*

P: 4cm (1½in) long; E: 3cm (1¼in) long

£95–120 **MG**

Antiqued gilt metal earrings with pink and white faux pearls and moulded green glass. *1950s*

4.5cm (1¾in) long

£65–100 **LB**

Floral bow pin in sterling silver with peridot, rose quartz, jonquil, and amethyst crystal rhinestones. *1940s*

10cm (4in) wide

£200–220 **CRIS**

Bracelet and pin with flower, fruit, and bow motifs in vermeil and antiqued vermeil sterling silver. *1940s*

B: 17.75cm (7in) circ; P: 6.5cm (2½in) wide

£100–135 **BY**

Silver-tone metal earrings with dark and light blue paste cabochons and clear rhinestones. *1960s*

2.5cm (1in) wide

£20–25 **TR**

Heart pin in vermeil sterling silver with a large square-cut faux amethyst centre. *1940s*

6.5cm (2½in) long

£250–280 **CRIS**

Unsigned necklace and earrings with rose motifs and bow in vermeil sterling silver, metallic faux pearls, and a white-on-red carved cameo. *1940s*

N: 40cm (15½in) circ; Cameo: 4.5cm (1¾in) long; E: 3.75cm (1½in) wide

£335–400 **BY**

FLORAL PINS

Hobé is best-known for the exquisite floral pins it produced in the 1940s. Made in antiqued sterling or vermeil sterling silver with pastes or semi-precious stones, the pins are either in the form of floral sprays set in baskets or, as here, bouquets of stemmed blooms entwined with ribbons and bows.

Rose bouquet pin in vermeil sterling silver with crystal rhinestones. *1940s. 15.5cm (6in) wide* **£600–700 CRIS**

Joseff of Hollywood

EUGENE JOSEFF
1905–48

1905 Born in Chicago

1923–26 Works as a graphic artist in Chicago advertising agency. Designs jewellery in his spare time

1927 Moves to Los Angeles to escape the Great Depression. Starts training as a jewellery designer

1931–35 Some of his early pieces used in Hollywood films

1935 Opens Sunset Jewelry in Hollywood and founds "Joseff of Hollywood"

1937 Now a leading supplier of costume jewellery to Hollywood film studios, he develops his retail line for sale to the public

1948 Tragically killed in a plane crash

1950s onwards Joseff of Hollywood run by his widow, Joan Castle

In 1934 Eugene Joseff criticized the use of historically incorrect jewellery in Hollywood films. Premier costume designer Walter Plunkett responded: "Well, if you're so smart let's see what you can do!"

FOUNDATIONS OF SUCCESS

Of Austrian heritage, Eugene Joseff was born in Chicago in 1905. Following a spell in advertising he moved to California in the late 1920s to pursue a passion for jewellery design in one of the few growth industries of the Great Depression: Hollywood. Rapid elevation to leading designer and supplier of costume jewellery to the major studios – which endured beyond his death in 1948 through to the 1960s – was fuelled by Joseff's artistic creativity and commercial acumen.

In addition to developing a camera-friendly substitute for gold (*see opposite*), Joseff had the ability to accurately research and simplify specific historical styles of jewellery that immediately conveyed the appropriate period ambience on the "Silver Screen". Together with his wife, Joan Castle, he also adopted a policy of leasing, rather than selling, pieces to the studios for a specific film, and thereby accumulated an archive of nearly three million pieces available for rehire. In addition, from 1937 they developed a massively successful line of jewellery for retail to the star-struck public, much of which was copied from, or inspired by, pieces originally designed for the cinema. It is these latter pieces that are the most readily found today.

STAR PROVENANCE

Joseff's jewellery is never nondescript – it always makes a strong visual statement. However, its popularity is most certainly linked to its Hollywood connections. The vast list of films for which Joseff designs were commissioned includes: *A Star is Born* (1936); *The Wizard of Oz* and *Gone With The Wind* (both 1939); *Casablanca* (1942); *Easter Parade* (1949); *Singing in the Rain* (1952); *To Catch a Thief* (1955); *Ben*

> *"If you want to start a collection, start with a brooch because you will find most use for it. It can be pinned on a suit lapel, collar, or pocket, on a hat, belt, or evening gown."*
> *Eugene Joseff*

Above: Bee pin, Russian gold plated. *1940s*
4cm (1½in) wide **£40–50 CRIS**

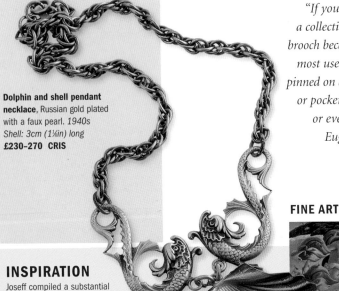

Dolphin and shell pendant necklace, Russian gold plated with a faux pearl. *1940s*
Shell: 3cm (1⅛in) long
£230–270 CRIS

FINE ART

Joseff studied fine art for authentic period motifs. Seashells, as in Botticelli's *The Birth of Venus* (c.1485), recur in classical mythology and feature in some of the jewellery he designed for Roman and Biblical epics.

INSPIRATION

Joseff compiled a substantial collection of rare antiquarian books on costume and jewellery, which provided inspiration and reference for many of his historically authentic designs.

ALL THAT GLITTERS IS NOT GOLD

Joseff's status as Hollywood's leading supplier of costume jewellery was partly founded on his development of a visually effective substitute for gold. Known as Russian gold plating, its semi-matte, copper-gold finish minimized the traditional problem of flare from over-reflective jewellery when filming real gold, or other gold substitutes, under powerful studio lights. It proved a popular material aesthetically, too, and many of Joseff's retail line pieces were also created from this new metal.

Semi-matte Russian gold plating

Crescent moon and cherub pin, Russian gold plated with faux pearl drops. From Joseff's retail line, modelled on a a pin and earrings worn by the actress Virginia Mayo. *1940s. 4cm (1½in) long* **£70–100 CRIS**

Sun god pin, one of Joseff's most distinctive pieces, is of Russian gold and has clear rhinestone eye tremblers. It is also shown being modelled by the Hollywood actress Pier Angeli. *1940s. 7.5cm (3in) wide* **£240–280 CRIS**

Hur (1959); *Breakfast at Tiffany's* (1961); *Cleopatra* (1963); and *My Fair Lady* (1964). The list of stars who wore the jewellery is equally impressive, ranging from Greta Garbo, Vivian Leigh, and Grace Kelly, to Clark Gable, Errol Flynn, and Tony Curtis.

Typical objects include pins, bracelets, buckles, necklaces, pendants, and earrings – sometimes produced in parures or demi-parures. Diverse styles include Art Nouveau, Art Deco, 1940s retro, oriental, and Middle-Eastern, as well as astrological, and animal, fish, bird, and insect imagery.

Decoratively, Russian gold pieces are either plain or embellished with faux pearls and clear or coloured crystal – the latter hand cut, rather than pressed, on the best pieces. There are also a number of black, ivory, or red Bakelite examples.

IDENTIFICATION AND CONDITION

Identification is quite straightforward as most pieces are stamped "Joseff" or "Joseff of Hollywood" – exceptions being one-offs made for celebrity clients. However, collectors should note that some of the pieces made in the late 1930s and 40s have been reissued by the Joseff company in recent years to meet increased demand. Recent examples are still very collectable but you can expect to pay slightly less than you would for an original piece. Bear in mind that much of the attraction of Russian gold jewellery lies in its subtle, semi-matte finish, which acquires a darker, more mellow patina over time. Be wary, therefore, of overly bright examples – usually the result of abrasive polishing, which renders them almost worthless.

Bow motif châtelaine pin of solid and pierced Russian gold, with prong-set rhinestones. *1940s. 7cm (2¾in) long* **£150–180 CRIS**

EGYPT

Inspiration for the Joseff jewellery worn by Elizabeth Taylor in *Cleopatra* (1963), included pieces found in Tutankhamen's tomb in 1922. These Russian gold coiled snake earrings incorporate red glass cabochons. *1940-65 8.5cm (3⅜in) long* **£180–220 CRIS**

ROMANCE

Star motifs featured in the Joseff jewellery worn by Norma Shearer in *Marie Antoinette* (1938). Later they were a hit in Joseff's retail line. These Russian gold star pendants have rhinestone centres. *1940s 7cm (2¾in) long* **£80–120 CRIS**

Floral motif pin with aquamarine crystal lozenges and clear rhinestones set in Russian gold plated metal. *1940s*

11.5cm (4⅝in) wide

£800–900   **SUM**

Russian gold plated tassell pin of Middle-Eastern inspiration. (Also made with a faux silver finish). *1940s*

16.5cm (6½in) long

£350–450   **SUM**

SWARM OF BEES

Joseff's Russian gold plated bee pins were originally made in the 1940s and 50s, but are being reproduced today. Originals range from £25 to £70, depending on size. They are worn either individually or as a small swarm.

Bee pins in various sizes. *Large: 5.5cm (2⅛in), medium: 4.5cm (1¾in), small: 2.5cm (1in) wide* **£25–70 CRIS**

Turban head pendants necklace, Russian gold plated. One of a number of variations of Joseff turban head motifs. *1940s*

Heads: 1.25cm (½in) long

£180–220   **CRIS**

Floral motif pendant necklace and earrings, Russian gold plated with faux topaz and clear rhinestones. *1940s*

Floral pd: 7.5cm (3in) wide; E: 7cm (2¾) long

£500–600   **SUM**

Unusual floral motif necklace and earrings, Russian gold plated with navette-cut ruby and round-cut clear rhinestones. *1940s*

Longest Pd & E: 9cm (3½in) long

£800–900   **SUM**

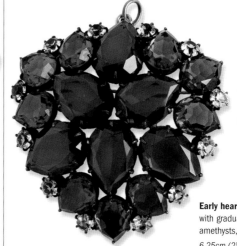

Joseff's faux precious stone pieces are particularly desirable to collectors.

Early heart-shaped floral pendant with graduated teardrop and round faux amethysts, and clear rhinestones. *1930s*

6.25cm (2½in) long

£120–180   **ROX**

American eagle and flag pin, Russian gold plated with prong-set ruby, sapphire, and clear coloured rhinestones. *1940s*

5.75cm (2¼in) wide

£100-150   **CRIS**

Moon god with ruff pin, Russian gold plated with clear rhinestone eye tremblers. Extremely rare. *1940s*

6.25cm (2½in) wide

£270-300   **CRIS**

Floral pin, Russian gold plated with central ruby red cabochon and navette-cut clear rhinestones. *1940s*

9cm (3½in) wide

£250-300   **SUM**

Crown pin with clear rhinestone finial, Russian gold plated and signed "Joan Castle" (Joseff's wife). *1950s*

5cm (2in) wide

£250-300   **CRIS**

Leaf and berry "C-cutter" pin, Russian gold plated and very rare. *1940s*

15.5cm (6⅛in) long

£650-750   **CRIS**

Faux pearl pendant earrings, Russian gold plated, as worn by Grace Kelly in the film *High Society*. Mid *1950s*

10cm (4in) long

£150-200   **SUM**

Cherub earrings, Russian gold plated with prong-set round clear rhinestones and inverted teardrop clear rhinestone pendants. *1940s*

3.75cm (1½in) long

£120-150   **PC**

Pendant owl head earrings, Russian gold plated and suspended from a gold-tone faux pearl. *1940s*

5cm (2in) long

£140-160   **CRIS**

Swarm of bees châtelaine pin, Russian gold plated with two large and three small bees. *1940s*

Large bees: 5cm (2in) long

£230-270   **CRIS**

Large floral pin with pendant tassel. Russian gold plated with three large pear-cut clear rhinestones. *1940s*

15cm (6in) long

£300-350   **SUM**

Good, Better, Best

In addition to rarity and condition, the price of Joseff pins is primarily determined by subject matter, quality of design, and wearability.

£180–220

A 1940s Russian gold plated **bee and flower pin**. Robustly styled with good attention to detail and a collectable motif. Worth £350–400 if sold with matching earrings.
7cm (2¾in) wide **CRIS**

£200–250

A 1940s Russian gold plated **lily of the valley pin**. Rarer than the bee and flower pin *(see above)* with a more fluid, stylized sense of movement. Ultimately, more overtly feminine and wearable.
7.5cm (3in) wide **CRIS**

£550–650

A 1940s **Russian gold plated leaf pin** with three hand-cut, aquamarine lead crystal stones in basket settings. Very rare, naturalistic, and displaying exceptional standards of craftsmanship. The largest and most visually striking of the three pieces. *15cm (6in) wide* **CRIS**

Charging bull pin, Russian gold plated with three basket-set, rectangular-cut sapphire, emerald, and red crystals. *1940s*
10cm (4in) wide

| £100–150 | CRIS |

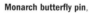

Pair of wolves pin, Russian gold plated with ruby, chalcedony, amber, and sapphire crystal cabochons. *1940s*
6.25cm (2½in) long

| £100–150 | CRIS |

Insects, animals, and fish are recurring motifs in Joseff's jewellery designs.

Monarch butterfly pin, Russian gold plated with prong-set clear, emerald, and amethyst rhinestones. *1940s*
9cm (3½in) long

| £240–280 | CRIS |

Châtelaine camel pin, Russian gold plated with ruby, emerald, citrine, jade, and aquamarine crystal cabochons. *1940s*
3cm (1⅛in) wide

| £240–280 | CRIS |

"Kitty kat" pin, Russian gold plated with prong-set, navette-cut emerald rhinestone eyes. *1940s*
7.5cm (3in) wide

| £150–200 | CRIS |

Crab and seashell pin, Russian gold plated with a faux pearl. *1940s*
5cm (2in) wide

| £75–100 | CRIS |

Pendant earrings of French bulldogs with ruffs, Russian gold plated. *1940s*
7cm (2¾in) long

| £85–100 | CRIS |

Retro design châtelaine pin, Russian gold plated with square and rectangular basket-set clear crystal stones. *1940s*

12cm (4¾in) wide

£550–600   CRIS

Twin-tassel pendant necklace, Russian gold plated with oriental figures. *1940s*

107cm (42in) long

£175–200   CRIS

Large, rare scrolling leaf and flower pin, Russian gold plated with basket-set ruby red crystal petals and a central round clear rhinestone. *1940s*

14cm (5½in) long

£650–750   CRIS

Art Deco Egyptian-style earrings, Russian gold plated with ruby red crystal cabochons. *1940s*

6.25cm (2½in) long

£75–100   CRIS

Oak leaf and acorn pendant necklace, Russian gold plated. The original was designed for the actress Carol Lombard. *1940s*

Pd: 9cm (3½in) long

£450–500   CRIS

Russian gold plated earrings of butterfly wings and leaf motifs with faceted amethyst crystals. *1940s*

5cm (2in) long

£80–120   CRIS

Pendant stars bar pin, Russian gold plated with clear rhinestone centres. *1940s*

11cm (4⅜in) wide

£325–375   CRIS

Multiple fish pendant-hoop earrings, Russian gold plated with topaz crystal cabochons. *1940s*

9cm (3½in) long

£120–150   CRIS

Fish scatter pins, Russian gold plated with ruby red crystal cabochon eyes. *1940s*

4cm (1½in) wide

£25–30 each   CRIS

Art Deco Egyptian-style triple pendant necklace and earrings. Russian gold plated with amethyst crystal stones. *1940s*

Pd & E: 9cm (3½in) long

£550–600   CRIS

Horses heads châtelaine pin, Russian gold plated with emerald crystal cabochon eyes and trailing cowboy motifs. *1940s*

Heads: 2.5cm (1in) long

£150–180   CRIS

Kenneth Jay Lane

"Wearing costume jewellery is like wearing glass slippers. You can feel like you're going to the ball, even if you're not." (Kenneth Jay Lane's "Cinderella" philosophy, from his autobiography, *Faking It*.)

KENNETH JAY LANE
c.1930–present

c.1930 Born in Detroit, USA

Mid 1950s Begins work in *Vogue*'s art department

Late 1950s–early 60s Designs shoes for Roger Vivier studio at Dior, then shoes and jewellery for Arnold Scaasi

1963 Founds K.J.L. company in New York and soon establishes a clientele that includes first ladies, royalty, and movie stars

Mid 1980s Begins designing jewellery lines for Avon

Late 1990s Begins selling his jewellery on QVC

FOR THE RICH AND NOT SO RICH

Detroit-born Kenneth Jay Lane began his illustrious career in the mid 1950s in New York. His work in the art department at *Vogue* was championed by the legendary editor Diana Vreeland and she featured his designs in the magazine. Lane went on to create shoes for Dior, and shoes and earrings for Arnold Scaasi. After such a prestigious start, 1963 saw the foundation of K.J.L., his enormously successful costume jewellery company. Almost immediately a highly enviable clientele was knocking at the door for his bold and exquisitely made designs. High-profile admirers included Jackie Kennedy Onassis, Audrey Hepburn, Elizabeth Taylor, Raquel Welch, Ivana Trump, Nancy Reagan, Barbara Bush, and Diana, Princess of Wales. Equally, however, lack of social standing or wealth have been no bar to owning a piece of K.J.L. His prices have always been accessible to most, recently evidenced by the volume sales achieved via the QVC shopping channel.

INVENTIVE STYLING

Always bright, bold, and elegant, Lane's jewellery is characterized by distinctive combinations of materials and by creative, and often witty reworkings of many traditional styles, including Greco-Roman, Egyptian, Medieval and Renaissance, through to Art Deco and Asian (*see below*). His brilliant clear stones are always the best Swarovski crystals, while his coloured stones and faux pearls display exceptional depth and luminosity of colour. Pieces made up until the late 1970s (the most collectable) are signed "K.J.L"; thereafter they are signed "Kenneth Jay Lane" or "Kenneth Lane".

Above: Big Cat with Indian goddess pendant pin, gold-plated with faux coral, emerald, turquoise, and jet cabochons, and a faux pearl. *1960s. 13cm (5⅛in) long* **£315–380 ROX**

Pendant necklace with Buddha and snakes. Gold-plated with faux mother-of-pearl, emerald cabochons, jade, and coral. *1980s. N: 62cm (24⅖in) circ; P: 14cm (5½in) long* **£100–115 JJ**

ASIAN INFLUENCE

Motifs and imagery of Asian origin have been recurring themes in the designs of Kenneth Jay Lane. They were particularly prevalent in the late 1960s and early 70s, when Eastern mysticism, religion, and ornament captured the imagination of many travellers. Examples include extravagant Maharajah-style earrings, pins, and pendants of gilt base metal encrusted with faux precious stone cabochons and drops. Favourite figural subjects include snakes, warriors, dancers, gods and goddesses, and religious teachers – most notably Buddha. Lane's 1960s' series of "Big Cat" pins also displays his enthusiasm for Asian imagery.

A giant seated stone Buddha in the grounds of a ruined temple at Ayuthaya, Thailand. Buddhism, Hinduism, and other religions of Asian origin have been a rich source of figural imagery for Kenneth Jay Lane's jewellery designs.

Flower earrings of gilt base metal with large French jet cabochon centres encircled by small clear rhinestone highlights. *1970s*

2.5cm (1in) long

£25–35 TR

"Catwalk" pendant chain necklace of gilt base metal with faux emerald and ruby oval cabochons. *1970s*

N: 73cm (29in) circ; Pd: 14.5cm (5¾in) long

£200–235 JJ

Chain necklace of gold-plated base metal set with four faux deep sapphire oval glass cabochons. *1950s*

63.5cm (25in) circ

£45–65 TR

Gilt earrings with large pink cabochon centres encircled by small clear rhinestones and faux turquoise cabochons. *1960s*

2.5cm (1in) long

£115–130 TR

Pendant pin and earrings with large coloured Czechoslovakian crystal cabochons encircled by small clear rhinestones. *1960s*

P: 4cm (1½in) long; E: 2cm (¾in) long

£630–665 TR

Faux precious earrings of gilt metal with prong-set faux jade and diamond cabochons above rows of clear rhinestone baguettes. *1970s*

6.25cm (2½in) long

£55–80 ABIJ

Textured gilt base metal bangle with large faux amber and smaller French jet cabochons. *c.1980*

8.25cm (3¼in) wide

£265–300 TR

Multiple-pendant "catwalk" necklace of silver-gilt base metal set with clear rhinestones. *Late 1960s*

Longest pd: 20cm (7⅞in) long

£600–665 TR

Dragon pin of gilt base metal with black and white enamelling, faux emerald and French jet cabochons, and clear rhinestones. *Late 1960s*

6.5cm (2½in) wide

£100–125 CRIS

Link bracelet of rectangular and round gilt base metal links banded with clear rhinestone highlights. *1970s*

2.5cm (1in) wide

£110–125 TR

LEA STEIN
1931–present

1931 Born in Paris, France

1957 Having trained as an artist, establishes her own textile design company

1965 Begins designing and making buttons for the fashion industry

1967 Starts making buttons from laminated rhodoid – a process developed by her husband

1969–81 Designs costume jewellery from laminated rhodoid, and experiments with fabric and metallic inclusions to produce variations of texture and colour. At the peak of its expansion, the company employs up to 50 people

1981 The company closes and a costume jewellery dealer purchases most of the remaining stock and begins selling Lea Stein pieces in the United States. For the first time, her designs begin to achieve recognition outside France

1988–present Lea Stein returns to designing and making laminated rhodoid costume jewellery. Each year she introduces at least one new and eagerly awaited design

Lea Stein

From the late 1960s to the early 80s, when she first produced her unique rhodoid jewellery, Lea Stein was barely recognized outside France. Recently, however, her work has become international hot property.

INNOVATIVE MATERIAL

Having trained as an artist, and run a textile design company from the late 1950s, Parisian-born Lea Stein began making costume jewellery in 1969. The material she used was superficially similar to Bakelite, but was actually developed by her husband Fernand Steinberger and consisted of laminated layers of coloured rhodoid (multiple, bake-bonded sheets of cellulose acetate). This process also allowed for the inclusion of layers of other material – most notably metallic elements and textured fabrics, such as lace. By cutting or shaping the resulting composition into different shapes, Lea Stein was able to produce polychromatic "plastic" jewellery with marked or subtle variations of both colour and texture.

The pieces she made from 1969 to 1981 included rings, bangles, and earrings, but mostly pins. Figural subjects ranged from cats, dogs, birds, and insects, to children, portraits, and Joan Crawford and Elvis Presley look-a-likes. Other favourite imagery included cars, stars, hats, hearts, rainbows, eyes, and flowers.

BELATED RECOGNITION

Although they sold well in her native France up until the company's demise, Lea Stein's pieces only became appreciated overseas when, in 1981, a dealer bought most of the remaining stock and began selling it in the United States. By the late 1980s, demand from collectors was such that Lea Stein returned to designing her unique rhodoid pins, and has subsequently introduced at least one new instant collectable each year. All pieces are marked "Lea Stein Paris". However, dating specific pieces as "first" or "second" generation isn't always easy, so buying Lea Stein pieces from a reputable dealer is advisable.

Above: "Felix Brothers" cat pin made of red, black, grey, and blue laminated rhodoid. *Late 1980s* 8.5cm (3⅜in) long **£80–95 CRIS**

GONE WITH THE WIND

The visual splendour of *Gone With The Wind*, in particular the costumes and jewellery, was the influence behind this beautiful Lea Stein pin (*left*). Officially known as the Ballerina pin, its similarity to Scarlett's infamous dress made from red velvet drapes has earned it the title "Scarlett O'Hara" pin and it is by far one of Lea Stein's most sought-after pieces.

Ballerina (or "Scarlet O'Hara") pin, made of red, white, and grey laminated rhodoid with lace inclusions. *c.1980.* 6.5cm (2½in) long **£80–95 CRIS**

Vivien Leigh as Scarlett O'Hara in *Gone With The Wind*, the film that was the influence behind Lea Stein's "Ballerina" pin.

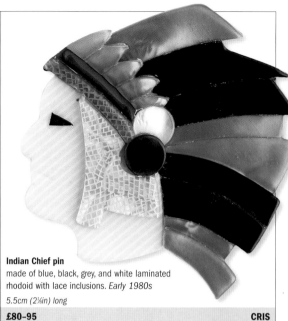

Penguin pin made of red, orange, terracotta, black, cream, and faux mother-of-pearl laminated rhodoid. *2001*

9cm (3½in) long

£80–95   CRIS

Black Cat and Ball pin made of black, grey, and faux mother-of-pearl laminated rhodoid. *Late 1980s*

7cm (2¾in) wide

£60–70   CRIS

"Ric the Dog" pin made of blue, grey, brown, and white laminated rhodoid with metallic inclusions. *Late 1980s*

9cm (3½in) long

£40–60   CRIS

Indian Chief pin
made of blue, black, grey, and white laminated rhodoid with lace inclusions. *Early 1980s*

5.5cm (2⅛in) long

£80–95   CRIS

"Buba the Owl" pin made of brown, yellow-ochre, and turquoise laminated rhodoid. *Early 1990s*

6cm (2⅜in) long

£40–60   CRIS

"Bacchus" cat head pins made of orange, peach, red, grey, black, and white laminated rhodoid. *Early 1990s*

6cm (2⅜in) wide

£40–60   CRIS

Edelweiss flower pin made of red, pink, orange, brown, green, and white laminated rhodoid. *Late 1980s*

8.5cm (3⅜in) long

£80–95   CRIS

"Colorette" pin made of dark blue, ice blue, black, and faux pearl laminated rhodoid. *Early 1980s*

5.5cm (2⅛in) wide

£60–70   CRIS

Panther pin made of mottled brown and orange laminated rhodoid. *Late 1990s*

10cm (4in) wide

£60–70   CRIS

"Egyptian Eye" pin made of red, black, and iridescent white laminated rhodoid. *Late 1970s*

8cm (3⅛in) wide

£60–70   CRIS

FOX PINS

Instantly recognizable, Lea Stein's 3-D fox pins have acquired the status of a signature piece. They have been made in numerous colourways and textures, variations of which are produced by fabric or metallic inclusions. No Lea Stein collection is complete without at least one of these fabulous fox pins.

3-D fox pins made of mottled coloured laminated rhodoid.
Left: early 1990s; Centre and right: late 1980s
10cm (4in) long **£40–60 each CRIS**

1904 D. Lisner and Company founded in New York City, USA

1920s Sells good-quality jewellery marked "Lanvin's Violet"

Mid 1930s Becomes the authorized US agent for Elsa Schiaparelli. The "Lisner" mark, in block letters, is used for the first time on its own pieces

1938 "Lisner" mark in script is introduced

1950s Production at its most prolific

1960s onwards Most pieces are marked "Lisner" in block letters together with an elongated "L"

1978 The company merges into the Lisner-Richelieu Corporation

1979 Production ceases

Lisner

In the late 20th century, Lisner jewellery was largely overlooked by collectors. This is no longer the case. Its distinctive designs, especially those from the 1950s and 60s, are becoming increasingly sought after.

DISTRIBUTOR AND MAKER

The early years of the Lisner company are not well documented. Founded in New York City in 1904, it spent approximately the first three decades of its existence selling jewellery that didn't bear its company name, and distributing jewellery for others. Lisner is best known as the authorized US importer and distributor for Elsa Schiaparelli's Parisian jewellery (*see pp.108–111*) prior to World War II. It began to gain a higher profile in the mid 1930s, following the introduction of the "Lisner" mark on its own designs. However, it took until the 1950s for the pieces most sought after by today's collectors to emerge.

QUALITY AND VALUE

Coloured Lucite, crisply moulded into either geometric or organic shapes, is the most prevalent material in Lisner pieces (*see below*). However, clear and coloured rhinestones – notably *aurora borealis* – were also used, usually as accents, as were larger, more exotic lava stones. Settings, links, and clasps were mostly chromed or silver-plated, although black japanned metal was also employed in the 1960s. Lisner jewellery was traded for very low sums up until the late 1990s. Subsequently, however, there has been a significant rise in the price of Lisner jewellery as its pieces become increasingly popular with modern collectors.

Above: "C-scroll" pin with green lava stones and *aurora borealis* crystal rhinestones set in silver-plated metal. *Mid 1950s. 5cm (2in) wide* **£60–70 CRIS**

ACRYLIC PLASTIC

Many costume jewellery makers enthusiastically adopted DuPont's acrylic plastic, Lucite, when it was launched in 1937. Lisner's extensive and impressive use of coloured Lucite, especially in its 1950s and 60s pieces, is only now being fully appreciated by collectors. Much of the attraction lies in the wonderful range of colours and pretty combinations Lisner employed.

Necklace, bracelet, circular pin, and earrings parure of hand-looped silver-plated metal with pink, mauve, blue, and white Lucite heart motifs. *Late 1950s N: 35.5cm (14in) circ; B: 17.75cm (7in) circ; P: 3.75cm (1½in) wide; E: 2cm (¾in) wide* **£180–200 CRIS**

Necklace, bracelet, and earrings with silver-plated metal, Lucite, and rhinestones. *1950s*

N: 38.75cm (15¼in) circ; B: 18.5cm (7¼in) circ; E: 3cm (1⅛in) long

£100–125   **CRIS**

Necklace, bracelet, and earrings of gold-plated metal set with navette-cut pink, brown, and amber Lucite leaf motifs. *Late 1950s*

N: 40cm (15½in) circ; B: 19cm (7½in) circ; E: 4cm (1½in) long

£100–125   **CRIS**

Gold-tone metal chain necklace set with Rivoli cabochons and clear crystal rhinestones. *1960s*

40.5cm (16in) circ

£105–120   **JJ**

Sprig of leaves and berries pin in silver-tone metal with prong-set blue *aurora borealis* rhinestones. *1950s*

5cm (2in) long

£10–15   **MILLB**

Necklace, bracelet, and earrings of gold-tone metal with Lucite leaf motifs and crystal rhinestone highlights. *Late 1950s*

N: 42cm (16½in) circ; B: 17.75cm (7in) circ; E: 3.75cm (1½in) long

£150–175   **CRIS**

Floral motif bracelet of gold-tone metal with white Lucite petals and clear crystal rhinestone highlights. *1950s*

17cm (6⅝in) circ

£15–25   **MILLB**

Leaf motif bracelet of gold-tone metal set with dark and pale green Lucite. *1950s*

16.5cm (6½in) circ

£20–40   **ECLEC**

Maison Gripoix

For three generations, Maison Gripoix created *haute couture* jewellery for Chanel, Dior, Yves St Laurent, and other leading fashion houses. The pieces it produced in its own name are equally impressive.

MAISON GRIPOIX
c.1870–present

1870s Company starts life as a wholesaler of glass buttons and beads

1895 Suzanne Gripoix (above) born in Paris

Mid-1920s Produces costume jewellery for Chanel

1940s Produces pieces for Dior

1980s Produces pieces for YSL

1990s Histoire de Verre line introduced

FROM BUTTONS AND BEADS

Founded in Paris in about 1870, Maison Gripoix's primary business for 30 years was the manufacture and wholesale of glass beads and buttons. However, at the turn of the century, it began to establish a reputation for making costume jewellery, by creating inexpensive copies of the flamboyant Art Nouveau-style pieces worn by the actress Sarah Bernhardt. Soon afterwards it began producing pieces for Piguet, a leading Parisian couturier, and in the mid 1920s, it started working for Chanel (see pp.56–59). Other eminent clients followed, such as Worth, Jacques Fath, and Christian Dior (see pp.60–65) – the most notable pieces for the latter being those that were worn with his 1940s "New Look" collection (see p.60). More recent prestigious clients have included Yves St Laurent, Balmain, Ungaro, and Guy Laroche.

Throughout this long association with *haute couture*, Gripoix continued to create jewellery in its own name and, from the 1990s, under the Histoire de Verre brand (see below). It is known above all for its fabulous *pâte-de-verre* work, produced in both subtle and vibrant colours of varying degrees of translucency and opacity. Provided the pieces are in good condition – fine crazing in the glass is acceptable, but chips are not – they continue to fetch high prices from admiring collectors.

Above: Maison Gripoix flower pin with *pâte-de-verre* leaves and turquoise, emerald, and black glass cabochons in an antiqued gilt metal frame. *1940s. 8.25cm (3¼in) long* **£600–700 SUM**

HISTOIRE DE VERRE

In the early 1990s, Josette Gripoix's son Thierry became head of Maison Gripoix. The pieces the company subsequently produced, branded "Histoire de Verre", are dominated by floral, leaf, and fruit imagery. While materials such as faux pearls are sometimes used, *pâte-de-verre* remains Maison Gripoix's signature material. Handcrafted, and highlighted with crystal rhinestones, Histoire de Verre pieces uphold Gripoix's reputation for style and craftsmanship of the highest order.

Histoire de Verre flower pin with a gold-plated brass stem, stamens, and leaf and petal borders, sapphire blue and emerald green *pâte-de-verre* petals and leaves, and clear crystal rhinestone stigmas. *1990s. 8.25cm (3¼in) long* **£180–220 CRIS**

Histoire de Verre floral necklace and earrings with amethyst and jonquil *pâte-de-verre* petals and amethyst glass bead centres in gold-plated brass wire frames. *1990s N: 54cm (21¼in) circ; E: 5cm (2in) wide* **£950–1,000 CRIS**

A FAMILY BUSINESS

Maison Gripoix has always been a family-run firm. Born in 1895, Suzanne Gripoix (*shown opposite*) – reverentially known in the jewellery world as "Madame Gripoix" – led the company from the mid 1920s throughout its long associations with Chanel, Dior, and other leading French fashion houses. After World War II, she was assisted by her daughter Josette (*shown right*), who took over the running of the company from Suzanne in 1969 and who was still at the helm in the 1980s.

Histoire de Verre flower necklace and earrings with *pâte-de-verre* petals and cabochon centres encircled by clear crystal rhinestones in gold-plated brass wire frames. *1990s. N: 51cm (20⅜in) circ; E: 5.75cm (2¼in) wide* **£800–950 CRIS**

Good, Better, Best

Different materials, colour, and complexity of composition determine the desirability of these Histoire de Verre necklaces.

£150–175

Made in the 1990s, this **single-strand faux baroque pearl necklace** has been given an interesting modern twist by having just four – rather than all – of the pearls capped with filigree gilt metal, also employed in the small clasp. *82cm (32¼in) circ* **CRIS**

£180–220

This 1990s' **leaf and petal necklace** is of red, pink, amethyst, topaz, and amber *pâte-de-verre* set in gilt brass. As both the imagery and materials employed are more representative of Gripoix's work than those in the piece on the left, this necklace commands a slightly higher price. *48.25cm (19in) circ* **CRIS**

£600–700

The flowers and leaves of this 1990s **floral necklace** are in amethyst, black, and emerald green *pâte-de-verre*, set in gilt metal. Like the leaf and petal necklace shown left, this is a classic and easily recognizable Gripoix design. Its layered composition is complex and its dark, rich palette conveys substance and sophistication. These qualities enhance considerably both the desirability and value of the piece. *51.25cm (20½in) circ* **CRIS**

Flowers and leaves modelled in opaque or, as here, translucent pâte-de-verre, are characteristic of Maison Gripoix's jewellery designs.

Maison Gripoix glass flower necklace with amber and topaz *pâte-de-verre* petals set in japanned metal frames, and clear crystal rhinestone stigmas. *c.2001*

Largest flower: 7cm (2¾in) wide

£450–500   **RITZ**

Maison Gripoix spray of flowers pin with *pâte-de-verre* petals and leaves set in gilt wire, and clear crystal rhinestone highlights. *1980s*
8cm (3¼in) wide

£200–240   **RITZ**

Maison Gripoix green flower pin with *pâte-de-verre* petals and leaves set in gilt wire and with a ruby glass centre. *c.2001*

7cm (2¾in) wide

£200–240   **RITZ**

Histoire de Verre floral pin with red and green *pâte-de-verre* and glass beads in a gilt brass frame. *1990s*
9cm (3½in) wide

£140–180   **CRIS**

Maison Gripoix wreath of berries necklace with green *pâte-de-verre* leaves and cherry *pâte-de-verre* beads. *1980s*
45cm (17½in) circ

£450–550   **RITZ**

PLANT ORNAMENTS

In the 1950s, Maison Gripoix produced decorative plant ornaments made from the same materials – notably *pâte-de-verre* – that it used in its jewellery. Primarily intended as window displays for retailers, the ornaments were set in antiqued gold-tone metal pots or baskets. Most were 12–20cm (5–8in) tall, but some larger trees were up to 90cm (3ft) high. Fairly scarce, these pieces rarely come on to the market.

Maison Gripoix basket of flowers ornament in antiqued gold-tone metal with emerald *pâte-de-verre* leaves and faux baroque pearl drops. *1950s. 16cm (6⅜in) high*   **£600–650 CRIS**

L'Atelier de Verre

At the end of the 1990s, four ex-Maison Gripoix workers set up their own small costume jewellery studio: L'Atelier de Verre. For a brief period – until early 2003, when Chanel acquired it – the studio designed and manufactured high-quality costume jewellery in keeping with the spirit and style of Gripoix and Gripoix for Chanel pieces. Marked "L'Atelier de Verre", its refined, mostly floral compositions of *pâte-de-verre*, lustrous faux pearls, shimmering crystal rhinestones, and gilt metal were sold through prestigious outlets such as Nyman Marcus and Saks Fifth Avenue in the United States, Galeries Lafayette in France, and Harrods in England.

L'Atelier de Verre floral pin and earrings, with emerald green *pâte-de-verre* leaves and pavé-set clear crystal rhinestone petals in gilt metal settings. *c.2000*

P: 7.5cm (3in) long; E: 5cm (2in) long

£650–850   **SUM**

L'Atelier de Verre four-strand bracelet with dark amethyst *pâte-de-verre* beads and a *pâte-de-verre* pansy clasp. *c.2000*

20cm (8in) long

£250–300   **SUM**

L'Atelier de Verre flower pin in gold-plated metal with *pâte-de-verre* petals and leaves, and rhinestone stigmas. *c.2000*

6.5cm (2½in) long

£250–300   **SUM**

L'Atelier de Verre green flower earrings with *pâte-de-verre* petals in gold-plated settings, outlined with clear crystal rhinestones. *c.2000*

5.5cm (2⅛in) long

£200–250   **SUM**

L'Atelier de Verre pendant rose necklace with faux pearls and emerald *pâte-de-verre* and mother-of-pearl leaves. *c.2000*

N: 39cm (15¼in) circ; Pd: 7cm (2¾in) drop

£400–500   **SUM**

L'Atelier de Verre pendant necklace with faux pearls, *pâte-de-verre* petals, and glass cabochons and rhinestones in the centre. *c.2000*

N: 41cm (16in) circ; Pd: 6.5cm (2½in) long

£250–300   **SUM**

MARCEL BOUCHER
(BOUCHER ET CIE)
1937–72

Marcel Boucher

Late 1910s Marcel Boucher starts work for Cartier, in Paris

1922 Boucher transfers to Cartier's New York workshops

Early 1930s Cartier cuts its workforce and Boucher leaves the company to work with other New York jewellers

1937 Forms his own company, Boucher et Cie in New York

1939 Saks Fifth Avenue places an order for Boucher designs

1949 French designer Sandra Semensohn joins the company and later becomes Boucher's second wife

1965 Boucher dies. Semensohn takes over the company

1972 Boucher et Cie sold to American watch manufacturers, Dovorn Industries

French by birth, Marcel Boucher became one of America's finest costume jewellery designers and makers. His superbly crafted and colourful pieces are often mistaken for precious jewellery.

FROM PRECIOUS BEGINNINGS

Marcel Boucher's reputation for producing costume jewellery that was, and still is, often mistaken for "real" jewellery, dates from the early stages of his career.

An apprentice model-maker with Cartier in Paris during the late 1910s and early 20s, he was transferred to its New York branch in about 1922 and continued working in fine jewellery until the Wall Street crash of 1929. Fortunately for costume jewellery collectors, the Great Depression of the 1930s forced Boucher to transfer his considerable talents to costume jewellery, a burgeoning industry that employed more affordable materials. After initially designing for Mazer Brothers (*see pp. 96–97*), Boucher felt sufficiently confident to establish his own small company, Boucher et Cie, in 1937. Just two years later, a lucrative order from Saks Fifth Avenue for a run of six, innovative, three-dimensional bird

pins gave Boucher the financial boost to substantially expand his operation.

The jewellery produced by Boucher et Cie before Boucher's death in 1965, and up until the early 1970s under the control of his second wife, designer Sandra Semensohn, was of exceptional quality. Often innovative, it is characterized by exquisite metalwork, fabulous rhinestones in hues and cuts that bear a striking resemblance to real gemstones, and wonderfully colourful enamelling. Marked either "MB" or" "Marboux" (earlier pieces), or signed "Marcel Boucher" or just "Boucher" (later pieces), most pieces are currently competitively priced – even undervalued. As such they represent an excellent investment.

Above: Sterling silver earrings with prong-set, emerald crystal cabochons, faux pearls, and pavé-set clear rhinestones. *1940s 2.5cm (1in) long* **£55–65 TR**

Retro style fan motif clip earrings made from a single casting of bright-finish, gold-tone base metal. *Late 1940s 2.5cm (1in) long* **£20–25 CRIS**

Marcel Boucher et Cie's "Illusion" pins are advertised in a 1955 edition of *Vogue*. The pins are made from textured gold- and rhodium-plated metals, crystal rhinestones, and faux pearls.

Necklace, bracelet, and earrings of rhodium-plated metal with prong-set aquamarine and clear crystal rhinestones. *Early 1950s*

N: 35.5cm (14in) circ;
B: 17.75cm (7in) circ;
E: 3cm (1⅛in) long

£500–600   CRIS

Circular floral and bow motif pin and earrings of rhodium-plated metal with prong-set sapphire blue and pavé-set clear crystal rhinestones. *1950s*

P: 5cm (2in) wide; E: 2.5cm (1in) wide

£80–90   CRIS

Ballerina pin of rhodium-plated metal with gilt highlights and round-cut and pavé-set clear crystal rhinestones. *c.1950*

5cm (2in) long

£100–115   ABIJ

Sheaf of wheat pin in silver-plated metal with green enamelling and emerald and clear crystal rhinestone highlights. *c.1940*

10.75cm (4¼in) long

£200–250   CRIS

Scrolling forms pin in sterling silver with clear crystal rhinestone highlights around a faux ruby paste. *1930s*

5.75cm (2¼in) long

£135–165   ABIJ

Gold-plated metal bracelet with ruby, emerald, and sapphire crystal cabochons, edged with clear crystal rhinestones. *1950s*

17.75cm (7in) circ

£200–250   CRIS

Floral motif pin of antiqued silver-tone metal with pale blue round and striated crystal cabochons. *1960s*

6.25cm (2½in) long

£50–55   ABIJ

Fruit tree pin with ladder and basket, in rhodium- and gold-plated metal with faux pearls, turquoise paste cabochons, and clear crystal rhinestones. *1950s*

3.75cm (1½in) long

£50–60   CRIS

CREATURE PINS

Marcel Boucher designed hugely popular animal pins. Rare examples from the late 1930s and 40s include birds of paradise, praying mantises, and other stylized insects. Produced in greater numbers, his 1950s elephant, poodle, donkey, and kitten pins, like Boucher et Cie's late 60s to early 70s bird and turtle pins, are more commonly found.

Turtle pin of textured gold-tone metal with clear crystal rhinestone highlights. *1970s. 3.75cm (1½in) long* **£25–30 JJ**

Bird pin of gold-tone metal with blue enamelling and rhinestones. *1970s* 6.25cm (2½in) long **£45–55 JJ**

Plant form pin and earrings of gold-plated metal castings with pavé-set clear crystal rhinestones. *1950s*

P: 10cm (4in) long;
E: 3.75cm (1½in) long

£70–85   CRIS

Mazer Brothers and Jomaz

Made from fine-quality materials, Mazer Brothers and Jomaz jewellery was competitively priced. For current collectors it remains an affordable investment in excellent craftsmanship and interesting design.

JOSEPH AND LOUIS

Mazer Brothers was founded by Joseph and Louis Mazer in New York City in 1927, and rapidly established a reputation for making remarkably good, affordable simulations of precious jewellery. Its early pieces, many of which were designed and made by Marcel Boucher before he established his own company in 1934 (*see p.94*), were mostly classic floral, foliate, or ribbon and bow motif designs, accented with fine "Sea-Maze" faux pearls or the best Austrian crystal rhinestones – the latter often intricately cut in sophisticated settings. The same standard of materials and craftsmanship was also evident in the pieces Mazer produced during the late 1930s and 40s. Usually made from sterling or vermeil sterling silver, these included opulent cocktail necklaces, bracelets, and earrings, as well as a series of Duette pins and crown jewel pins – both of which echoed similar lines produced at that time by Trifari (*see pp.118–129*) and Coro (*see pp.68–71*).

Above: Mazer Bros. bow pin in vermeil sterling silver with clear crystal rhinestones and faux ruby glass cabochons. *1940s. 7.5cm (3in) long* **£150–180 RG**

JOSEPH GOES IT ALONE

Mazer Brothers continued making jewellery until 1977. However, in 1946, Joseph Mazer left the company to set up a new and totally separate business, Joseph J. Mazer & Co. This new company produced jewellery until 1981, marked either "Joseph Mazer", "Mazer" or, more commonly, "Jomaz". Testament to the creative skills of designers such as Andre Fleuridas (in the 1950s) and Adolfo (in the 1970s), its pieces were also of high quality and reasonably priced. Combinations of textured metals (*see opposite*) with pavé-set rhinestones and colourful pastes, were typical of many innovative and unusual compositions – some of which are stylistically similar to those made by Boucher et Cie (*see pp.94–95*).

Mazer Bros. pendant necklace and earrings of rhodium-plated metal set with clear crystal rhinestones. *1940s. N: 38cm (15in) circ; Pd: 6.25cm (2½in) long; E: 4.5cm (1¾in) long* **£150–180 RG**

Advertisement from *Harper's Bazaar*, November 1948, promoting a Mazer Bros. parure of necklace, bracelet, pin, and earrings set with faux emerald, ruby, sapphire, amethyst, aqua, topaz, and clear crystal rhinestones.

TEXTURED METALS

While silver- and rhodium-plated metal were regularly used in Mazer Bros. and Jomaz jewellery, gold-plating and gold-tone metal alloys also featured. In the 1960s, these often had fashionable textured finishes, in contrast to the smooth gold-plating that had been in vogue during the 1940s and early 50s.

Jomaz gold-tone leaf pin with faux turquoise and lapis stones and clear crystal rhinestone highlights. *1960s*
7cm (2¾in) long **£60–80 RG**

Rhodium-plated Mazer Bros. pin set with round- and baguette-cut clear crystal rhinestones. *1930s*
7½cm (3in) long
£120–140 RG

Mazer Bros. crown pin of sterling and vermeil sterling silver with amethyst glass cabochons and crystal rhinestones. *1940s*
5.75cm (2¼in) long
£250–300 CRIS

Mazer Bros. floral bow pin of rhodium-plated metal with prong-set glass stones and clear crystal rhinestones. *1930s*
7cm (2¾in) long
£150–200 RG

Jomaz chandelier-pendant earrings of gold-plated metal with cranberry glass cabochons and clear crystal rhinestones. *1960s*
7cm (2¾in) long
£50–75 RG

Silver Jomaz necklace, bracelet, and earrings with glass cabochons, faux pearls, and rhinestones. *1960s*
N: 35cm (14in) circ;
B: 18cm (7in) circ;
E: 2cm (¾in) long
£250–350 RG

Mazer Bros. gold-plated bangle and earrings with glass cabochons and crystal rhinestones. *1950s*
B: 19cm (7½in) circ;
E: 2.5cm (1in) wide
£200–250 CRIS

Mazer Bros. pendant earrings with leaves pavé-set with crystal rhinestones, and turquoise glass cabochon berries. *Late 1950s*
5cm (2in) long
£120–135 CRIS

Mazer Bros. caterpillar earrings of rose-gold-plated metal with faux amethyst glass stones and clear crystal rhinestones. *Mid 1950s*
3cm (1¼in) long
£60–75 CRIS

Jomaz leaf pin and earrings of brushed gold-tone metal with clear crystal rhinestones (some pavé-set). *c.1960*
P: 5cm (2in) long; E: 3cm (1⅛in) long
£45–50 ABIJ

Jomaz pin and earrings of textured, gold-plated metal with faux emerald and lapis glass cabochons and clear crystal rhinestones. *1960s*
P: 7.5cm (3in) wide; E: 2.5cm (1in) long
£80–120

Prong-set faux precious cabochons are often a feature of Jomaz designs.

RG

Miriam Haskell

Together with Coco Chanel and Elsa Schiaparelli, Miriam Haskell elevated the status of costume jewellery to an accessory as prestigious, and even more fashionable than, its precious equivalent. Her innovative pieces are among the finest ever made.

MIRIAM HASKELL
1899–1981

1899 Born in Indiana, USA

1924 Moves to New York and opens shop in the McAlpin Hotel

1926 Establishes Miriam Haskell Company with Frank Hess as chief designer

1930s Establishes retail outlets at Saks Fifth Avenue in New York and Harvey Nichols in London

1940s Starts trademarking jewellery

1960 Robert F. Clark becomes chief designer

1970s Larry Vrba becomes chief designer

1981 Miriam Haskell dies

A PIONEER OF FASHION

Miriam Haskell's energetic and hugely successful career from the mid-1920s to the late 1940s introduced new standards of glamour to the world of fashion. In doing so she did for the women of the United States what her contemporary Coco Chanel (*see pp 56–59*) had done for the well-dressed ladies of Paris: namely, establish costume jewellery as a fashionable and valued art form in its own right. For that alone, costume jewellery collectors of today have much to thank her for.

Born in 1899 to a modest, American family in Cannelton, Indiana, Miriam Haskell moved to New York in 1924 and opened her first costume jewellery shop the same year in the prestigious McAlpin Hotel. Although not a designer herself – she had majored in education at the University of Chicago – her skill lay in spotting the potential in others and in choosing which of their designs should go into production. Recognizing the latent talents of Frank Hess, a window dresser at Macy's, and appointing him Chief Designer of the Miriam Haskell Company, which she founded in 1926, was her first stroke of genius. Hess, who retained his position until 1960, rapidly established a precedent for stylish and innovative designs, which was maintained subsequently under the aegis of other hugely talented head designers, namely Robert Clark and Peter Raines in the 1960s, Larry Vrba in the 1970s (*see p.180*), and Millie Petronzio from 1980 onwards.

Above: Multiple-strand bracelet with pink and pearl poured glass beads. *1940s. Clasp: 3.75cm (1½in) wide*
£100–165 ROX

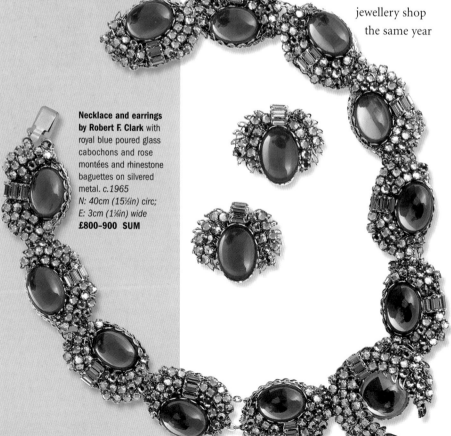

Necklace and earrings by Robert F. Clark with royal blue poured glass cabochons and rose montées and rhinestone baguettes on silvered metal. *c.1965*
N: 40cm (15½in) circ; E: 3cm (1⅛in) wide
£800–900 SUM

Floral necklace and earrings by Miriam Haskell with faux seed pearls and clear rhinestones, advertised in American *Vogue* and *Harper's Bazaar* in October 1958.

FOUNDATIONS OF SUCCESS

Haskell pieces are of innovative design and rarely replicate the classic forms of precious jewellery, which does much to explain why her jewellery has consistently struck a chord with show business (*see opposite*), retail clients, and current collectors alike. Nevertheless, other equally important factors have contributed to its desirability. Haskell's ground-breaking aquisition of a front-of-store retail outlet in Sak's Fifth Avenue in New York, and a similar arrangement with Harvey Nichols in London, elevated both her profile and prestige. The employment of highly skilled emigré European craftsmen during the late 1920s and 30s also ensured that the innovative and often complex designs were executed to the highest standards.

Above all, however, it is the choice and standard of materials used in Haskell jewellery that has proved so compelling. Both Haskell and Hess, and subsequent head designers, regularly travelled abroad to source the best materials. Notable among these are glass beads from Murano; faceted crystals from Austria, including flat-backed rose montées mounted in pierced metal cups (a Haskell favourite); lustrous faux pearls from Japan (*see below*); and, during the restrictions of World War II, wood, feathers, and plastics. Invariably hand-wired, often combined with filigree antiqued gilt metal, and presented in unusual and striking colour combinations, Haskell pieces have proved continuously irresistable. However, collectors should note that good condition is very important: missing coloured Austrian rhinestones, and chipped or eroded faux pearls are hard to replace and therefore detract substantially from the value of a piece.

Floral pin of gilt metal with coral poured glass beads, faux seed and baroque pearls, and clear rose montée highlights. *c.1940* *10cm (4in) long.* **£650–750 SUM**

SHOW BUSINESS

Haskell jewellery has often appeared on stage and in film and television. Florenz Ziegfeld bought pieces for his Ziegfeld Follies, Lucille Ball often wore Haskell in her TV shows, and in more recent times the company has provided the jewellery for Broadway hits such as The Phantom of the Opera.

JOAN CRAWFORD

Hollywood actress Joan Crawford, seen above wearing a cascading bib necklace with earrings, regularly bought Haskell jewellery from the early 1930s to the late 60s. In 1978, the year after she died, Crawford's extensive collection was sold at auction amid much publicity by the Plaza Art Gallery in New York.

JAPANESE PEARLS

Of all the high-quality components Haskell's craftsmen employed in her jewellery, it is the faux pearls that have been the most consistently admired. Traditionally, the primary source of fine-quality imitation pearls was Gablonz, in Bohemia (also famed for its Bohemian glass). However, in the late 1930s Japan became an alternative and highly competitive supplier, and one enthusiastically adopted by Haskell after the hiatus of World War II. Multiple immersions in *essence d'orient*, a solution of cellulose, fish scales, and various resins, gave Haskell's Japanese faux seed and baroque pearls – the latter supplied exclusively to her – a deep, lustrous finish unrivalled by European equivalents and highly prized by collectors of her costume jewellery.

Sorting faux pearls at a Japanese factory c.1947. In addition to white pearls, other colours were produced including champagne, pink, brown, and various shades of grey.

Faux baroque pearls

Edwardian-style pendant necklace with multiple-looped and interlaced strands of baroque pearls; the clasp and head of the pendant encrusted with rings of tiny baroque pearls and rose montées. *c.1950. Pd: 10cm (4in) long* **£1,550–1,750 SUM**

Necklaces

Regardless of style, all Miriam Haskell necklaces are extremely desirable. The best-known are those with single or multiple strands of lustrous faux pearls in shades ranging from white and champagne, through pink and grey, to dark brown. Other examples with exquisite combinations of high-quality materials such as Murano beads, pressed and poured French glass, seed pearls, and rose montées, are equally admired. Often finished with elaborately decorated clasps, Haskell's necklaces are nothing less than costume jewellery classics.

Floral necklace and earrings with amber and citrine poured glass cabochons, glass oval beads, and rhinestones. *c.1950*

N pd: 7cm (2¾in) long; E: 3cm (1⅛in) long

£1,150–1,250　　　　SUM

Pendant necklace, two pins, and earrings parure with black resin beads and cabochons and square-cut clear rhinestones. *c.1960*

N: 38cm (15in) circ; Round P: 8cm (3⅛in) wide; Long P: 9.5cm (3¾in) long; E: 5cm (2in) long

£2,500–2,750　　　　SUM

Two-strand faux pearl necklace with floral pendant of glass beads, seed pearls, rose montées, and poured glass leaves. *c.1960*

N: 35.5cm (14in) circ; Pd: 9cm (3½in) wide

£1,500–1,700　　　　SUM

Necklace and hoop earrings with baroque pearls, poured glass beads, and cabochons encircled with clear rose montées. *c.1960*

E: 5cm (2in) long; N: 51cm (20in)

£1,000–1,200	SUM

Floral pendant necklace of gilt metal with amber and coral glass beads (smooth and rough), and amber poured glass leaves. *1940s*

Pd: 5cm (2in) long

£165–265	ROX

Gilt metal chain necklace with clear rhinestone navettes, faux and seed pearls, and clear rose montées. *c.1960*

Pd: 9.5cm (3¾in) long

£900–1,000	SUM

Pendant fruit drop necklace and earrings with faceted citrine glass beads, filigree gilt findings, and clear rose montées. *c.1950*

N: 37.5cm (14¾in); E: 5.75cm (2¼in) long

£800–900	SUM

Festoon necklace of filigree gilt metal, clusters of faux seed pearls, and round-cut clear rhinestones. *1950s*

Longest pd: 9cm (3½in) long

£1,600–1,700	SUM

Floral wreath necklace and earrings with smokey poured glass petals and leaves, and gilt findings. *c.1960*

N: 40.5cm (16in) circ; E: 3cm (1⅛in) long

£1,000–1,200	SUM

Multi-strand necklace of amber poured glass beads, and a filigree gilt metal clasp with glass cabochons. *1940s*

51cm (20in) circ

£165–265	ROX

Good, Better, Best

When comparing Haskell necklaces made from similar materials, price difference is mostly determined by the styling and degree of elaboration of features such as clasps and pendants.

£135–200

This 1940s to early 50s **triple-strand necklace** has two strands of faux baroque pearls with a single strand of chalcedony poured glass beads. The colour of the glass beads is echoed in the sapphire blue rhinestone in the clasp. *51cm (20in) circ* **ROX**

£250–315

This 1940s **flowerhead pendant necklace** has two strands of faux pearls and a pendant of antiqued gilt metal with seed pearls, rose montées, and faux pearl centres. It commands a high price because of its striking pendant. *45.75cm (18in) circ* **ROX**

£850–950

This 1960s **"Shooting Star" necklace** by Robert F. Clark has strands of baroque pearls and a wheatear pendant of antiqued metal with rose montées and tassels of filigree-capped baroque pearls. Its elaboration and dynamic shape make it the best piece. *45.75cm (18in) circ* **WAIN**

Pink glass necklace and earrings with gilt metal wirework and clear and amethyst rose montées, and the necklace strands of oblong pink glass beads. *c.1950*

N: 51cm (20in) circ; E: 2.5cm (1in) wide

£165–230   **ROX**

Five-strand necklace of faux pearls in various sizes; the strands are of graduated length, and the clasp of gilt metal plates with small, faux pearl floral motifs. *c.1950*

26.5cm (10½in) circ (to lowest strand)

£550–600   **SUM**

Twin-strand necklace and pendant earrings of white, turquoise, and marbled turquoise glass beads, white poured glass, and small turquoise beads. *1950s*

E & N Pd: 4.5cm (1¾in) long

£200–265   **ROX**

Gilt metal chain necklace with faux baroque pearls, and an ornament with a central faux pearl flanked by pearlized horns. *1940s*

40.5cm (16in) circ

£140–160   **RG**

Necklace and pendant earrings with baskets of tubular gilded metal and emerald, amber, and ruby oblong glass beads. *1940s*

*N: 40.5cm (16in) circ;
E: 5.75cm (2¼in) long*

£265–400   **ROX**

Pearlized parure of necklace, bracelet, and hooped pendant earrings in gilt metal with faux baroque pearls, and pearlized horns. *1940s*

N: 40.5cm (16in) circ; B: 20.25cm (8in) circ; E: 6.25cm (2½in) long

£300–350   **RG**

Multiple-strand necklace of pink and white poured glass beads and a gilt metal clasp with gilt balls. *1960s*

40cm (15¾in) circ

£115–150   **ROX**

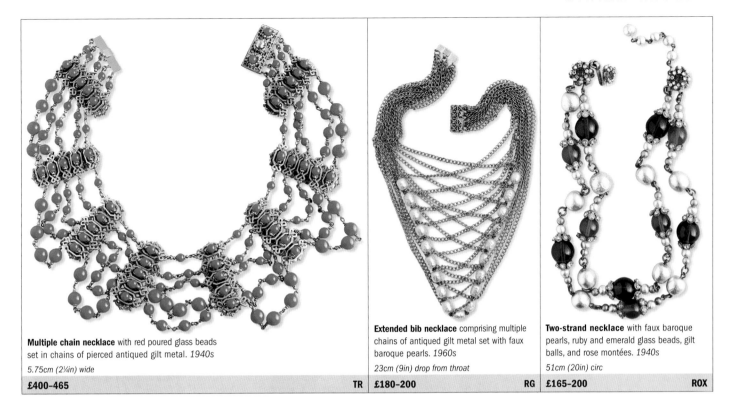

Multiple chain necklace with red poured glass beads set in chains of pierced antiqued gilt metal. *1940s*

5.75cm (2¼in) wide

£400–465   **TR**

Extended bib necklace comprising multiple chains of antiqued gilt metal set with faux baroque pearls. *1960s*

23cm (9in) drop from throat

£180–200   **RG**

Two-strand necklace with faux baroque pearls, ruby and emerald glass beads, gilt balls, and rose montées. *1940s*

51cm (20in) circ

£165–200   **ROX**

Bracelets

Most Haskell bracelets are of plain and antiqued gilt or silvered metal. Decoration with faux pearls and glass beads and stones is usually colourful, invariably elaborate, and often incorporates delicate filigree work. A matching pin or earrings usually enhances the desirability and price.

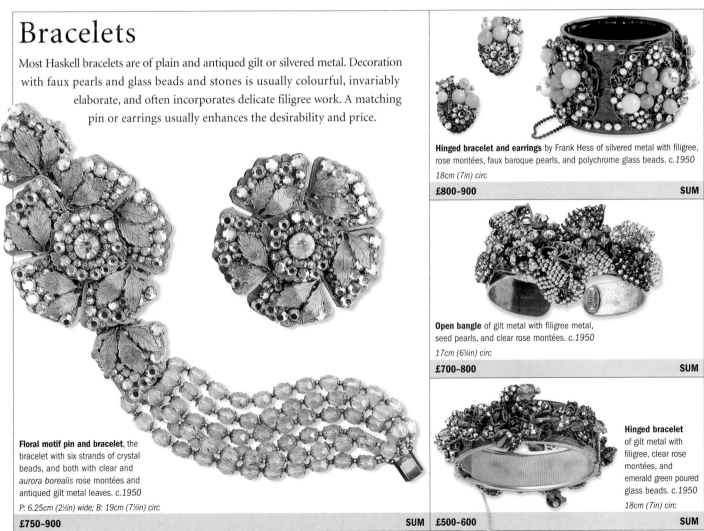

Floral motif pin and bracelet, the bracelet with six strands of crystal beads, and both with clear and *aurora borealis* rose montées and antiqued gilt metal leaves. *c.1950*

P: 6.25cm (2½in) wide; B: 19cm (7½in) circ

£750–900   **SUM**

Hinged bracelet and earrings by Frank Hess of silvered metal with filigree, rose montées, faux baroque pearls, and polychrome glass beads. *c.1950*

18cm (7in) circ

£800–900   **SUM**

Open bangle of gilt metal with filigree metal, seed pearls, and clear rose montées. *c.1950*

17cm (6⅝in) circ

£700–800   **SUM**

Hinged bracelet of gilt metal with filigree, clear rose montées, and emerald green poured glass beads. *c.1950*

18cm (7in) circ

£500–600   **SUM**

Pins

The majority of Haskell pins are complex compositions of metal, crystal, and paste made to exceptionally high standards of craftsmanship. Floral and foliate subjects and shell motifs are common, and figurals, especially turtles and exotic birds, are also in evidence – either featured prominently or secreted within a design.

Leaves are a recurring motif in Haskell jewellery. Many are highly naturalistic, particularly those in gilt metal, but others, especially in glass, can be quite stylized.

Floral motif pin with dark amber poured glass petals set under an antiqued gilt metal shell motif, and with five pendants comprising amber and dark amber poured glass beads of various shapes (some capped with filigree gilt metal findings) and finished with textured poured glass amber leaves. *1930s*

16cm (6¼in) long

£200–250   **SUM**

French jet cabochon pin of antiqued gilt metal with rings and clusters of clear rose montées. *1940s*

8.5cm (3⅜in) long

£500–600   **SUM**

Two-tier pendant pin of antiqued gilt metal with clusters of clear rose montées and three faux baroque pearl drops. *c.1950*

9.5cm (3¾in) long

£500–600   **SUM**

Floral motif pin of antiqued gilt metal with lavender, amethyst, and moonstone glass cabochons and clear rose montées. *1950s*

10cm (4in) long

£450–550   **SUM**

Floral motif pin with ringed clusters of faux seed pearls with faux baroque pearl centres, set in antiqued gilt metal. *1940s*

8.25cm (3¼in) long

£135–200   **ROX**

Grapes and leaves pin with rose montées and white poured glass beads in various sizes. *1940s*

7.5cm (3in) long

£100–165   **ROX**

Floral and foliate pin with antiqued gilt metal leaves and chained petals, and clear rose montées. *c.1950*

9.5cm (3¾in) long

£600–700   **SUM**

FILIGREE METAL

Like the beads and faux pearls of the pin below, most decorative components of Haskell jewellery are painstakingly hand-wired to a filigree metal backing. Although ultimately functional, these backings have an aesthetically pleasing architectural quality.

Fruit and floral motif pin with silvered faux "black" baroque and seed pearls on a filigree gilt metal casting. *1950s* 5cm (2in) long **£100–140 PC**

A filigree antiqued gilt metal back with horseshoe-shaped signature plaque as used in the 1940s.

Floral pin with pressed glass, glass beads, and rhinestones in fuchsia and shades of pink. *1940s*

6.25cm (2½in) long

£185–250 — ROX

Floral pin of antiqued gilt metal with rings and rows of faux seed and baroque pearls and clear rose montées. *c.1950*

5.75cm (2¼in) wide

£390–450 — SUM

Floral and foliate pin of antiqued gilt metal with melon-cut emerald beads and clear rose montées. *c.1960*

7.5cm (3in) long

£450–500 — SUM

Floral pin of antiqued textured and filigree gilt metal with prong-set blue and green poured glass cabochons. *1940s*

7.5cm (3in) long

£85–150 — ROX

This pin displays the signature Haskell combination of faux pearls and rose montées.

Faux pearl pin with alternating bands of antiqued gilt metal and small faux baroque pearls, flanked by large baroque pearls and topped with gilt metal leaves and clear rose montées. *c.1960*

7.5cm (3in) long

£500–600 — SUM

Floral motif stick pin with bird and turtle figures, of antiqued gilt metal with clear crystal beads and rose montées. *c.1960*

9.5cm (3¾in) long

£500–600 — SUM

Bird of paradise stick pin of antiqued gilt metal with sapphire, emerald, and pink glass beads. *1940s*

7.5cm (3in) long

£50–70 — SUM

Floral motif stick pin with antiqued gilt metal leaves and faux baroque pearl centres and drop, and three small faux pearl highlights. *1950s*

7cm (2¾in) long

£90–120 — CRIS

Art Nouveau style floral motif bracelet of antiqued gilt metal bordered with clusters of faux seed pearls. *c.1950*

16cm (6¼in) circ

£500–600 — SUM

Floral motif pin of filigree antiqued gilt metal studded with faux pearls and clear rose montées. *c.1950*

8.25cm (3¼in) wide

£450–550 — SUM

Earrings

Haskell earrings were produced in myriad designs, sometimes as part of a demi-parure with matching pin. Mostly floral, foliate, or fruit motifs, all are collectable, although the classic combination of gilt metal, faux pearls, and clear rose montées commands a higher price.

Pin and matching earrings of cast antiqued gilt metal with clear rose montées and faux baroque pearls; some of the pearls linked on the pin with antiqued gilt metal chains. *c.1950*

P: 7.5cm (3in) long; E: 2.5cm (1in) wide

£200–335　　　　**ROX**

Pin and pendant earrings with white poured glass petals, centres, and drops, and small coloured glass beads. *1950s*

P: 5cm (2in) wide; E: 3.75cm (1½in) long

£100–135　　　　**ROX**

Floral pin and matching earrings of gilt metal with clusters of faux seed pearls and centres of rose montées encircling a faux pearl topped with an amber glass bead. *c.1960*

P: 6.25cm (2½in) long; E: 2.5cm (1in) wide

£135–200　　　　**ROX**

Large floral motif earrings with seed pod and foliate pendants of filigree and textured silvered metal. *1970s*

10.5cm (4⅛in) long

£65–85　　　　**ABIJ**

Antiqued gilt metal earrings with marbled emerald poured glass and clear rose montées. *1940s*

2.5cm (1in) wide

£80–120　　　　**ROX**

French glass bead earrings of antiqued gilt metal with clear rose montées. *1940s*

3cm (1⅛in) long

£140–160　　　　**CRIS**

Pink pressed glass earrings with tiny faux baroque pearls. *1950s*

3cm (1⅛in) long

£140–160　　　　**CRIS**

Good, Better, Best

The most desirable Haskell earrings and pins are the classic 1940s and 50s designs incorporating signature components. More recent and overtly "modern" examples are currently less expensive but are equally well crafted and worth collecting.

£115–165

These 1960s **fruit and foliate earrings with matching pin** have clusters of seed pearls and metallic coloured beads above pewter glass drops; the pin also has five faux baroque pearls. Their modern style and colouring currently commands lower prices than the more classic Haskell designs.
P: 9cm (3½in) wide; E: 4.5cm (1¾in) long **ROX**

£180–220

These late 1940s **faux pearl and amber earrings with matching pin** feature hand-wired faux pearls with amber-coloured rose montées and poured glass beads. The exotic, variegated colouring of the beads combined with the greater complexity of the composition explains the higher price band.
P: 6.25cm (2½in) wide; E: 2.5cm (1in) wide **ROX**

£265–335

These 1940s **cherry motif earrings and matching pin** are considered by current collectors to be a classic example of Haskell design. Antiqued gilt metal, clusters of faux seed pearls, and bands of clear rose montées are all signature Haskell components. The colouring of these pieces is stylized, but in much of their detail they are exquisitely naturalistic.
P: 7cm (2¾in) long; E: 5cm (2in) long **ROX**

Floral earrings of antiqued gilt metal with pink poured glass centres, rose montées, and emerald and sapphire rhinestones. *1940s*
3cm (1⅛in) long

£80–130	ROX

Seed pearl earrings of antiqued gilt metal with centres of rose montées and a faux pearl. *1940s*
3.75cm (1½in) long

£120–145	ROX

Clear rose montée earrings of antiqued gilt metal with prong-set clear rhinestone centres. *1940s*
3.75cm (1½in) long

£120–150	ROX

Floral earrings with yellow pressed glass flower heads, sapphire, pink, and clear rhinestones and rose montées. *1940s*
3cm (1⅛in) long

£120–150	ROX

Antiqued gilt metal earrings with clusters of small faux baroque pearl beads and prong-set clear rhinestones. *c.1950*
5cm (2in) long

£250–300	SUM

ELSA SCHIAPARELLI
1890–1973

1890 Born in Rome, Italy

1920s Establishes her first *maison couture* on the Rue de la Paix in Paris. Becomes a rival of Coco Chanel and befriends Dadaist and Surrealist artists such as Salvador Dali

1936 Introduces "shocking pink" in a collection. This becomes her signature colour

1940 Moves to New York to seek refuge from the war

1945 Returns to her fashion house in Paris where future couturiers Hubert de Givenchy and Pierre Cardin train as assistants

1949 Opens a retail ready-to-wear outlet in New York and licenses DeRosa to make her jewellery stamped or tagged "Designed in Paris–Created in America"

1954 Closes her French fashion house and returns to New York to concentrate on costume jewellery designs

Late 1950s Production ceases

1973 Elsa Schiaparelli dies

INSPIRATION

Schiaparelli's main sources of inspiration were the forms of nature and Surrealism, the latter also evident in her love of unusually cut or coloured fantasy gemstones.

Schiaparelli

In pushing costume jewellery to the cutting edge of fashion, flamboyant couturier Elsa Schiaparelli created a legacy of Surrealist-inspired designs that shocked critics in the 1930s, then became fashion statements, and still receive admiration today.

ROME, NEW YORK, AND PARIS

Born in Rome in 1890, Elsa Schiaparelli moved to New York in the early 20th century to become a script writer. However, her career soon gravitated to her first loves – fashion and the arts – and she established her *maison haute couture* in Paris in the early 1920s. Like her Parisian contemporary Coco Chanel (*see pp. 56–59*), Schiaparelli believed costume jewellery as not only a vital art form in its own right, but also an integral component of costume. Stylistically, however, these often bitter rivals were miles apart.

> *"Fashion is born by small facts, trends, or even politics, never by trying to make little pleats and furbelows, by trinkets, by clothes easy to copy, or by the shortening or lengthening of a skirt."*
>
> Elsa Schiaparelli

In contrast to Chanel's elegant, classic designs, many of Schiaparelli's pieces dating from the 1920s and 30s were unusual and quirky. For example, some incorporated circus

imagery and others astrological motifs. Where more natural imagery was employed (*see below*), the floral or faunal subjects were usually either particularly exotic, or were highly stylized. Bizarre examples include pea-pod pendant necklaces and human eye pins.

Underpinning many of these seemingly light-hearted subjects, however, were the artistic and political philosophies of Dadaism and Surrealism, whose leading exponents were close friends of Schiaparelli and who designed a number of pieces for her (*see opposite below*). The influence of Surrealism on Schiaparelli's work was most evident in her dramatic "Shocking Pink" collection of 1936 (*see opposite above*).

Above: Stylized flower earrings with amber and olivine glass stones encircling *aurora borealis* rhinestones. *c.1950* 4.5cm (1¾in) wide **£150–200 SUM**

FORMS OF NATURE

Flora and fauna are recurring themes in Schiaparelli's jewellery. The fantastic sea coral shapes of a glass and rhinestone necklace and bracelet in this 1952 advertisement are typical, as are the foliate forms of this pin and earrings set, made of pale pastel green and pink Lucite, and gold-plated metal. *1950s.* P: 9cm (3½in) long; E: 4.5cm (1¾in) long **£275–350 PC**

SHOCKING PINK

Elsa Schiaparelli's dramatic injection of "shocking pink" at a time when a black cocktail dress was still *de rigueur* was entirely in keeping with the artistic principles of her Dadaist and Surrealist social set (*see below*). The rapturous reception to what rapidly became her signature colour ensured its translation into the exotic stones used in many pieces of her jewellery, such as this necklace, and also into the hugely successful Shocking perfume and range of cosmetics. As the accompanying advertisement implies, this was Schiaparelli wearing her Surrealist heart on her sleeve.

Lava rock necklace with staggered rows of shocking pink lava stones suspended from a rhinestone studded collar. *c.1940* *38cm (15in) circ* **£400–500 CRIS**

Surrealist-style advertisement from *Vogue*, November 1938, promoting Schiaparelli's Shocking range of cosmetics. The torso was purportedly inspired by the actress Mae West.

As ground-breaking as Christian Dior's "New Look" collection after World War II (*see pp.60–63*), Schiaparelli's collection confirmed her ability to both shock and, at the same time, win over even the most conservative critics.

A NEW FOCUS

Having sought refuge from the war in New York, Schiaparelli returned to her fashion house in Paris in 1945 and, in 1949, set up one of the first ready-to-wear *couture* retail outlets back in New York. After selling her business in Paris in 1954 – much to the dismay of her assistants Hubert de Givenchy and Pierre Cardin – she returned to New York and to the second major phase of her career. Focusing on costume jewellery, she produced during the course of the 1950s a series of fabulous abstract, floral, and faunal designs characterized by the use of unusual and often very colourful stones and glass. It is these, and her 1940s pieces, that collectors are most likely to come across today (examples from the 1930s being all too rare).

Would-be collectors should note that most early French Schiaparelli pieces are unsigned, although some carry her name in block lettering on a rectangular plate. In contrast, most of the later French and all of the American pieces bear her signature. However, forgeries (and legitimate reproductions from the 1980s) are not unknown. Consequently, purchasing Schiaparelli pieces via a specialist dealer or reputable auction house is strongly advisable.

SURREALISM

The Surrealist artists Salvador Dali (pictured left posing in the village of Port Lligat in Spain in 1951), Jean Cocteau, and Christian Bérard were close friends of Schiaparelli. In addition to designing some pieces for her, their Surrealist concept of art and imagery pervaded her often playful, sometimes shocking designs.

Fantasy stone bracelet and earrings of abstract design, composed of shaped and faceted red pastes, and Swarovski's iridescent *aurora borealis* rhinestones. *1950s. B: 19cm (7½in) circ; E: 3.75cm (1½in) long* **£350–400 CRIS**

Necklace, bracelet, and earrings with rhodium-plated links, prong-set blue and green glass stones, and *aurora borealis* rhinestones. *1950s*

N: 38cm (15in) circ; B: 19.5cm (7⅝in) circ; E: 2.5cm (1in) long

£1,000–1,200 **CRIS**

Necklace, bracelet, and earrings of gold-plated metal with prong-set smoked topaz and amber crystal stones and beads. *1950s*

N: 40.5cm (16in) circ;
B: 24cm (9½in) circ;
E: 3.75cm (1½in) long

£400–450 **CRIS**

Necklace, bracelet, and earrings with gilt metal links and prong-set glass stones and rhinestones. *1950s*

N: 37cm (14½) circ;
B: 18.5cm (7¼in) circ;
E: 4.5cm (1¾in) long

£900–1,000 **SUM**

Necklace and earrings with gilt metal links, faux pearls, prong-set lilac, amethyst, and dusty pink pastes, and *aurora borealis* rhinestones. *1950s*

N: 37cm (14½in) circ; E: 3cm (1⅛in) long

£300–400 **SUM**

PERFUME FLACON PINS

Like other couturiers, Schiaparelli produced house perfumes retailed in very distinctive flacons. Miniature examples in the form of lapel pins were also made. As well as the "Success Fou" flacon below, other rare and collectable examples include a "Sleeping" candlestick (1938), and a "Shocking" torso (*see p.109*).

Perfume bottle pin, made for the perfume "Success Fou", in antiqued gilt metal with glass cabochons. *1945* 4.5cm (1¾in) high **£1,100–1,300 WAIN**

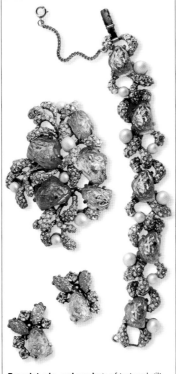

Bracelet, pin, and earrings of textured gilt metal with lava rock stones, faux pearls, and tiny turquoise cabochons. *1950s* B: 18cm (7in) circ; P: 8.25cm (3¼in) long; E: 3.5cm (1¾in) long

£900–1,000   **SUM**

Bracelet, pin, and earrings of silver-plated metal with prong-set baby blue and chalcedony crystal cabochons. *1950s* B: 18.5cm (7¼in) circ; P: 7cm (2¾in) long; E: 3cm (1⅛in) long

£500–600   **CRIS**

Bracelet and earrings with antiqued gilt metal discs set with faux amethyst glass stones and *aurora borealis* rhinestones. *1950s* B: 18cm (7in) circ; E: 3.75cm (1½in) long

£425–475   **CRIS**

Good, Better, Best

Complexities of composition and the size, colours, and cuts of the stones determine the prices of these Schiaparelli bracelets.

£225–275

Made in the 1950s, this is a very pretty and elegant **rhinestone bracelet**. It combines carved white, faux "baby tooth" pearls with prong-set aquamarine and *aurora borealis* rhinestones. 16cm (6¼in) long **CRIS**

£325–375

The dense, complex combination of stones in this pretty 1950s **seashell motif bracelet** commands a higher price than the bracelet above. Set with white glass shells, faux pearls, and cabochons. 18cm (7in) long **CRIS**

Octagon-cut "black diamonds"

£425–475

For Schiaparelli collectors this **1950s paste bracelet** is the most desirable of the three bracelets. Bold yet elegant, it incorporates large pastes in a characteristic fantasy colour similar to smoky quartz and sometimes referred to as "black diamonds", and small *aurora borealis* rhinestones that are prong-set with gold-plated metal. 18.5cm (7¼in) long **CRIS**

Stanley Hagler

Described as "the Picasso of jewellery", American designer, Stanley Hagler, created pieces that were unique, colourful, seemingly larger than life, and often outrageous.

STANLEY HAGLER
1923–96

1923 Stanley Hagler is born in the United States

Late 1940s Works briefly as a business advisor to Miriam Haskell

Late 1950s Hagler begins creating his own designs. His signature is "Stanley Hagler" until 1983

1968 Hagler wins the Swarovski Design Award for the first time

1979 Mark Mercy joins as a contributing designer

1983 The company relocates to Florida. Signature changes to "Stanley Hagler N.Y.C."

1989 Ian St. Gielar joins as Chief Designer, remaining until 1993

1993 Hagler retires

1996 Stanley Hagler dies. After his death, jewellery continues to be produced under Stanley Hagler & Company

DESIGNER TO THE STARS

For a man who apparently launched his jewellery career on a whim, Stanley Hagler was remarkably successful, creating and selling costume jewellery throughout the second half of the 20th century. He was equally successful at cultivating a glittering client list, drawn largely from the ranks of the rich and famous.

Hagler specialized in faux pearl jewellery, using individually strung pearls to highlight their quality. This was in marked contrast to other makers of faux pearl jewellery who grouped them together to hide individual flaws and inconsistencies. His baroque pearls were hand-blown glass beads dipped in pearl resin up to 15 times to achieve maxium luminosity.

Opulent and complex, Stanley Hagler's jewellery combines contemporary design with antique components. He always used the finest materials, such as hand-blown glass, Swarovski crystals, and Russian gold plated filligree. Pieces were wired by hand, with stones and crystals prong-set into place rather than glued. His work has a strong architectural style and pieces look equally good whether they are viewed from the front or from the back. He also created some outstanding Christmas Tree pins (*see pp.172–175*).

MULTI-PURPOSE DESIGN

One of the intriguing features of Stanley Hagler's jewellery is that it is often multi-purpose. The clasp of a necklace can be transformed into a hair ornament or a pin, necklaces can become double bracelets, and certain earrings can be given an alternative look, simply by adding or removing various components.

During the course of his career, Hagler won 11 Swarovski awards for "Great Designs in Jewellery". He always designed jewellery he thought was "just plain pretty", although his earlier pieces were less complex than later ones.

Above: Flower pin with red and green Murano glass leaves and petals and a yellow glass cabochon centre. *1960s. 10cm (4in) wide* **£180–220 CRIS**

Floral pendant necklace and earrings with faux coral glass beads and cabochons hand-wired to a filigree gold-plated backing. *1980s N: 40cm (15¾in) circ; E: 3.75cm (1½in) wide* **£500–600 CRIS**

INSPIRATION

Stanley Hagler followed Miriam Haskell's lead, creating intricately designed handcrafted costume jewellery. Flowers are a recurring motif in his work, as are oriental and figural motifs, such as butterflies. The twice yearly Fashion Press Week was another major source of inspiration.

UPTOWN STYLE

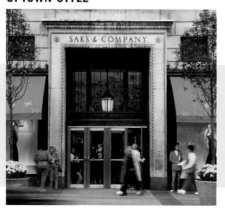

Hagler produced jewellery for a range of middle and upmarket retail outlets, most notably Saks Fifth Avenue, Lord & Taylor, Bergdorf, and Goodman. He started off selling through a prestigious west coast fashion group called Joseph Magnin.

JEWELS FIT FOR A DUCHESS

Famed for her legendary jewellery collection, the stylish Duchess of Windsor (*right*) enjoyed wearing both faux and genuine pieces. So, when one of Stanley Hagler's friends remarked that he would never succeed as a jewellery designer, Hagler rose to the challenge and declared he would create something "fit for a queen". In fact, his first piece was designed for the woman whose husband famously gave up the British throne for her: the Duchess of Windsor. Stanley Hagler sent her the result, a bracelet, and she became the first in a long and illustrious line of clients.

Gold-plated bangle with polychrome moulded glass and glass bead floral motifs, and clear crystal rhinestones. The original version of this bangle was made with seed pearls in the 1950s for Wallace Simpson. *1970s. 19cm (7½in) circ* **£500–600 CRIS**

Hagler also gave much thought to how, when, and where a woman wears jewellery: earrings had to hang perfectly, while a necklace should lie in a particular way so as to be flattering. Although his jewellery was often large in scale, he varied the size according to current fashions. The name tags were also smaller or larger, depending on the size of the piece.

As well as his own jewellery, Hagler produced various designs for other companies, including jewelled swimming flippers, wigs, and jewellery that matched a prestigious range of luggage.

ABOUT IDENTIFICATION

Three designers were associated with the company: Stanley Hagler from the 1950s, Mark Mercy from 1979, and Ian St. Gielar from 1989. The marks from the 1950s had "Stanley Hagler" printed straight across an oval disc. On moving to Florida, Hagler added "N.Y.C." to read "Stanley Hagler N.Y.C." on the curve of the oval. Jewellery bearing the tag "Stanley Hagler NYC", with no period, has been designed by Ian St. Gielar since Hagler's death in 1996.

Vase of flowers pin in gilt metal with blue, green, red, and pink glass petals and beads. *1980s. 7cm (2¾in) long* **£120–150 CRIS**

COLOURED PEARLS

Faux pearls were first dipped in opalescent dyed coating before being incorporated into a design, as in this stylized floral pin. It has pink champagne and lime-green coloured faux pearls and mother-of-pearl petals, hand-wired to a filigree gold-plated backing. *1980s 7.5cm (3in) wide* **£150–195 CRIS**

Faux coral flower necklace and earrings with glass beads, cabochons, and drops hand-wired to filigree gold-plated backings. *1980s*
N: 57cm (22½in) circ; E: 6.25cm (2½in) long

£500-600   CRIS

Blue and gold flower pendant necklace and earrings of gilt metal with lapis glass cabochons, and cobalt-blue glass beads, hand-wired to filigree gold-plated backings. *1980s*
N: 51cm (20in) circ; E: 3.75cm (1½in) wide

£500-600   CRIS

Pendant necklace and earrings with moulded glass beads wired to filigree gold-plated backings. *1960s*
N: 56cm (22in) circ; E: 3cm (1⅛in) long

£300-350   CRIS

Flower necklace and earrings of moulded amethyst glass beads and drops, hand-wired to filigree gold-plated backings. *1980s*
N: 40cm (15¾in) circ; E: 5cm (2in) long

£500-600   CRIS

Buddha necklace with ivory Buddha and flower petals and French jet beads hand-wired to filigree gold-plated backings. *1960s*
N: 48.25cm (19in) circ; Buddha: 7.5cm (3in) long

£400-500   CRIS

Flower necklace and earrings with faux pearls and floral clusters of Murano glass and glass beads. *1970s*
N: 76cm (30in) circ; E: 2.5cm (1in) long

£500-600   CRIS

Flower necklace and earrings with Murano glass and glass beads hand-wired to filigree gold-plated metal backings. *1980s*
N: 76.25cm (30in) circ; E: 2.5cm (1in) wide

£500-600   CRIS

FAUX SEED PEARLS

Many of Stanley Hagler's imaginative pieces feature tiny faux seed pearls of Japanese origin. Made of glass, and produced in numerous colours, they are mostly hand-wired into floral and foliate motifs. The intricacy of these compositions is typical of Hagler's craftsmanship and counterbalances the boldness of his designs.

Necklace and earrings with floral rosettes of hand-wired, coral-coloured faux seed pearls, crystal rhinestones, and faux coral cabochons. *1980s*
N: 45cm (17¾in)) circ; E: 2.5cm (1in) wide **£350-400 CRIS**

Faux pearl necklace with an ornament of faux pearls and rose montées. *1970s*

40cm (15¾in) circ

£200–250 **CRIS**

Floral pin and earrings of faux and seed pearls and clear crystal rhinestones hand-wired to filigree gold-plated backings. *1990s*

P: 7.5cm (3in) wide; E: 3.75cm (1½in) long

£100–180 **PC**

Floral pin and earrings with petals and leaves of pressed glass and glass beads on filigree gold-plated backings. *1980s*

P: 9.5cm (3¾in) long; E: 3.5cm (1⅜in) wide

£100–150 **CRIS**

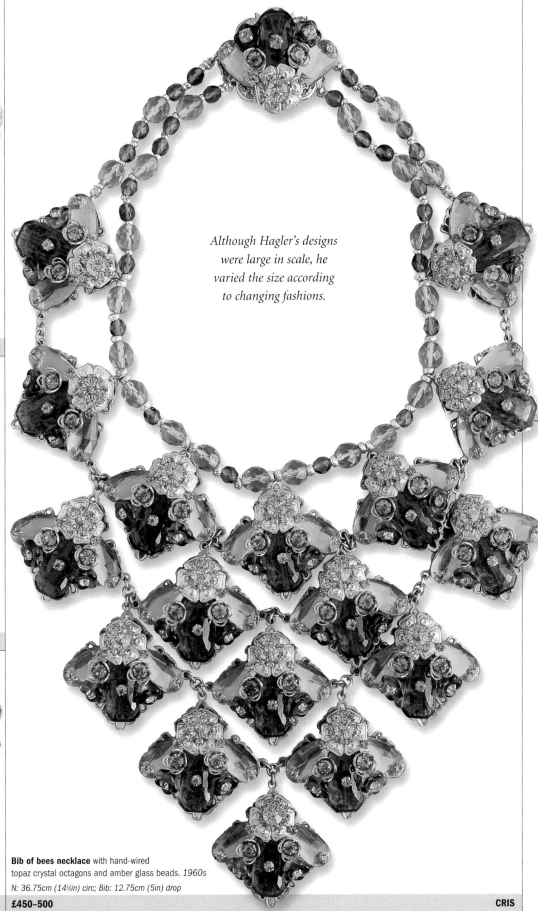

Although Hagler's designs were large in scale, he varied the size according to changing fashions.

Bib of bees necklace with hand-wired topaz crystal octagons and amber glass beads. *1960s*

N: 36.75cm (14½in) circ; Bib: 12.75cm (5in) drop

£450–500 **CRIS**

115

Flowers are recurring motifs in Hagler's jewellery designs.

Floral pin with petals and leaves of gilt metal, clear crystal rhinestones, and blue and turquoise pressed glass and faux seed pearls. *Late 1960s*

6cm (2⅜in) long

£60–70   **CRIS**

Orchid pin with faux coral composite petals and amber and smokey topaz rhinestones. *1960s*

7.5cm (3in) long

£150–200   **CRIS**

Reverse of pin

Floral and foliate pin with pink Murano glass petals and carved plastic leaves. *1960s*

10cm (4in) long

£130–150   **CRIS**

Floral pin with grey faux seed pearls, green poured glass, and jade glass beads. *1980s*

9.5cm (3¾in) wide

£200–250   **CRIS**

Fruit and leaf pin with fruits and leaves in cherry red, yellow, black, and green Murano glass. *1960s*

5.5cm (2⅛in) long

£100–120   **CRIS**

Floral pin with orange pressed glass and glass beads, coral faux seed pearls, and clear crystal rhinestones. *1980s*

7.5cm (3in) wide

£100-150   **CRIS**

Cameo floral pin with butter faux seed pearls and jonquil rhinestones around a carved ivory cameo. *1960s*

7.5cm (3in) long

£125-150   **CRIS**

Stylized camelia pin with pearlized metal blue petals, pressed red glass, red faux seed pearls, and clear crystal rhinestones. *1960s*

8.25cm (3¼in) wide

£200-250   **PC**

Panda and leaf pin with amethyst pressed glass, green and amethyst faux seed pearls, rhinestones, and ivory pandas. *1980s*

6.5cm (2½in) long

£200-250   **CRIS**

Flower and leaf pin with yellow and green pressed glass and yellow, red, and green faux seed pearls. *1980s*

12.75cm (5in) long

£250-300   **CRIS**

Turquoise pressed glass flower with powder blue faux seed pearls and a blue glass cabochon. *1970s*

7.5cm (3in) wide

£120-150   **CRIS**

Butterfly pin with white and peach pressed glass, yellow and peach glass beads, and seed pearls. *1980s*

9.5cm (3¾in) wide

£200-250   **CRIS**

Good, Better, Best

Age and rarity are significant, but the different prices these Hagler pins command is ultimately determined by their visual impact.

£75-100

This 1980s **floral pin** is a classic Hagler composition incorporating white, pink, and red pressed glass petals, green seed pearls, Venetian glass drops, and filigree gilt metal. *10.75cm (4¼in) long* **CRIS**

£150-200

This 1960s **vase of flowers pin** is in gold-tone metal with carved shell leaves, mother-of-pearl petals, and clear crystal rhinestones. Its rarity commands a high price. *9cm (3½in) long* **CRIS**

£200-250

This 1980s **head and flowers pin** features a central carved ivory oriental head encircled by rose quartz and green faux seed pearl leaves, rose quartz and violet pressed glass petals, and jade green rhinestones. It fetches the highest price because the inclusion of the head makes the composition more dramatic than that of the vase of flowers pin. *6.25cm (2½in) wide* **CRIS**

TRIFARI
1918–present

1904 Gustavo Trifari emigrates from Naples to New York and works with his uncle making costume jewellery

c.1910 The company Trifari and Trifari is founded, and becomes just Trifari after two years

1918 Trifari and Krussman founded a year after Leo Krussman joins as sales manager

1925 The company becomes Trifari, Krussman and Fishel (T. K. F.) after Carl Fishel joins as salesman

1930 Alfred Philippe joins as chief designer. The company expands to become the second largest US producer of costume jewellery

1954 Trifari wins a legal case against Coro that establishes fashion jewellery as copyright works of art

1964 Gustavo Trifari, Jnr., Louis Krussman, and Carlton Fishel succeed their fathers as owners

1994 Trifari becomes part of the Monet Group, which is bought by Liz Clarborne in 2000

Trifari

Trifari has long been one of the United States' pre-eminent costume jewellery makers. Covering diverse styles and a full spectrum of price points, its pieces invariably display imaginative design and quality craftsmanship.

ITALIAN ORIGINS

Like many American costume jewellers, Trifari was founded on the skills of a newcomer to the country. Gustavo Trifari was born in Naples, Italy in 1883 and, prior to his arrival in New York in 1904, had trained as a goldsmith under his grandfather, Luigi. After initially working for an uncle, with whom he formed Trifari and Trifari in about 1910, Gustavo branched out on his own to make high-quality pieces under the name Trifari. The arrival of sales manager Leo Krussman in 1917, and the formation of Trifari and Krussman a year later, brought embryonic commercial success – further enhanced when salesman Carl Fishel came on board in 1923.

Two years later the three founded Trifari,

Krussman and Fishel (T. K. F.), and the rest is history. Some seven decades on, T. K. F. – still best-known as Trifari – remains one of the United State's largest and most prestigious designers and manufacturers of costume jewellery.

FOUNDATIONS OF SUCCESS

An essential part of Trifari's enduring success has been the powerful mix of glamorous clientele and prestigious publicity. From the 1930s onwards, Trifari's creation of exclusive designs for Broadway musicals, such as *Roberta*, and for numerous stars of stage and screen, highlighted the desirability of its jewellery. This status was further enhanced by Trifari's commissions in the 1950s from First Lady Mamie Eisenhower. More recently, Madonna wore Trifari in the Hollywood blockbuster *Evita*.

Above: Patriotic American eagle pin of sterling silver with red enamelling, white clear rhinestones, and blue Lucite belly. *1940s. 4.5cm (1¾in) long* **£130–200 ROX**

Rare and fabulous plant motif pin of sterling silver with green and brown enamelling and a profusion of pavé-set clear crystal rhinestones. *1940s 18cm (7in) long* **£1,200–1,300 SUM**

Modern and sophisticated is how this late-1950s advertisement promotes a Trifari "Comet" necklace and earrings in gold Trifanium with clear crystal rhinestones.

Of course, such commissions would never have been forthcoming if the jewellery hadn't been of sufficient quality. In terms of materials and techniques, chief designer Alfred Philippe set the tone from early on with his use of fine, skilfully hand-set Austrian rhinestones in extremely convincing imitations of expensive precious jewellery (*see below*). Subsequently, when 1940s wartime restrictions prohibited the use of white metals for retail, Trifari produced fabulous pieces in heavy sterling silver, often with a luxurious vermeil (gold-plated) finish. Other attractive and convincing materials have included the plastic Lucite, which closely resembles rock crystal and was used in Trifari's 1940s Jelly Bellies (*see below and p.127*). Post-war examples range from pressed or moulded glass, high-quality, milky coloured pastes in imitation of moonstones and chalcedony, superb faux pearls, and Trifanium, a non-tarnishing, gold-finish alloy named after the company.

DIVERSITY OF STYLES

Above all, however, it is the way in which such materials have been used that has guaranteed Trifari's reputation. The range of its pieces – always astutely launched in sympathy with the prevailing sentiment of the time – has been incredibly diverse and encompasses most styles fashionable since the 1920s. All are collectable, but among the most coveted are the Jelly Belly figural pins and Crown pins (especially those designed by Alfred Philippe during the 1940s), and the patriotic jewellery, including American flag and eagle pins, hailing the American armed forces of World War II. Faux pearls and paste gemstones from the 1950s have recently enjoyed a revival, as have combinations of pearls and brushed gold. However, due to their eminent wearability, it is the pieces incorporating floral and foliate imagery that have proved the most consistently popular.

A fur clip, in two-tone yellow and rose gold-plated silver and set with faux rubies and diamonds. *1940s 9cm (3½in) long* **£450–500 CRIS**

COMMISSIONS
In addition to producing retail costume jewellery, Trifari also created pieces for private and commercial clients, including Broadway theatres and Hollywood film studios. Undoubtedly the most prestigious, however, were those designed in the 1950s for Mamie Eisenhower.

FIRST LADY

This necklace and earrings set – part of a demi-parure of faux pearls, emeralds, and diamonds – was made to an original design by Alfred Philippe for US First Lady Mamie Eisenhower. Trifari made other pieces for Mrs Eisenhower, notably for the 1953 and 1957 Presidential Inaugural Balls. *1950s N: 38cm (15in) circ; E: 3cm (1⅛in) wide* **£400–500 CRIS**

ALFRED PHILIPPE – CHIEF DESIGNER

Much of Trifari's success can be attributed to Frenchman Alfred Philippe, who joined the company as its chief designer in 1930, and didn't retire until 1968. Significant contributions included his use of high-quality Swarovski crystals, which gave rise to the company's epithet: the Diamanté Kings. Having previously designed pieces sold via the prestigious jewellers Cartier and Van Cleef and Arpels, Philippe also introduced sophisticated techniques such as the invisible setting usually confined to high-end precious jewellery. However, his most enduring legacy resides in his imaginative and commercially successful designs. Notable among many are the much sought after 1940s Crown pins (*see p.129*) and Lucite Jelly Bellies (*see p.127*).

Poinsettia pin designed by Alfred Philippe with faux rubies and diamonds configured in imitation of the invisible setting technique developed by Van Cleef and Arpels. *1950s 7cm (2¾in) wide* **£600–700 CRIS**

Jelly Belly seal pin designed by Alfred Philippe, of vermeil sterling silver with clear Lucite belly, clear and ruby rhinestones (for the eyes), and a large prong-set sapphire rhinestone ball. *1940s. 6cm (2⅜in) high* **£400–500 CRIS**

EVITA

These "Jewels of India" pin and earrings are identical to those worn by Madonna when she starred in the film *Evita*. Of brushed gold finish with green and red cabochons and clear rhinestones, they were inspired by the Indian Mughal jewels popularized by Cartier during the 1920s. *1950s. P: 6cm (2⅜in) wide; E: 2.5cm (1in) wide* **£240–280 CRIS**

Necklaces, bracelets, and earrings

Numerous style influences are evident in Trifari necklaces, bracelets, and earrings, including neoclassical, Art Deco, romantic-historical, and oriental, to name but a few. With imagery ranging from floral to geometric to abstract, collectors have much to choose from.

Retro style floral motif necklace of vermeil sterling silver with round- and emerald-cut glass emeralds and clear rhinestones. *1940s*

Flower: 2½cm (1in) wide

£235–300   ROX

Floral pendant necklace, rose-gold-plated with a cluster of plum-black cabochons. *1950s*

Pd: 3.75cm (1½in) long

£80–95   TR

Pendant necklace and bracelet from the Princess Eugene series, of sterling silver and vermeil with rhinestones. *1940s*

Pd: 3.75cm (1½in) long; B: 18cm (7in) circ

£185–315   ROX

Necklace, hinged bracelet, and hoop earrings demi-parure, gold-plated and set with clusters of ruby red rhinestones. *1960s*

N: 37cm (14½in) circ; B: 18cm (7in) circ; E: 9cm (3½in) drop

£200–330   ROX

Ivy leaf necklace and earrings in sterling silver with pale blue chalcedony paste leaves. *1940s*

N: 1.25cm (½in) wide; E: 2½cm (1in) long

£150–215   ROX

Rhodium-plated necklace with white glass flowerheads and coral cabochon berries. *c.1940*

Flowers: 1.25cm (½in) wide

£185–315   ROX

Faux pearl necklace and earrings of vermeil sterling silver with large faux pearl cabochons. *1940s*

N: 27.5cm (10⅞in) circ; E: 2.5cm (1in) long

£185–250   ROX

Multiple-strand necklace with gun-metal links, tourmaline glass beads, and a gold-plated leaf motif clasp. *1960s*

Clasp: 6.25cm (2½in) wide

£100–150   TR

Star motif necklace and oriental mask-with-star earrings, both gold-plated with clear rhinestone highlights. *Early 1950s*

N: 43cm (17in) long; E: 2.5cm (1in) long

£120–150   ROX

Flowers, leaves, and berries necklace, silver-plated with ruby red and pale blue chalcedony cabochons, emerald green teardrops, and clear rhinestone highlights. *1930s*

Flowers: 2cm (¾in) wide

£200–335   ROX

Good, Better, Best

With or without earrings or a pin, early Trifari necklaces from the 1930s and 40s generally command higher prices than those made in the 1950s and 60s, with a few exceptions.

£95–100

This mid-1950s **glass and rose-gold necklace and earrings** set has carved, pale yellow glass flowerheads set in rose-gold-finish base metal. Their appeal lies in the simplicity of detail and clarity of form. *N: 38cm (15in) circ; E: 3.75cm (1½in) long* **CRIS**

£450–500

This 1940s **retro style twin-pendant necklace and bow pin** is of vermeil sterling silver with rhinestones which, together with greater intricacies of craftsmanship, command a substantially higher price. *Pd: 9cm (3½in) long; P: 5.75cm (2¼in) wide* **CRIS**

£600–700

This rare 1950s **floral garland necklace and earrings** with faux "baby's tooth" pearls and clear and black rhinestones on gold-plated castings, are brilliantly conceived and executed in both form and detail. *N: 38cm (15in) circ; E: 3cm (1⅛in) wide* **CRIS**

Necklace, bracelet, and earrings of vermeil sterling silver with turquoise cabochons and ruby red and blue rhinestones. *1940s*
N & B: 2cm (¾in) wide; E: 2.5cm (1in) wide

£200–335   **ROX**

Alfred Philippe necklace and earrings in vermeil sterling silver with carved coral glass leaves and clear rhinestone highlights. *1940s*
N: 40.5cm (16in) circ; E: 3.75cm (1½in) wide

£150–200   **RG**

Floral bracelet with clear navette-cut rhinestone flowerheads with faux pearl centres. *c.1950*
15cm (6in) circ

£150–250   **LB**

Jewels-of-India necklace and earrings of brushed gold alloy with navette-cut, square-cut, and round rhinestones. *1950s*
N: 2cm (¾in) wide; E: 2.5cm (1in) long

£185–250   **ROX**

Floral, foliate, and fruit pins

Trifari's flower, leaf, and fruit pins are a collecting field in their own right. Generally of more intricate design and craftsmanship, examples made during the 1930s and 40s almost invariably command higher prices than the simpler, albeit equally stylish pieces made thereafter.

Early, large, and rare sunflower pin, rhodium-plated with pavé-set clear and citrine rhinestones. *1930s*
9cm (3½in) wide

£400–500 CRIS

Early floral pin with trailing leaves, rhodium-plated with large blue baguettes and clear rhinestones. *1930s*
8cm (3⅛in) long

£185–250 ROX

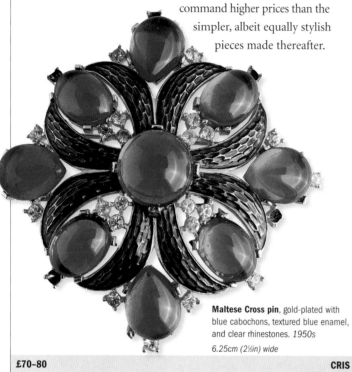

Maltese Cross pin, gold-plated with blue cabochons, textured blue enamel, and clear rhinestones. *1950s*
6.25cm (2½in) wide

£70–80 CRIS

Large flower pin with yellow, green, and orange enamel and clear rhinestones. *1930s*
10cm (4in) long

£300–435 ROX

Bouquet of flowers pin of vermeil sterling silver with red and clear rhinestones. *1930s*
8cm (3⅛in) long

£235–255 TR

Lily pin of vermeil sterling silver with semi-translucent white Lucite leaves and clear rhinestones. *Late 1930s*
10cm (4in) long

£1,200–1,500 ROX

Bouquet of flowers pin, rhodium-plated with sapphire blue pastes and clear rhinestones. *1930s*
9.5cm (3¾in) long

£135–185 ROX

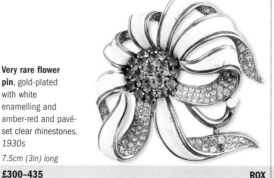

Basket of flowers pin, gold-plated with amethyst blue, jonquil, and rose pink rhinestones. *Mid 1950s*
4.5cm (1¾in) long

£35–40 CRIS

Very rare flower pin, gold-plated with white enamelling and amber-red and pavé-set clear rhinestones. *1930s*
7.5cm (3in) long

£300–435 ROX

Large rare bouquet of flowers pin, gold-plated with aquamarine pastes, amber, red, and clear rhinestones, and green enamelling. 1930s
12cm (4¾in) long

£1,000–1,335 ROX

Flower pin of rose-gold vermeil sterling silver with clusters of clear rhinestones. *1930s*

9cm (3½in) long

£200–335	ROX

Floral and foliate bouquet pin of vermeil sterling silver with rhinestones. *1930s*

10cm (4in) long

£235–365	ROX

Floral pin and earrings by Alfred Philippe, rhodium-plated with rose pink, caliber-cut pastes and pavé-set clear rhinestones. *1940s*

Flower heads: 3.5cm (1⅜in) wide

£400–670	ROX

Milky blue glass stones are convincing imitations of the mineral chalcedony.

Bouquet of flowers pin, gold-plated with green enamelling, milky blue glass stones, and clear rhinestones. *1930s*

9cm (3½in) long

£400–435	TR

Floral pin, rhodium-plated with sapphire navette and amethyst blue rhinestones. *1940s*

9cm (3½in) long

£115–150	ROX

Floral and foliate pin, matte-finish gold-plated with graduated white faux pearls. *1950s*

7.5cm (3in) long

£70–80	CRIS

Flower pin, rhodium-plated with small clear baguette and round rhinestones. *1930s*

10cm (4in) long

£135–200	ROX

Good, Better, Best

All these pieces are very stylish and highly collectable. However, their different prices are determined by factors such as weight, contrasts of colour, intricacy of workmanship, and the degree of naturalism.

£35–40

This late 1950s, silver-coloured alloy **tulip pin** is emminently wearable and its petals and leaves are fluently styled. The absence of contrasting-coloured materials gives it a nicely understated elegance. *8.25cm (3¼in) long* **CRIS**

£75–85

This mid-1950s, gold-plated **maple leaf pin** is set with bold red oval and teardrop coral cabochons. Boldly designed, it is, both visually and in weight, a more substantial piece than the tulip pin. *7.5cm (3in) long* **CRIS**

£450–550

This 1940s **hyacinths pin** is cold-enamelled and studded with pavé-set clear rhinestones. It is highly naturalistic, exquisitely detailed, old, and rare – a compelling combination that makes this by far the most desirable piece of the three. *11cm (4⅓in) long* **CRIS**

Foliate pin and earrings of vermeil sterling silver with rectangular emerald green and round clear rhinestones. *1940s*

P: 9cm (3½in) long; E: 2.5cm (1in) long

£200–270   **ROX**

Grapes and leaves pin of sterling silver with vermeil highlights and pavé-set clear rhinestones. *1930s*

7.5cm (3in) long

£135–200   **ROX**

Pin and earrings with emerald green, ruby red, and sapphire blue rhinestones set around clear rhinestone flower heads. *1930s*

P: 6.5cm (2½in) wide; E: 2.5cm (1in) wide

£185–250   **ROX**

Marine plant pin and earrings, gold-plated with fuchsia pink and faux moonstone cabochons and faux pearls. *1950s*

P: 9cm (3½in) long; E: 2.5cm (1in) long

£140–160   **CRIS**

Flower pin of green, purple, yellow, and pink enamel with clear rhinestone highlights. *1930s*

7cm (2¾in) long

£135–200   **ROX**

Foliate pin of sterling silver with "fruit salad" stones and clear and purple rhinestones. *1940s*

9cm (3½in) long

£150–170   **TR**

Alfred Philippe flower pin and earrings in sterling silver with invisible-set calibre-cut petals and green and clear rhinestones. *1940s*

P: 12.5cm (5in) long; E: 3cm (1⅛in) long

£370–570   **ROX**

Gold-plated leaf pin with pinkish red, blue, emerald green, and clear rhinestones. *1950s*

7cm (2¾in) long

£70–90   **RG**

Retro flower pin of pierced silver alloy with pear, navette, and round clear rhinestones. *1950s*

4cm (1½in) wide

£30–50   **ABAA**

Russian gold plating

Russian gold-plated leaf pin with chanel- and pavé-set clear rhinestones. *1950s*

20cm (7⅞in) long

£75–95   **LB**

Pea-pod pin of matte-finish white metal with turquoise cabochons for the peas. Naturalistic in form with stylized colour combinations, such pins are increasingly sought after. *1930s*

6.25cm (2½in) long

£115–185   **ROX**

Fruit pin with two pairs of matching earrings (one pair pendant), gold-plated with clusters of fuchsia pastes. *1960s*

P: 6cm (2⅜in) long; E (left): 2.5cm (1in) long; E (above): 6cm (2⅜in) long

£55–85 ROX

Bunch of grapes pin with deep purple glass beads and gold-plated leaves. *1930s*

3.75cm (1½in) long

£135–185 ROX

Gold-plated pea-pod pin with green cold enamel and faux pearls for the peas inside the pod. *1950s*

7cm (2¾in) long

£120–140 CRIS

Fruit motif pendant earrings in pierced, basket-weave patterned gold-plated base metal. *Mid 1950s*

4cm (1½in) long

£35–45 CRIS

Fruit pin and earrings of sterling silver, the fruits with ruby red rhinestones and clear rhinestone highlights, the leaves with pavé-set clear rhinestones. *1940s*

P: 4cm (1½in) long; E: 2cm (¾in) long

£350–550 ROX

MINI FRUITS

Trifari produced numerous miniature pins during the late 1950s and 1960s. They could be worn either individually, or scattered in groups of two, three, or more. Small fruits, as below, are particularly popular, but other ranges – notably their Heraldic motifs – are equally collectable.

Miniature fruit pins – the apple, pineapple, and bunch of grapes in matte-finish silver alloy; the strawberry in a gold-tone equivalent. *Late 1950s*

2–2.5cm (¾–1in) long **£20–25 each** CRIS

Gold-plated fruit pin, sliced to reveal clusters of emerald green rhinestones. *1950s*

6cm (2⅜in) long

£60–70 CRIS

Leaves and berries pin and earrings, the stalks and leaves of matte-finish gold alloy with graduated white faux pearls. *1950s*

P: 10cm (4in) long; E: 3.75cm (1½in) long

£140–160 CRIS

Gold-plated and pierced sponge earrings (with their original Trifari tag – not shown). *1960s*

2.25cm (⅞in) wide

£15–20 TR

Matte-finish gold alloy leaves and berries pin with elongated faux pearls. *1950s*

10cm (4in) long

£65–75 CRIS

Leaves and berries pin of matte-finish gold alloy with faux pearls and tiny pavé-set rhinestones. *1950s*

10cm (4in) long

£90–100 CRIS

Creature pins

Trifari produced numerous, eminently collectable animal, bird, and insect pins. Better-quality components and greater intricacies of design make its earlier 1930s and 40s pins the most desirable.

Angel fish pin, silver-plated with blue Lucite belly and clear and ruby red rhinestones (for the eyes). *1950s*

6cm (2⅜in) long

£165–235 ROX

Shoal of fishes pin of gold-plated casting with small ruby red cabochons for the eyes. *Late 1950s*

6.5cm (2½in) long

£75–85 ROX

Large hinged dragon's head watch ring set with clear rhinestones and green cabochon eyes. *1960s*

6.5cm (2½in) wide

£115–165 ROX

Jelly Belly crab pin of vermeil sterling silver with grey Lucite belly and clear rhinestone highlights. *1940s*

7.5cm (3in) wide

£600–670 TR

Châtelaine pin, gold-plated with faux pearls, enamel, and red cabochons. *1950s*

Coral: 3cm (1⅛in) long

£75–80 CRIS

Seahorse pin of matte-finish gold-plated casting with turquoise cabochons "belly" and ruby red glass cabochon eyes. *1950s*

11.5cm (4½in) long

£30–40 CRIS

Winged insect pin, rhodium-plated with emerald green cabochons, enamelling, and clear crystal rhinestones. *1930s*

4cm (1⅝in) long

£100–170 ROX

Fly pin, gold-plated with prong-set Lucite "belly", blue and aquamarine cabochons, ruby red baguettes, and clear rhinestones. *1940s*

4.5cm (1¾in) long

£115–165 ROX

Jelly Belly fly pin of vermeil sterling silver with grey Lucite belly and clear rhinestones. *1940s*

7.5cm (3in) long

£600–735 TR

Butterfly pin designed by Alfred Philippe of sterling silver with clear rhinestones and prong-set blue and red cabochons. *1940s*

6.25cm (2½in) long

£140–160 CRIS

Rare insect pin, gold-plated with blue navette paste body, and large and small red and emerald green cabochons. *1930s*

7.5cm (3in) long

£465–665 ROX

Exceedingly rare snail fur clip of vermeil sterling silver with black cold enamel, milky blue cabochons, and pavé-set rhinestones. *1940s*

7.5cm (3in) long

£900–1,000 CRIS

Bee pin with imperial purple enamelling over a gold-plated casting. *1950s*

3.5cm (1⅜in) wide

£30–40 CRIS

Jelly Belly beetle pin of vermeil sterling silver with grey Lucite "belly" and clear rhinestone highlights. *1940s*

5cm (2in) long

£600–665 TR

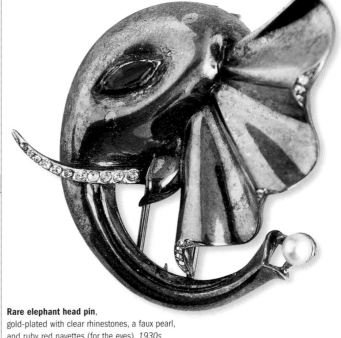

Coiled snake pin and earrings, gold-plated with inset faux ruby and emerald cabochons. *1950s*

P: 6.25cm (2½in) long; E: 2.5cm (1in) wide

£120–150 RG

Rare elephant head pin, gold-plated with clear rhinestones, a faux pearl, and ruby red navettes (for the eyes). *1930s*

5cm (2in) long

£200–265 ROX

Set of duck and baby duck scatter pins, gold-plated with ruby red, emerald green, aquamarine, and sapphire blue cabochons and clear rhinestones. *1930s*

Largest: 3.75cm (1½in) long; Smallest: 2.5cm (1in) long

£200–265 ROX

Perching birds pin, silver-plated with red and turquoise enamelling and clear rhinestones. *1930s*

5.75cm (2¼in) long

£200–335 ROX

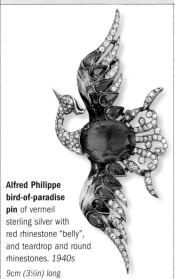

Alfred Philippe bird-of-paradise pin of vermeil sterling silver with red rhinestone "belly", and teardrop and round rhinestones. *1940s*

9cm (3½in) long

£200–250 RG

Grey Jelly Belly chick pin, gold-plated with pavé-set clear rhinestone head and coral cabochon eyes. *1930s*

5cm (2in) long

£735–865 TR

American eagle pin of vermeil sterling silver with red, white, and blue enamelling. *1940s*

5cm (2in) long

£120–135 TR

JELLY BELLY PINS

Trifari's famous Jelly Belly pins have risen in price dramatically over the last five years. The Lucite Jelly Bellies made in the 1940s (*see below*) are generally considered the most desirable. Price differences between them primarily depend on the rarity of the motif – poodles, for example, being scarcer than roosters.

Jelly Belly rooster pin, gold-plated with Lucite belly and red rhinestones. *1940s*
6.5cm (2½in) long **£400–500** CRIS

Jelly Belly poodle pin, gold-plated with Lucite belly and red rhinestones. *1940s*
5cm (2in) long **£500–600** CRIS

Miscellaneous pins

For many collectors the great appeal of Trifari pins lies in their sheer diversity. Bows, hearts, shells, and flags are the perennial favourites, but human-figural, architectural, pictorial, and abstract designs are also much sought after, and the most prestigious of all are its classic crown pins.

Heart pin of blue glass encased in vermeil sterling silver, with a rhodium-plated arrow and winged insect. *1940s*

7cm (2¾in) long

£135–200　　　　**ROX**

Shell and seaweed pin of gold-plated casting with green and coral enamelling and faux pearls. *1950s*

6.5cm (2½in) long

£120–140　　　　**CRIS**

The deep, lustrous shine of thick vermeil sterling silver is a recurring feature of Trifari pins made during the 1940s.

Heart pin and earrings of emerald green glass encased in scrolled vermeil silver with blue glass teardrops and clear rhinestones. *1940s*

P: 6.25cm (2½in) long; E: 3cm (1¼in) long

£180–200　　　　**CRIS**

Bow pin of gold vermeil over sterling silver, with ruby red baguette and pavé-set clear rhinestones. *1940s*

9cm (3½in) wide

£400–600　　　　**LYNH**

Rare swan and bridge pin with blue and dark ruby red enamelling and clear rhinestones on a sterling silver casting. *1940s*

7cm (2¾in) wide

£470–670　　　　**ROX**

Bow and fruit pin of vermeil sterling silver with large emerald green and small clear rhinestones. *1940s*

6cm (2⅜in) long

£100–130　　　　**RG**

Light weight gold plating

Vermeil sterling silver pin with bands of rope moulding alternated with blue enamelling, and with clear rhinestones. *1940s*

3.75cm (1½in) long

£100–120　　　　**CRIS**

Stars and Stripes flag pin with gold-plated staff, blue and red enamel, and clear rhinestone flag. *1940s*

6cm (2⅜in) long

£135–200　　　　**ROX**

Pendant pin with a single strand of thick, gold-plated wire looped into multiple, interlaced figure-of-eights above a large, ruby red glass pendant capped with gold-plated leaf motifs. *1950s*

7.5cm (3in) long

£60–80　　　　**CRIS**

Early and relatively rare duette pin of vermeil sterling silver with large emerald pastes, small red and emerald baguettes, and small clear rhinestones. *1930s*

8.5cm (3⅜in) long

£200–335 ROX

Toadstool pin of textured gold alloy with blue cabochons, clear rhinestones, and faux angel skin coral eggs. *1950s*

4cm (1½in) long

£45–65 CRIS

Shell pin in aquamarine and red cold enamel, with inset faux pearls, on a gold-plated casting. *1950s*

8cm (3⅛in) long

£120–130 CRIS

Sailor pin in white metal with clear rhinestones and flesh-tone enamelled head and pale blue enamelled globe. *1940s*

5.75cm (2¼in) long

£210–250 ROX

Balloon pin with heart-motif ballast, of satin finish gold-tone alloy. *1950s*

5.75cm (2¼in) long

£30–40 CRIS

Rare Chinese lantern pin with red, black, and white enamelling and clear rhinestones, on a gold-plated casting. *1930s*

7cm (2¾in) long

£400–535 ROX

Faux fabric bow-tie pin by Diane Love, who designed for Trifari from 1971 to 1974. *Early 1970s*

7cm (3in) wide

£40–50 TR

Figure-of-eight bow pin with small turquoise and ruby red cabochons on a gold-plated, rope-moulded casting. *1950s*

7.5cm (3in) wide

£160–190 CRIS

CROWN PINS

From the late 1930s to the 1950s, Trifari astutely produced a series of crown pins to coincide with a string of hugely popular romantic-historical movies that fired public interest in the lifestyle and trappings of European royalty. The inclusion of the crown silhouette in Trifari's trademark from around 1937 is testament to the commercial success of an enduring line that encompassed a wide range of fanciful designs, including the "Coronation Gems" launched in 1953. However, the most sought after pins are those designed by Alfred Philippe in the 1940s. Incorporating large cabochons on heavy vermeil sterling silver encrusted with rhinestones, they are opulent masterpieces of design. These 1940s vermeil silver examples should not be confused with Trifari's 1980s reissues in lighter-weight base metals, which command significantly lower prices.

Large crown pin designed by Alfred Philippe, of vermeil sterling silver with prong-set sapphire blue and ruby red cabochons, emerald green baguettes, and emerald green, ruby red, and clear rhinestones. *1940s. 4.5cm (1¾in) long* **£120–150** CRIS

Fleur-de-lys finial crown pin of sterling silver set with round-cut clear crystal rhinestones. The design is of medieval inspiration and comprises stylized foliate and floral forms topped with an heraldic fleur-de-lys finial. *1940s. 6.25cm (2½in) long* **£185–200** TR

Crown pin of vermeil sterling silver with emerald green, ruby red, and clear rhinestones, and a ring of faux pearls. *1940s*

5.5cm (2¼in) long **£180–200** TR

1944 Coro company first uses "Vendome" mark on some of its high-end jewellery

1953 Full Vendome line is introduced as the successor to the Corocraft line, and Vendome begins to operate as a subsidiary company

1957 Together with Coro, Vendome is purchased by the Richton International Corporation of New York

1960s onwards Helen Marion is appointed as Chief Designer and rejuvenates flagging sales

1979 Production ceases

Vendome

Originally Coro's top-of-the-range line, and later a semi-autonomous company, Vendome combined fine-quality materials and excellent craftsmanship with elegant and often highly innovative designs.

HAUTE JEWELLERY

Named after the Place de Vendôme, the centre of the Parisian *haute* jewellery trade, Vendome first appeared in 1944 as a mark on charm bracelets and faux pearl jewellery produced by the Coro company (*see pp.68–71*). Conceived as a replacement brand for Coro's top-end Corocraft range, and aimed at a wealthy American clientele aspiring to post-war Parisian chic, the full Vendome line was eventually introduced in 1953 – at which point Vendome was also established as a Coro company in its own right.

Vendome jewellery is characterized by the use of high-quality materials: silver- and gold-plated or gold-tone metals; crystal faceted beads and rhinestones of Austrian and Czechoslovakian origin; clear and coloured Lucite; lustrous faux pearls; and delicate enamelling. Prior to the 1960s, motifs and imagery were fairly traditional – mostly floral, but sometimes geometric. Thereafter, following the appointment of Helen Marion as Chief Designer and until the company ceased trading in the late 1970s, more radical designs were introduced. Notable among these were some sumptuous reinterpretations of ethnic jewellery and a series of fine art collage pins (*see opposite*). Regardless of style, however, all Vendome pieces are now avidly sought after by costume jewellery collectors.

Above: Floral motif earrings of gold-tone metal casting with clear and *aurora borealis* rhinestones and red faux stone centres. *1950s.* 5cm (2in) wide **£15–20 MILLB**

Bangle and earrings of highly polished silver-plated metal castings with prong-set aquamarine and sapphire blue crystal rhinestones, and powder blue prong-set crystal cabochons. *Late 1950s* B: 20cm (8in) circ; E: 4cm (1½in) wide **£200–300 CRIS**

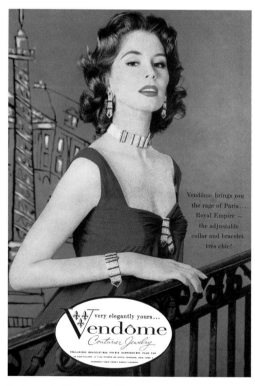

Vendome advertisement from *Harper's Bazaar*, November 1958, promoting a "Royal Empire" line parure, comprising an adjustable collar necklace, bracelet, pin, and pendant earrings.

Bouquet of flowers pin and earrings with rhinestone petals, emerald navette centres, and emerald and jade pendants. *1950s*

P: 8.25cm (3¼in) long

£120–140   **CRIS**

Floral motif pin and earrings with crystal rhinestones and faux pearls wired to filigree backs. *Mid 1950s*

P: 5cm (2in) wide; E: 2.5cm (1in) wide

£80–100   **CRIS**

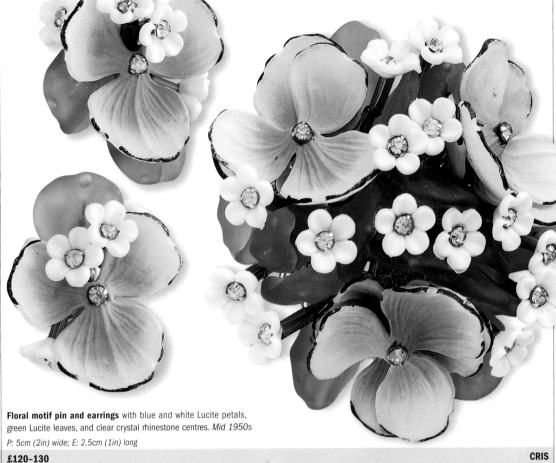

Floral motif pin and earrings with blue and white Lucite petals, green Lucite leaves, and clear crystal rhinestone centres. *Mid 1950s*

P: 5cm (2in) wide; E: 2.5cm (1in) long

£120–130   **CRIS**

AFTER GEORGES BRAQUE

Among many stylistic innovations conceived by Vendome designer Helen Marion was a series of six collage-like pins inspired by the work of Cubist artist, Georges Braque (1882–1963). Single pins surface from time to time, but complete sets are exceedingly rare and worth more than twice the sum of six individual pins.

"Georges Braque" pin with enamelling, rhinestones, and a cabochon. *1960s*

5.75cm (2¼in) long   **£200–250 CRIS**

Four-strand necklace of polychrome, clear, and *aurora borealis* crystal beads. *c.1960*

43cm (17in) long

£55–65   **ABIJ**

Link and hoop necklace of brushed gold-tone metal; half of the hoops with pale amethyst crystal rhinestone centres. *1970s*

45.75cm (18in) circ

£35–45   **ABIJ**

Extendable necklace with pin and earrings of gold-plated metal and polychrome crystal baguettes. *1965*

N: 40.5cm (16in) circ; P & E: 5cm (2in) long

£150–195   **WAIN**

Brushed gold-tone necklace set with magenta, white, and blue crystal rhinestones. *1960s*

40.5cm (16in) circ

£50–55   **ABIJ**

Watch with casing and bracelet of antiqued silver-tone chain-mail discs. *c.1970*

17.75cm (7in) circ

£65–80   **MILLB**

1942 Albert Weiss sets up his own jewellery company in New York City

1943 onwards Pieces are marked either "Weiss" in script or block letters, "Albert Weiss", or "AW Co." with the "W" shaped like a crown

1950s The company thrives and some of the work is contracted out to Hollycraft

1960s Albert Weiss retires and his son Michael takes over the business

1971 The company closes

Weiss

Admired by its contemporaries for its exquisite rhinestone work, Weiss has long been undervalued by collectors. Recent upward price trends indicate that this is now changing.

FROM A SMALL FISH IN A BIG POND

Albert Weiss honed his jewellery-making skills at the massive Coro company (*see pp.68–71*) during the 1930s, and left in 1942 to set up his own decidedly smaller Weiss enterprise in New York City. By the late 1940s, Weiss had begun to thrive, to the point where in the 1950s and 60s some of its output had to be contracted out for manufacture by Hollycraft (*see p.167*) in order to keep up with consumer demand. The majority of Weiss's designs are floral, foliate, fruit, or figural, although it also produced some geometric pieces, notably a range of Art Deco style necklaces, bracelets, pins, and earrings. Across all subject matters and styles, the materials used and the standards of craftsmanship were exceptionally high. Gold and silver metal or alloys were usually employed and sometimes enamelled or, especially in the 1960s, japanned. However, it is Weiss's Austrian crystal rhinestones that are most impressive.

QUALITY CRYSTALS

Whether citrine, aquamarine, sapphire, emerald, jade, ruby, or topaz, all Weiss rhinestones display exceptional purity of colour – a quality most clearly evident in the prong-set stones it used in its series of butterfly, insect, and single flower pins (sometimes with matching earrings) made in the late 1940s and 50s, and in its Christmas Tree pins of the 1950s and 60s (*see pp.172–175*). Weiss's reproductions of fine, German smokey quartz crystals, known as "black diamonds", were also highly convincing, and its enthusiastic use of Swarovski *aurora borealis* rhinestones from the mid 1950s onwards was often innovative (*see below*).

Above: Fleur-de-lys earrings of antique gold-tone metal casting with green round- and navette-cut crystal rhinestones. *1950s. 2.5cm (1in) long* **£15–20 MILLB**

Flower pin of gold-plated metal with prong-set navette-cut coloured Austrian crystal rhinestone petals and leaves, and a faceted sapphire blue crystal centre. *c.1950*
7.5cm (3in) long
£100–115 JJ

AURORA BOREALIS

Weiss was quick to exploit the decorative potential of the *aurora borealis* rhinestones that Swarovski developed with Dior in the mid 1950s. Named after the shimmering atmospheric phenomenon also known as the Northern Lights, the iridescent fantasy finishes of these stones were created with a polychrome metallic coating. In this pin (*right*), Weiss has made ingenious use of the stones, inverting them to display the more densely coloured undersides.

Fantasy coloured pin of gold-tone metal casting set with inverted, polychromatic, 3-D *aurora borealis* crystal rhinestones. *Early 1970s. 4.5cm (1¾in) wide* **£40–45 ABIJ**

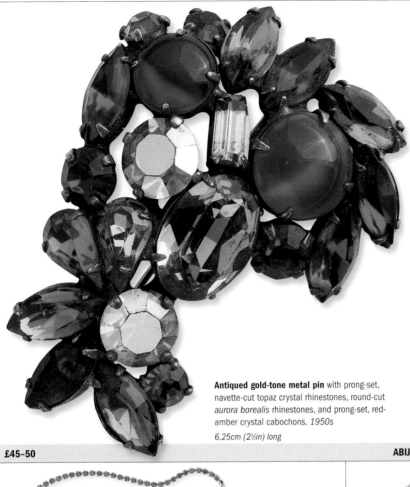

Antiqued gold-tone metal pin with prong-set, navette-cut topaz crystal rhinestones, round-cut *aurora borealis* rhinestones, and prong-set, red-amber crystal cabochons. *1950s*

6.25cm (2½in) long

£45–50 ABIJ

Strawberry earrings with ruby crystal beads and emerald crystal rhinestones in japanned metal settings. *1940s*

2.5cm (1in) long

£45–55 JJ

Floral pin and earrings set with clusters of yellow enamelled and rhinestone flowerheads. *1950s*

P: 3.75cm (1½in) wide;
E: 2.5cm (1in) wide

£50–55 JJ

FIGURAL PINS

Of the figural pins produced by Weiss, the most coveted by collectors are its 1950s butterflies and insects. Glittering compositions of crystal rhinestones hand-wired with gilt metal, they are now commanding high prices. More affordable are some excellent novelty figurals, such as this jack-in-the-box pin, made in the 1940s.

Jack-in-the-box pin of gilt metal with enamelling and rhinestones. *1940s*
5cm (2in) long **£60–65** JJ

Necklace, bracelet, and earrings of solid and meshed gold-tone metal with pink and *aurora borealis* crystal rhinestones. *1960s*

N: 38cm (15in) circ; B: 17.75cm (7in) circ; E: 2.5cm (1in) long

£80–85 JJ

Silver-tone white metal necklace set with Austrian crystal rhinestones. *1940s*

43cm (17in) circ

£60–65 JJ

Cross pin of japanned base metal set with "black diamond" Austrian crystal beads. *1970s*

6.25cm (2½in) long

£30–35 MILLB

Floral wreath pin and earrings in antiqued silver-tone metal with topaz, sapphire, and *aurora borealis* rhinestones. *1950s*

P: 9cm (3½in) wide; E: 4.5cm (1¾in) long

£45–50 ABIJ

Floral motif pin and earrings with smokey quartz and *aurora borealis* crystal rhinestones in antiqued gold-tone metal settings. *1950s*

P: 5cm (2in) wide; E: 3.25cm (1¼in) long

£45–50 ABIJ

Flower pin with white enamel petals and green enamel leaves and stem. *c.1970*

7.5cm (3in) long

£10–15 MILLB

A-Z of designers and makers

A gallery of highly collectable costume jewellery

The costume jewellery designers and makers profiled over the following pages are drawn from both sides of the Atlantic. Some of them are relatively large companies that have produced a huge number of diverse pieces, while others are much smaller enterprises, specializing in handcrafted, limited edition pieces. Some of the designers had already established a reputation by the start of the 20th century, while others are very much in the limelight now and have only recently risen to prominence. All of them, however, have their devotees, and collectively their work encompasses the extraordinary wealth of styles, materials, techniques, and prices available to contemporary costume jewellery collectors.

Accessocraft

Founded in the 1930s, Accessocraft produced tens of thousands of war relief pins in World War II, but then became known for its heavy, stylish jewellery and accessories. During the 1960s its distinctive gothic designs and blended antique gold-tone or bronzed metals with unusual stones, were particularly popular.

Many Accessocraft pieces have Renaissance, Victorian, or Art Nouveau touches.

Eagle and globe pin, the eagle casting of bright gold-tone metal; the globe of mottled red Lucite. *1940s*

7cm (2¾in) long

£30–50 BB

Bead necklace of pearlized brown plastic, clear Lucite with white inclusions, and clear rhinestone roundels. *c.1970*

40.5cm (16in) circ

£50–55 ABIJ

Alcozer

The Italian company, Alcozer & J. was founded in Florence in 1994 by designer Giampiero Alcozer. The company specializes in antique-style costume jewellery and accessories. Every piece is handcrafted from hypoallergenic gold-tone metal set with seed pearls, rhinestones, and semi-precious stones.

Vase of flowers pin with semi-precious stones, cultured pearls, and clear and ruby rhinestones on a rose-gold-plated casting. *Late 1990s*

11cm (4¼in) long

£180–200 CRIS

Basket of flowers pin with semi-precious stones, cultured pearls, beads, and rhinestones on a rose-gold-plated casting. *Late 1990s*

8.5cm (3⅜in) wide

£150–175 CRIS

Angela Hale

London-based jewellery designer Angela Hale creates feminine, delicate jewellery with a glamorous retro look. Inspired by the Victorian and Art Deco periods, each piece is handcrafted from hypoallergenic bronze and set with faux pearls and sparkling Swarovski crystals in myriad rainbow colours.

Pendant earrings of antiqued gold-tone metal with faux pearls and large prong-set oval rhinestones. *1990s*

3cm (1⅛in) long

£30–40 PC

Antiqued gold-tone metal earrings with clear and fuchsia rhinestones and mottled fuchsia navette pendants. *2000*

6.25cm (2½in) long

£40–50 PC

Alice Caviness

Costume designer Alice Caviness began making jewellery just after World War II, and her company, based in Long Island, New York, continued production following her death in 1983. Pieces range from parures and demi-parures to earrings and single pins, including carved cameos, fruits, and animal figurals. All her pieces are characterized by the use of high-quality materials, notably crystal stones of unusual colours. Mostly marked "Alice Caviness", they are relatively scarce and increasingly sought after by collectors.

Interwoven multiple-strand necklace and matching earrings of polychrome beads and seed pearls. *1970s*

N: 63.5cm (25in) circ; E: 2.5cm (1in) wide

£85–100   ABIJ

Necklace and matching bracelet of rhodium-plated metal set with graduated rows of lavender, pink, and black rhinestones. *1960s*

N: 42cm (16½in) circ; B: 17.75cm (7in) circ

£250–265   ABIJ

Japanned metal necklace and matching bracelet with olivine and ruby glass cabochons and prong-set rhinestones. *1960s*

N: 40.5cm (16in) circ; B: 19cm (7½in) circ

£235–250   ABIJ

Umbrella and turtle pin of white metal with prong-set ruby rhinestones, French jet teardrops, and a pink glass cabochon. *c.1980*

7cm (2¾in) long

£45–55   JJ

Umbrella and poodle pin of gilt base metal with prong-set pale and dark amber rhinestones and French jet teardrops. *c.1980*

7cm (2¾in) long

£55–60   JJ

Raspberry and raspberry leaf pin of textured gold-tone metal with pavé-set faux ruby cabochons for the berries. *1960s*

7cm (2¾in) long

£50–60   ABIJ

Andrew Logan

A contemporary British artist and sculptor of international repute, Andrew Logan creates vibrant jewellery from new and used glass. Each piece of jewellery is a miniature piece of sculpture, individually handmade from multicoloured mirrored glass and semi-precious stones set in a light and durable resin. Favourite motifs include hearts, fauna, flora, planets, and gods.

Egyptian scarab pin with a faceted red glass cabochon, glass beads, opaque red mirror glass, and clear rhinestones set in enamelling. *Late 1970s*

9cm (3½in) wide

£250–300　　　　　　　　　　　LB

Circular hoop earrings with segments of orange glass set in gold glittered metal castings. *1990s*

7cm (2¾in) wide

£140–160　　LB

Bow tie pin with broken segments of semi-opaque, clear mirror glass set in a black resin casting. *Late 1970s*

6.25cm (2½in) wide

£95–120　　LB

Plastic coated metal badge made to commemorate his "Alternative Miss World Contest". *Late 1970s*

5.75cm (2¼in) wide

£NPA　　　　　　LB

Argy-Rousseau

From 1921 to 1931, the glassworks Les Pâtes-de-verre d'Argy-Rousseau produced finely crafted glassware made from *pâte-de-verre* (poured glass), which was popular in the Art Nouveau and Art Deco periods. As well as highly collectable vases and bowls, Gabriel Argy-Rousseau created glowing pendants and pins depicting stylized fruit and flowers, butterflies, and figures drawn from mythology.

Art Nouveau belt buckle of stamped brass with bead moulding edges and three blue stone cameos carved with crab motifs. *c.1905*

12cm (4¾in) wide

£200–250　　　　　　　　　　　RITZ

Art

From the 1940s to the late 1960s, Art (also known as ModeArt) produced costume jewellery in a diverse range of styles, including replicas or reinterpretations of Renaissance, Victorian, and Art Deco pieces. While flower, fruit, and leaf motifs are most prevalent, figural imagery – especially animal subjects – was also employed. Characteristic materials and techniques include fine filigree metalwork, enamelling, carved or moulded polychrome plastics, and rhinestones – the latter often uniquely coloured and pavé-set in eye-catching clusters. Usually marked and displaying middle to high-end standards of craftsmanship, Art jewellery is increasingly sought after and prices have been rising accordingly.

Bouquet of flowers pin and earrings with pink, yellow, amber, and green Lucite petals, and clear rhinestone highlights, on gilt castings. *Mid 1950s*
P: 5cm (2in) long; E: 2cm (¾in) wide

£60–75   **CRIS**

Necklace, bracelet, and earrings demi-parure with antique gilt metal leaf motifs, ruby glass cabochons, and *aurora borealis* rhinestones. *Mid 1950s*
N: 39cm (15¼in) circ; B: 17cm (7in) circ; E: 3cm (1⅛in) long

£125–150   **CRIS**

Fruit pin and earrings with blue, green, and *aurora borealis* rhinestones on gun-metal castings. *Mid 1950s*
P: 4.5cm (1¾in) long; E: 3cm (1⅛in) long

£95–110   **CRIS**

Pear fruit pin of yellow and green enamel over a gold-plated casting. *Late 1950s*
3.5cm (1⅜in) long

£40–45   **CRIS**

Flower pin and earrings of silver and gilt metal; the surface of the leaves has an engraved "Florentine" finish. *1960s*
P: 5cm (2in) wide; E: 2.5cm (1in) wide

£30–35   **JJ**

Snake bangle, pin, and earrings of gilt metal with turquoise and red enamelling; the pin also has a turquoise plastic cabochon. *1960s*
B: 17.75cm (7in) circ; P: 5cm (2in) long; E: 3.75cm (1½in) long

£45–65   **JJ**

Atwood & Sawyer

Founded in England in 1956 by Horace Atwood (Sawyer was a silent partner), Atwood & Sawyer produced copies of 18th- and 19th-century precious jewellery, many pieces for the *Dallas* and *Dynasty* TV series, and glittering diamanté compositions for the Miss World competitions. In recent years, however, it is their exquisite Christmas jewellery (*see pp.172–175*) that has really proved popular with collectors.

Snowman pin with gold-plating, green and blue enamelling, and ruby and pavé-set clear rhinestones. *Late 1990s*

3.5cm (1⅜in) long

£35–40 (plus £20 if with original box)   CRIS

Auguste Bonaz

Innovative French designer Auguste Bonaz worked from the Bonaz Studios in France during the 1920s and 30s. Much of his jewellery is made from Bakelite or Galalith and has the simple lines, strong geometric shapes, and bold contrasting colours typical of the Art Deco period. Bonaz's pieces are among the rarest and most valuable of all Bakelite jewellery.

Crown tiara of faux tortoiseshell Galalith – a plastic similar to Bakelite made from formaldehyde and a derivative of sour milk. *1900*

14cm (5½in) wide

£150–250   LB

Avon

The American company Avon was founded in 1886 as the California Perfume Company. In the late 1920s it introduced the Avon line of jewellery and subsequently changed its name to Avon Products, Inc. Avon has been very successful at introducing reasonably priced, good-quality jewellery to American housewives. The jewellery is not particularly valuable, but is of interest to those who collect Avon memorabilia.

Paisley motif earrings of gold-tone metal casting with three shades of pink enamelling. *1980s*

3.75cm (1½in) long

£10–15   MILLB

Apple pendant necklace of antiqued gold-tone metal with semi-opaque clear plastic pendant. *1970s*

N: 68.5cm (27in) circ;
Pd: 3.75cm (1½in) wide

£15–20   MILLB

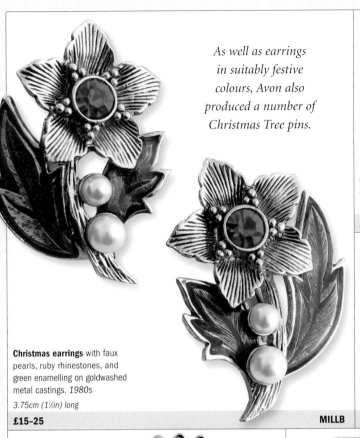

As well as earrings in suitably festive colours, Avon also produced a number of Christmas Tree pins.

Christmas earrings with faux pearls, ruby rhinestones, and green enamelling on goldwashed metal castings. *1980s*

3.75cm (1½in) long

£15–25   **MILLB**

Geometric form open bangle of silver-tone white metal. Originally promoted as part of a silver and gold pair. *1980s*

16.5cm (6½in) circ

£15–25   **MILLB**

Knotted rope earrings made from moulded faux white ivory plastic. *Late 1970s*

3cm (1⅛in) long

£10–15   **MILLB**

New Millennium clock pin of polished silver-tone metal casting with sapphire rhinestone star centres and a paper-under-glass clock-face. *2000*

4.5cm (1¾in) long

£10–15   **MILLB**

Perfume basket pin (with hinged lid) of goldwashed metal casting with clear rhinestone highlights. *c.1980*

3.75cm (1½in) long

£15–25   **MILLB**

Perfume owl pin (with hinged head) of goldwashed metal casting with emerald green rhinestone eyes. *c.1980*

5cm (2in) long

£20–25   **MILLB**

Christmas present earrings of goldwashed metal casting with clear rhinestone highlights. *1990s*

1.25cm (½in) long

£15–20   **MILLB**

Goldwashed metal chain necklace and antiqued goldwashed pendant with faux white and pink pearls and a pink plastic cabochon. *Late 1970s*

N: 60cm (24in) circ; Pd: 5cm (2in) long

£15–25   **MILLB**

B.S.K.

Little is known about B.S.K. other than that it was based in New York and was in business from about 1950 to the early 1980s. The letters stand for the first initials of the three owners' names, Benny Steinberg, Slovitt, and Kaslo. Some B.S.K. jewellery is interesting in design, but much of it is of average quality. It was produced initially as the demand for affordable jewellery boomed in the early 1950s. The line was reasonably priced and was sold through department stores such as Woolworths.

Bust of an oriental lady pin in gold-tone metal casting with faux pearl drop earrings. *1970s*

5cm (2in) long

£20–25   JJ

Oriental man pin of gold-tone metal casting with faux jade sacks. *1970s*

3cm (1¼in) high

£20–25   JJ

Balenciaga

The famous Spanish couturier Cristóbal Balenciaga founded his *haute couture* line in 1919 and opened the House of Balenciaga in Paris in 1937. The simple lines of his costume jewellery were designed to complement the classical elegance of his clothes, and were often inspired by indigenous Spanish forms and motifs.

Couture choker with four interwoven strands of faceted black glass beads, and a gilt metal clasp with turquoise glass cabochons and clear rhinestones. *c.1960*

N: 38cm (14¾in) circ; Clasp: 3.75cm (1½in) wide

£1,500–1,600   SUM

Barry Parman

Originally a theatre set designer, London-based Barry Parman turned his creative talents to jewellery design for just a few years prior to his death in the late 1980s. The distinctive and superbly modelled pieces he originally designed for leading costume jewellery dealers such as Linda Bee are rare, and are now hot collectables.

1920s "flapper" pin in shades of grey and black plastic with enamelled make-up and clear rhinestone highlights. *c.1975*

9cm (3½in) long

£100–150   LB

Beaujewels

Beaujewels was run by Bowman & Foster from the late 1940s to the early 1970s. Flowers and leaves are recurring motifs, often portrayed in rich colours and unexpected colour combinations. Although reasonably priced, the jewellery incorporated fruit salad stones that were popular in the more expensive jewellery of the day.

Floral wreath pin and earrings with faux baroque pearls and *aurora borealis* rhinestones set in gold-tone metal. *c.1960*
P: 6.25cm (2½in) wide; E: 3.75cm (1½in) long

£45–55   JJ

Twin leaf pin of bold naturalistic design in brushed matte sterling silver and signed "Beau Sterling". *1950s*
5cm (2in) long

£30–35   BBG

Floral pin and earrings with pink *aurora borealis* and fuchsia pink rhinestones set in gold-tone metal. *1940s*
P: 5cm (2in) long;
E: 3cm (1¼in) long

£45–55   JJ

Bettina von Walhof

Contemporary designer Bettina von Walhof, based in California, is known for her imaginative jewellery. Her whimsical figural pins feature motifs such as lobsters, parrots, and whales, as well as flowers. Each piece is unique, handcrafted from vintage glass beads, poured glass leaves and flowers, and sparkling Swarovski crystals.

Flowers, animals, and birds are recurring motifs in Bettina von Walhof's jewellery designs, all crafted with minute attention to detail and a sense of fun.

Floral pin with hand-wired yellow, green, and clear poured glass leaves and flowers, and jonquil crystal rhinestones set above a carved red and black medallion. *c.1980*
8.5cm (3⅜in) long

£450–550   SUM

Billy Boy

An American company with workshops and a small team of assistants in Paris, Billy Boy has produced jewellery in diverse and interesting styles. These include a range of strongly coloured resin pieces inspired by Schiaparelli's work, and a number of "barbaric" tribal designs. Other examples recall the geometric forms of ancient amulets, necklaces, and belts executed in rough-textured metals with square and pyramid-form glass beads.

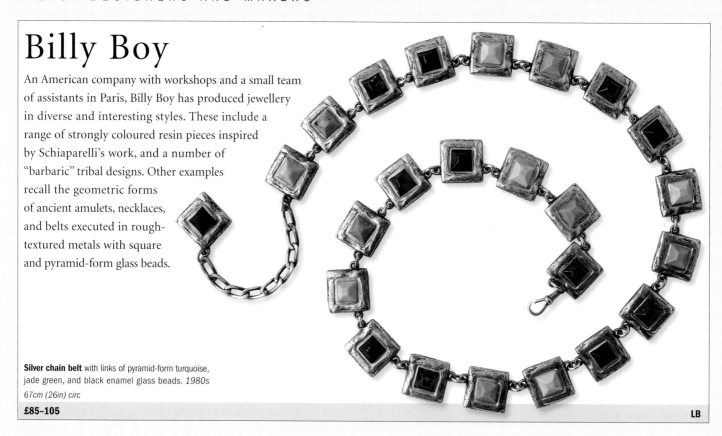

Silver chain belt with links of pyramid-form turquoise, jade green, and black enamel glass beads. *1980s*
67cm (26in) circ

£85–105   **LB**

Blackinton

Founded in 1862, in North Attleboro, Massachusetts, R. Blackinton & Co. produced silver and gold jewellery, and accessories such as compacts and cigarette cases. Although not well known, the company produced many fine pieces at the end of the 19th century, often influenced by Art Nouveau designs.

Goldwashed sterling silver bangle with graduated bead moulding and turquoise glass cabochons. *c.1895*
7.5cm (3in) wide

£160–175   **CGPC**

Scrolling leaf motif bangle of goldwashed sterling silver with amethyst glass cabochons. *c.1895*
7.5cm (3in) wide

£225–240   **CGPC**

Bogoff

Throughout the 1950s and 60s, the Bogoff Spear Novelty Company, based in Chicago, made elegant and interesting costume jewellery that imitated high-cost designer jewellery. Crafted from good-quality materials, the pieces usually had rhodium backings and hand-set stones.

Gold-tone metal necklace with clear round crystal rhinestones and three large clear teardrop rhinestones. *1960s*
N: 45.75cm (18in) circ; Pd: 5cm (2in) wide

£45–55   **BB**

Butler & Wilson

After selling antique jewellery from London market stalls, Nicky Butler and Simon Wilson opened a shop in the early 1970s and started marketing their own jewellery based on reproductions of period styles. By the late 1980s, they were selling their jewellery all around the world. Butler and Wilson's 1980s pieces are glitzy and diamanté-studded, harking back to the Art Deco period. Their lizard and spider pins became classics, and their early 1970s designs in particular are now highly collectable.

Glittering clusters of pavé-set rhinestones feature in many Butler & Wilson designs from the 1980s and 90s.

Dancing couple pin with prong-set clear paste and black and clear rhinestones. *1980s*

12cm (4¾in) long

£40–50   **PC**

Three-strand faux pearl necklace, champagne-coloured with gilt metal clasp. *1980s*

42cm (16½in) circ

£30–40   **PC**

Oriental dragon pin with blue and green metallic enamelling, pavé-set clear crystal rhinestones, and ruby red cabochon eyes set in a gold-plated casting. *Mid 1990s*

11cm (4¼in) long

£95–120   **CRIS**

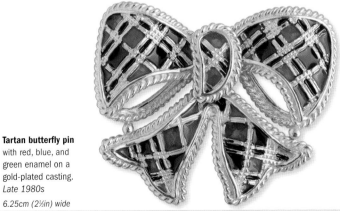

Tartan butterfly pin with red, blue, and green enamel on a gold-plated casting. *Late 1980s*

6.25cm (2½in) wide

£35–40   **CRIS**

Charm bracelet of antiqued gold-tone metal with pendant crowns, fleur-de-lys motifs, and faux pearl drops. *1980s*

18cm (7in) circ

£40–50   **PC**

Austrian Fruits

Made in Austria almost exclusively for export to the United States, these exquisite glass fruit pins have become highly collectable. All marked "Austria", the pins come in a wide variety of fruits, as well as a wonderful range of rich and glowing colours.

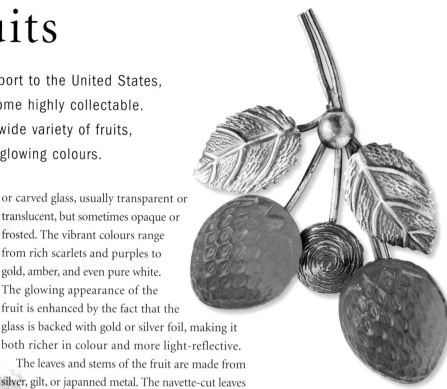

OLDE WORLD APPEAL IN A TIME OF CHANGE

Austrian fruit pins were created during the 1940s and 50s and represent the more traditional side of costume jewellery during the postwar period. The pins were made at different factories in Austria, but some earrings are marked "Germany". None of the fruit is marked with the name of a designer or manufacturer.

The pins are mostly single, although some have matching earrings. Strawberries, cherries, pears, and bunches of grapes are the most common motifs. Reminiscent of delicate Christmas tree decorations, the fruit pins are made of moulded or carved glass, usually transparent or translucent, but sometimes opaque or frosted. The vibrant colours range from rich scarlets and purples to gold, amber, and even pure white. The glowing appearance of the fruit is enhanced by the fact that the glass is backed with gold or silver foil, making it both richer in colour and more light-reflective.

The leaves and stems of the fruit are made from silver, gilt, or japanned metal. The navette-cut leaves are often enamelled or have crystal highlights, adding to the lasting appeal of these desirable pieces.

Strawberries pin of red glass with stamped silver alloy leaves and stalks. *1950s 6.5cm (2½in) long* **£85–100 CRIS**

Strawberries pin and earrings of red glass with green glass and gilt leaves, and gilt metal stalks. *1940s. P: 7cm (2¾in) long; E: 3.25cm (1¼in) long* **£55–80 ROX**

Pears pin of blue and yellow glass with japanned metal stalks and a crystal rhinestone. *1950s. 7cm (2¾in) long* **£45–55 BY**

Bunches of grapes pin of clear and yellow glass, metal stalks, and a crystal rhinestone. *1950s. 5.75cm (2¼in) long* **£40–45 BY**

Cherries pin with black and green glass, japanned metal, and a crystal rhinestone. *1950s. 5cm (2in) long* **£40–45 BY**

Pear pin of opaque green glass, enamelled leaves, gilt metal stalks, and crystal rhinestones. *1950s. 5.75cm (2¼in) long* **£40–45 BY**

Pears pin of clear and yellow glass, japanned metal stalks, and a crystal rhinestone. *1950s. 6.5cm (2½in) long* **£45–55 BY**

Cherries pin of red and yellow glass, japanned metal, and a red crystal rhinestone. *1950s. 5.75cm (2¼in) long* **£70–80 CRIS**

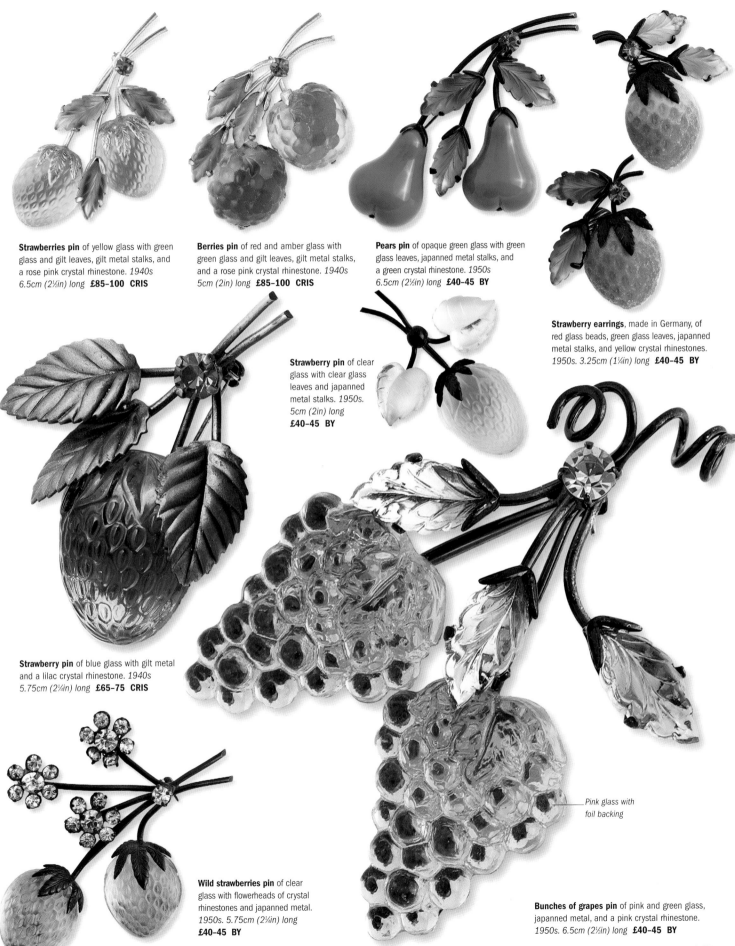

Strawberries pin of yellow glass with green glass and gilt leaves, gilt metal stalks, and a rose pink crystal rhinestone. *1940s 6.5cm (2½in) long* **£85–100 CRIS**

Berries pin of red and amber glass with green glass and gilt leaves, gilt metal stalks, and a rose pink crystal rhinestone. *1940s 5cm (2in) long* **£85–100 CRIS**

Pears pin of opaque green glass with green glass leaves, japanned metal stalks, and a green crystal rhinestone. *1950s 6.5cm (2½in) long* **£40–45 BY**

Strawberry earrings, made in Germany, of red glass beads, green glass leaves, japanned metal stalks, and yellow crystal rhinestones. *1950s. 3.25cm (1¼in) long* **£40–45 BY**

Strawberry pin of clear glass with clear glass leaves and japanned metal stalks. *1950s. 5cm (2in) long* **£40–45 BY**

Strawberry pin of blue glass with gilt metal and a lilac crystal rhinestone. *1940s 5.75cm (2¼in) long* **£65–75 CRIS**

Pink glass with foil backing

Wild strawberries pin of clear glass with flowerheads of crystal rhinestones and japanned metal. *1950s. 5.75cm (2¼in) long* **£40–45 BY**

Bunches of grapes pin of pink and green glass, japanned metal, and a pink crystal rhinestone. *1950s. 6.5cm (2½in) long* **£40–45 BY**

Carolee

The American company Carolee was founded in 1972 and is still in business today, creating classic, high-quality jewellery. Most of the pieces are made of sterling silver, sometimes gold-plated with faux or cultured pearls and rhinestones. A popular 1980s line called the "Duchess of Windsor" is considered highly collectable.

Crystal bracelet with round-cut clear crystal rhinestones set in white metal castings. *c.1980*

17.75cm (7in) circ

£105–110 | JJ

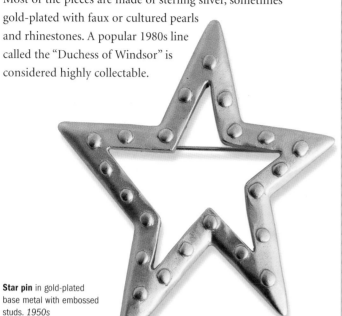

Star pin in gold-plated base metal with embossed studs. *1950s*

7.75cm (3in) wide

£50–65 | MILLB

Pearls, both faux and cultured, play a key role in Carolee's jewellery collections.

Chain necklace of antiqued gold-tone metal and a single strand of faux pearls. *c.1990*

40.5cm (16in) circ

£15–20 | MILLB

Castlecliff

Founded in New York by Clifford Furst in 1945, Castlecliff created bold but intricate jewellery made from good-quality materials. Its designs show an imaginative use of stones, and styles range from Art Deco to Gothic and Native American. Large signed pieces that have stood the test of time are the most sought after.

Pendant necklace and earrings with gold-plated Mesoamerican heads and motifs, and polychrome semi-precious stone beads and drops. *Late 1940s*

Pd: 12cm (4¾in) drop; E: 5cm (2in) long

£200–250 | RITZ

Floral motif earrings set with bands and rings of ruby red crystal rhinestones. *1950s*

2.5cm (1in) wide

£65–100 | LB

Native American-style pin of gold-plated metal with green enamelling and a faux green agate stone. *1960s*

7cm (2¾in) wide

£40–50 | RG

Ciner

The Ciner Manufacturing Company was founded in 1892 by Emanuel Ciner to produce fine jewellery. Since 1931, the company has manufactured classic, upmarket costume jewellery. Ciner pieces look like fine jewellery, but are set with rhinestones rather than jewels. Swarovski crystals are often used, hand set in gold-tone metalwork. Early pieces are often unmarked, but most pieces after 1945 were marked "Ciner".

Ciner jewellery uses small, delicate stones, in a glittering array of rainbow colours.

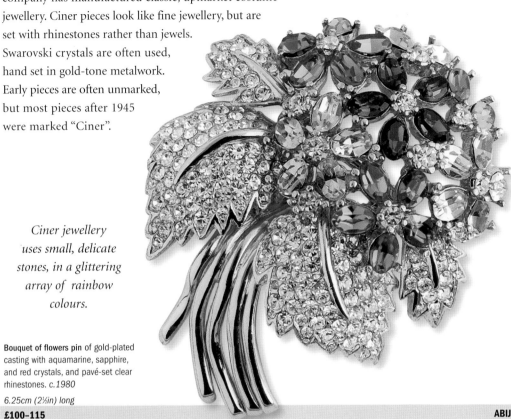

Bouquet of flowers pin of gold-plated casting with aquamarine, sapphire, and red crystals, and pavé-set clear rhinestones. *c.1980*

6.25cm (2½in) long

£100–115   **ABIJ**

Flower pin of gold-plated casting with green and pavé-set clear Swarovski crystal rhinestones. *Mid 1960s*

7cm (2¾in) long

£80–90   **WAIN**

White metal earrings with navette-cut clear crystal rhinestones and Japanese luminescent faux pearl drops. *1970s*

6.25cm (2½in) long

£105–115   **JJ**

Cow and dog pin of gold-plated castings set with small turquoise glass cabochons and larger ruby glass cabochons. *1950s*

3cm (1⅛in) long

£140–160 for the pair   **CRIS**

Starburst motif bracelet of vermeil and rose vermeil sterling silver set with clear and jonquil crystal rhinestones. *1940s*

18cm (7in) circ

£215–220   **CBU**

Woven gold-plated metal bracelet with interwoven bands of clear crystal rhinestones. *1980s*

20.25cm (8in) circ

£80–85   **JJ**

Floral motif bracelet of gold-plated castings set with turquoise, aquamarine, ruby, emerald, and black crystal cabochons. *1950s*

19cm (7½in) circ

£190–220   **CRIS**

Cristobal

Founded in London in 1986, Cristobal is an internationally renowned retailer of 20th-century costume jewellery. In addition, in the late 1990s owners Steven Miners and Yai Thammachote launched their own limited-edition designs, currently divided into four series: the "Butterfly Collection", the "Secret Garden Collection", the "London Collection" (comprising necklaces and earrings), and the "X-mas Collection" (including some Christmas Tree pins shown on pp172–175). Increasingly sought after by collectors in Britain and overseas, these distinctive pieces use only the highest-quality Austrian crystals (mostly dating from the 1940s and 50s) hand-set in gorgeous, eye-catching colour combinations.

Bouquet of flowers pin from the "Secret Garden Collection" of polychrome French poured glass and clear rhinestones set in a brass wire frame. *Late 1990s*

9cm (3½in) long

£300–350   CRIS

Bib necklace and pendant earrings from the "London Collection" with citrine, topaz, and *aurora borealis* rhinestones in gun-metal settings. *Late 1990s*

N: 45.5cm (18in) circ; Bib: 7.5cm (3in) drop; E: 7.5cm (3in) drop

£100–150   CRIS

Apple pin from the "Secret Garden Collection", with 1950s ruby, fuchsia, aquamarine, amethyst, and emerald rhinestones. *Late 1990s*

9.5cm (3¾in) long

£90–120   CRIS

Rhinestone necklace of 1950s amber and topaz rhinestones in a ruthenium-plated casting. *Late 1990s*

39cm (15⅜in) circ

£100–150   CRIS

Butterfly pin from the "Butterfly Collection", ruthenium-plated with navette-cut blue and clear rhinestones. *Late 1990s*

9.5cm (3¾in) long

£85–100   CRIS

Butterfly pin from the "Butterfly Collection", ruthenium-plated with sapphire, lime green, and *aurora borealis* rhinestones. *Late 1990s*

7.5cm (3in) long

£50–70   CRIS

Sunflower pin from the "Secret Garden Collection", ruthenium-plated and set with Swarovski jet, emerald, peridot, and rainbow rhinestones. *Late 1990s*

12cm (4¾in) long

£50–70   CRIS

Czech Jewellery

From the 1890s to the late 1930s, the jewellery makers of Gablonz in Czechoslovakia produced a distinctive and romantic style of costume jewellery. Glass stones in rich purples and delicate pastels were set into filigree backings. Pins were usually set with multi-coloured pastes. Necklaces and bracelets are rarer and the more complex the piece, the more collectable it is. Czech jewellery is usually unsigned, but is sometimes marked "Czech" or "Czechoslovakia".

Floral pin and earrings with crystal rhinestones prong-set in a gilt metal casting. *c.1930*

P: 2.5cm (1in) long; E: 2cm (¾in) long

£55–80   **MILLB**

Multiple-pendant necklace of gilt metal with sapphire blue rhinestones and a large, dark amethyst cabochon. *Early 1900s*

N: 57cm (21in) circ; Pd: 11.5cm (4½in) long

£80–100   **JJ**

Pale pink necklace with a chain of silvered metal and pink beads, and a pendant with a glass cabochon and rhinestones. *1920s*

N: 51cm (20in) circ; Pd: 7.5cm (3in) long

£55–85   **MILLB**

Stylized floral motif pin with ruby, jade, amethyst, and sapphire crystal rhinestones of various cuts set in a filigree gilt metal backing. *1940s*

6.25cm (2½in) wide

£25–45   **LB**

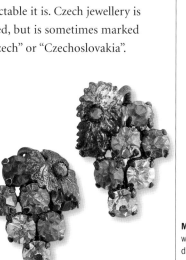

Rectangular pin with a filigree gilt metal backing set with numerous crystal rhinestones of various cuts and gemstone colours. *Early 1900s*

6.25cm (2½in) wide

£50–65   **JJ**

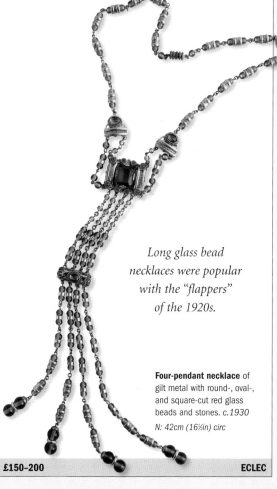

Long glass bead necklaces were popular with the "flappers" of the 1920s.

Scrolled cartouche triple-pendant pin of gilt metal with large prong-set Burmese-ruby coloured oval cabochons. *1930s*

9cm (3½in) wide

£130–145   **JJ**

Heart-shaped pin with filigree blackened steel backing and dark and light sapphire blue crystal rhinestones. *1930s*

6.25cm (2½in) wide

£25–45   **LB**

Four-pendant necklace of gilt metal with round-, oval-, and square-cut red glass beads and stones. *c.1930*

N: 42cm (16½in) circ

£150–200   **ECLEC**

DRGM

Although also applied to numerous other items ranging from clocks and corkscrews to cameras and toys, jewellery stamped with the German patent mark DRGM – *Deutsches Reichs Gebrauchsmuster* – is a collecting field in its own right. Used from about 1891 until the early 1950s by various, and often now anonymous, German jewellery makers, the DRGM mark is commonly associated with pieces incorporating clear crystal rhinestones set in zinc alloys, which are often rhodium-plated. The majority of pieces are of geometric Art Deco design, although earlier Art Nouveau forms can also be found.

Most German DRGM jewellery displays the streamlined geometric forms of the Art Deco movement and the Machine Age.

Rhodium-plated chain and bib necklace set with clear crystal rhinestones and a central cluster of rhinestones configured in a floral motif. *c.1930*

N: 37cm (14½in) circ;
Bib: 4.5cm (1¾in) wide

£250–290   **LB**

"Woven" alloy link bracelet with highly polished rhodium-plated clasp. *c.1930*

19cm (7½in) circ

£175–250   **LB**

Art Deco bracelet with safety chain in rhodium-plated alloy set with clear crystal rhinestones. *1920s*

18cm (7in) circ

£60–100   **MARA**

Art Deco geometric form bracelet in rhodium-plated alloy set with clear crystal rhinestones. *1920s*

18cm (7in) circ

£60–100   **MARA**

Danecraft

In 1939, Danecraft was founded by Victor Primavera in Providence, Rhode Island. The company is now known as the Felch-Wehr Company, but it continues to manufacture silver and vermeil jewellery, which it markets under the name of Danecraft to the better department stores. Danecraft specializes in quality sterling silver. Reminiscent of Scandinavian jewellery design, its pieces have a handcrafted look.

Sterling silver bracelet with die-stamped seashell motifs and bands of pink enamelling. *1950s*

20cm (7¾in) circ

£25–30	BBG

Umbrella pin of white metal with selected gilding, iridescent blue enamelling, and emerald green rhinestones. *1980s*

4.5cm (1¾in) long

£30–35	JJ

Sterling silver bracelet with vermeil sterling silver links and medallions, the latter with large faceted purple pastes. *1940s*

17.75cm (7in) circ

£80–85	JJ

David-Andersen

Goldsmith David Andersen founded his company in Christiana (now called Oslo), Norway, in 1876, and it is still trading today. The company produces beautifully designed silver jewellery decorated with fine enamelwork and has commissioned work from many talented designers. Marks on the jewellery include "David-Andersen" and "D-A".

Seahorse pin of vermeil sterling silver casting with blue and turquoise enamelling. *1940s*

5cm (2in) high

£115–120	MAC

De Nicola

Founded by Jerry De Nicola in 1957, De Nicola produced beautifully crafted, fine-quality costume jewellery during the late 1950s and early 60s. It then became part of the Capri Jewelry Company, before ceasing operations altogether in 1973. Signed De Nicola pieces are now rare and are therefore highly collectable.

Floral pin with six gilt metal flowers with faux turquoise cabochon centres encircled by tiny clear rhinestone highlights. *1950s*

5cm (2in) wide

£65–75	MG

DeRosa

Founded by Ralph DeRosa in New York in about 1935, DeRosa was one of the first manufacturers of good-quality costume jewellery to use local craftsmanship. Its pieces are striking in design, featuring richly coloured stones with unusual cuts, and high-quality enamelwork. The floral pieces are especially good, particularly those in the retro style of Hollywood precious jeweller Paul Flato. Unfortunately, many DeRosa pieces are not marked. The signed pieces, however, are very collectable and command high prices.

Vermeil sterling silver pin with prong-set cranberry glass cabochons encircling clear crystal rhinestones and a dark blue glass cabochon centre. *1940s*

5.75cm (2¼in) wide

£95–105   MG

Bowl of flowers pin with vermeil sterling silver bowl and leaves, and red enamelled roses. *1940s*

5cm (2in) long

£225–240   ROX

Vermeil sterling silver bracelet with three black enamelled roundels set with clear crystal rhinestones. *1940s*

17.75cm (7in) circ

£150–180   RG

DeRosa's crystals display exceptional depth and purity of colour.

Floral fur clip of vermeil sterling silver with ruby red crystals, rose montées, and clear crystal rhinestones. *1940s*

7.5cm (3in) long

£200–250   RG

Gold-plated bangle and earrings with black enamelling and pavé-set clear crystal rhinestones. *1950s*

B: 20.25cm (8in) circ; E: 2.5cm (1in) long

£80–85   MG

Sterling silver pin with two faux sapphire cabochons, and clear and jonquil crystal rhinestones. *1940s*

5cm (2in) wide

£80–110   RG

Dinny Hall

One of Britain's leading jewellery designers, Dinny Hall opened her first boutique in 1992 in London. Her elegant, modern designs feature colourful stones in pared-down settings that reflect simple, natural forms, such as leaves and starfish. Each piece is handcrafted using fine materials and following traditional techniques.

Dinny Hall's impressive list of celebrity clients include Madonna, Uma Thurman, Kristin Scott-Thomas, and Liz Hurley.

Gold-plated silver earrings in the form of elongated, stylized leaf motifs. *2001*

3.5cm (1⅜in) long

£80–100   PC

Large circular hoop earrings in silver (also produced in gold-plated silver). *2001*

3.5cm (1⅜in) long

£60–70   PC

Mauve icicle earrings with handcrafted, antiqued silver in Classical scrolling forms with three icicle-form pendants of mauvish-blue resin. *2002*

6.5cm (2½in) long

£60–80   PC

Pendant earrings with gold fishhooks and pendant caps with semi-translucent white resin drops. *Late 1990s*

4cm (1½in) long

£50–60   PC

"Diffusion Line" necklace and earrings with silver chain, fishhooks, pendant caps, and semi-translucent white resin drops. *Late 1990s*

N: 46cm (18in) circ; E: 4cm (1½in) long

£90–100   PC

Pendant necklace with silver chain and pendant cap with semi-translucent blue resin drop. *1992*

N: 46cm (18in) circ; Pd: 3cm (1⅛in) long

£80–90   PC

"Diffusion" Line necklace and earrings with gold chain, fishhooks, and scrolling hoops with baroque pearl drops. *Mid 1990s*

N: 40cm (15¾in) circ; E: 3cm (1⅛in) long

£90–110   PC

155

Eisenberg

American clothing company Eisenberg Original was founded in 1914 and, in 1930, began accessorizing its dresses with its own pins. These pins soon proved so popular that they were sold separately – and are still produced to this day. Incorporating fine materials such as Swarovski rhinestones, Eisenberg pieces are large and display a boldness and clarity of design. The early 1940s figurals are now particularly sought after. Pieces from 1930 to 1945 are marked "Eisenberg Original", and thereafter, marked "Eisenberg Ice".

Eisenberg Original Russian dancer pin in vermeil sterling silver with red enamel and prong-set Swarovski crystal rhinestones. *Early 1940s*
9cm (3½in) long

£800–900 CRIS

Eisenberg Original stylized floral pin of rhodium-plated metal with sapphire, turquoise, and clear Swarovski crystal rhinestones. *Early 1940s*
7.5cm (3in) wide

£165–200 ABIJ

Eisenberg Original pin of sterling silver set with clear Swarovski crystal rhinestones and champagne and grey faux pearls. *1930s*
7.5cm (3in) long

£500–565 TR

Eisenberg Original bow tie pin of rhodium-plated metal set with unfoiled Swarovski clear crystal rhinestones. *Early 1940s*
9cm (3½in) wide

£165–200 ABIJ

Eisenberg Original flower pin of gilt metal with emerald poured glass, an Austrian crystal cabochon, and four ruby crystal rhinestones *c.1940*
10cm (4in) wide

£650–750 SUM

Eisenberg Original pin of rhodium-plated metal with Swarovski crystal rhinestones, a round faux pearl, and nine faux pearl drops. *Late 1930s*
7.5cm (3in) long

£115–150 ABIJ

Eisenberg Original fur clip with tiered scrolls of sterling silver and prong- and bezel-set Swarovski crystal rhinestones. *Early 1940s*
5.75cm (2¼in) long

£165–200 ABIJ

Eisenberg Original fur clip of rhodium-plated metal with prong- and bezel-set Swarovski emerald and clear crystal rhinestones. *1940s*
7.5cm (3in) long

£200–250 ABIJ

Fischel and Nessler

Founded in New York in the late 19th century, Fischel and Nessler produced costume jewellery until it ceased trading in 1937. It is best known for its Art Deco style necklaces and earrings made in the late 1920s and 30s. Marked with a fish motif with an "L" at its nose, these elegant and highly desirable pieces are almost invariably made in silver and set with high-quality Austrian crystal rhinestones, beads, or cabochons.

Sterling silver necklace with carved tubular and round emerald moulded glass beads, and a carved pendant of jade green glass. *1930s*
Pd: 6.5cm (2½in) wide

£150–200　　　　　　　　　　　　　**RG**

Necklace and pendant earrings of sterling silver with round- and baguette-cut clear crystal rhinestones, and prong-set cranberry glass beads. *1920s*
N: 45.75cm (18in) circ; E: 7cm (2¾in) long

£350–450　　　　　　　　　　　　　**RG**

Florenza

Daniel Kosoff set up Florenza in the late 1940s in New York where it continued in business until 1981. Along with costume jewellery, Florenza also made enamelled and jewelled boxes and picture frames, often for other companies. Many pieces reflect Renaissance and Victorian styles, and typical components include antiqued gold-tone metal, enamelling, carved cameos, and frosted and *aurora borealis* rhinestones. Most pieces are marked "Florenza".

Intricate filigree work features strongly in Florenza jewellery, and is often combined with coloured rhinestones.

Shield-shaped pin of scrolled gold-tone metal with green enamelling, clear and emerald rhinestones, a ring of faux pearls, and a faux pearl drop, with gold-tone metal chains. *Late 1970s*
9cm (3½in) long

£55–60　　　　　　　　　　　　　**JJ**

Gold-tone metal bracelet with floral motif clusters of faux pearls and rhinestones, and a central white-on-pink carved cameo. *c.1970*
16.5cm (6½in) circ

£80–85　　　　　　　　　　　　　**JJ**

Clover motif earrings of antiqued gold-tone metal with jade green beads, faux pearls, and round-cut *aurora borealis* rhinestones. *1960s*
2.5cm (1in) wide

£25–35　　　　　　　　　　　　　**JJ**

Floral bow pin of antiqued silver-tone metal set with rows of small turquoise glass cabochons. *1950s*
6.5cm (2½in) long

£35–40　　　　　　　　　　　　　**ABIJ**

Bakelite

Fashionable in the 1920s and 30s, Bakelite jewellery was seemingly "old hat" by the end of World War II. The successful sale of Andy Warhol's Bakelite jewellery collection in 1988 at Sotheby's in New York proved otherwise.

A THOUSAND USES

Preceded by 19th-century celluloid and Galalith, and supplanted by mid-20th-century innovations such as Lucite, Bakelite was neither the first nor the last "plastic" to be used in costume jewellery. Its popularity, however, can be gauged by the fact that it is frequently employed as a catch-all term for early plastic jewellery. For example, the open bangle opposite would often be labelled Bakelite, but is actually made from a more translucent Lucite.

Patented in 1907 by Dr. Leo Baekeland, Bakelite was used initially as an electrical insulator but, tagged "the material of 1,000 uses", it was soon utilized for numerous useful and decorative wares – notably radio and clock casings, and kitchenalia. Enthusiastically adopted by the costume jewellery industry from the 1920s to the 1940s, it was exploited for its attractive colouring and the fact that it could be carved on a lathe into diverse shapes. Geometric Art Deco forms dominated the late 1920s and early 30s, while figural subjects later became more prevalent. Typical colours, often embellished with rhinestones or chromed steel, include black, white, and shades of red, brown, and yellow, two or more of which were often combined in the same piece.

Egyptian-style motif pin in iridescent pink, red, and taupe with a small, central mauve cabochon. *Early 1930s. 8cm (3in) long* **£50–70 ABAA**

Art Deco belt buckle of mirror-image stylized leaves in black and amber-red. *1930s 9cm (3½in) wide* **£40–50 ABAA**

Red Bakelite bead

Carved Egyptian Revival pendant necklace with red beads and black tassel. *Late 1920s Pd: 17cm (6⅝in) long* **£220–250 RBRG**

Brown scrolling pin of geometric form encrusted with clear rhinestones. *c.1930 6cm (2⅜in) long* **£20–30 ABAA**

Egyptian Revival camel pin typical of the animal figurals popular in the 1920s and 30s. *c.1930. 4cm (1½in) high* **£25–35 ABAA**

Stylized feather pin with gold edging, incised linear decoration, and clear rhinestones. *1930s. 7cm (2¾in) long* **£50–70 ABAA**

Brown swinging monkey pin with baby monkey on the branch above. *1930s 7cm (2¾in) long* **£25–35 ABAA**

Art Deco stylized twin-leaf pin in blue with grey linear incisions. *1930s 7cm (2¾in) long* **£25–35 ABAA**

Extremely rare head pin of "apple juice" colour with headress in green, red, blue, and black. *c.1940. 7cm (2¾in) long* **ROX**

Victorian-style red hand pin with lace cuff of brass and brass wire. *c.1930 5cm (2in) long* **£25–35 ABAA**

Art Deco flower pin with black stem and translucent white petals with incised linear decoration. *1930s 10cm (4in) long* **£25–35 ABAA**

Dice cufflinks of "apple juice" and white Bakelite. *1940s. 2cm (¾in) wide* **£25–35 PC**

Green and gold lapel pin or hat pin, with tiny brass beads and rhinestones. *1930s. 13.5cm (5¼in) long* **£30–40 ABAA**

Black and ivory snake bangle with clear rhinestones and tiny inset brass beads. *1930s. 23cm (9in) circ* **£25–35 ABAA**

Rare open bangle of translucent "apple juice" colour with shoal-of-fish decoration. *1940s 6.5cm (2½in) wide* **£670–1,340 ROX**

Art Deco geometric pin of chromed steel with red Bakelite insert and clear rhinestone highlights. *1930s. 6.5cm (2½in) long* **£30–40 ABAA**

Black hoop-pendant clip earrings encrusted with clear rhinestones and tiny faux pearls. *c.1930. 7cm (2¾in) long* **£20–30 ABAA**

Black Scotty dog figural pin with a red collar and tongue. *Early 1930s 5cm (2in) wide* **£25–35 ABAA**

Brown Art Deco loop and buckle pin with clear rhinestones. *c.1930 5cm (2in) wide* **£20–30 ABAA**

Dark green cuff links with gilt links, by Birkby's of Liversedge, England. *1920s Face: 2cm (¾in) long* **£20–30 MHC**

Black stylized scrolling leaf pin with a row of clear rhinestones. *1920s 4cm (1½in) long* **£20–30 ABAA**

"Five and six" oversize dice cufflinks of black and white Bakelite set in gilt metal. *Early 1950s. Face: 2cm (¾in) wide* **£50–80 CVS**

Stretching black cat pin with mauve collar and ruby red glass eyes. *Early 1930s 4cm (1½in) long* **£25–35 ABAA**

Brown stylized shoe-shape pin encrusted with clear rhinestones. *1920s. 6cm (2⅜in) long* **£20–30 ABAA**

Chromed base metal sails and mast

Dark blue schooner pin with chrome-plated base metal sails and mast. *1930s 5cm (2in) long* **£30–40 ABAA**

Black fan-shaped pin with clear rhinestones and partly edged with tiny brass balls. *c.1930. 7cm (2¾in) long* **£20–30 ABAA**

Clear rhinestone and brass ball highlights

Black leaf and flower bud pin with clear rhinestones and tiny brass balls. *c.1930. 11cm (4⅜in) long* **£20–30 ABAA**

Black folded neckscarf pin with clear rhinestones. *Early 1930s 5cm (2in) wide* **£20–30 ABAA**

Black triple-bow pin with incised linear decoration and rows of clear rhinestones. *c.1930. 6.5cm (2½in) wide* **£20–30 ABAA**

Black hoop pendant earrings with clear rhinestones. *c.1930 3.5cm (1⅜in) wide* **£20–30 ABAA**

Stylized elongated heart pin with clear rhinestones. *Early 1930s 9cm (3½in) long* **£20–30 ABAA**

Dark brown bow tie pin with decorative loops and clear rhinestones. *c.1930 6cm (2⅜in) wide* **£25–35 ABAA**

Black Art Deco shield-shaped pin with rows of clear rhinestones. *c.1930 4.5cm (1¾in) long* **£20–30 ABAA**

Double-knot pin of black Bakelite with clear rhinestones and of unusual design. *c.1930. 8cm (3⅛in) long* **£20–30 ABAA**

Black stylized scrolling hair pin with rows of clear rhinestones and tiny brass balls. *Early 1930s. 8cm (3⅛in) long* **£20–30 ABAA**

Black stylized leaf motifs on a white background

Black torchier and buckle pin with gold incisions and edging and, on the lower edge of the buckle, a row of stylized leaf motifs set on a white background. *c.1930 11cm (4⅜in) long* **£30–40 ABAA**

Fred A. Block

Based in Chicago, Fred A. Block Inc. made costume jewellery from the 1930s to the 1950s, initially to promote and accessorize its *prêt-à-porter* clothing lines. Many of its rare, collectable, and increasingly expensive pieces – especially its whimsical figural pins – are made in high-quality vermeil sterling silver with colourful enamelling and large rhinestones or beads.

Strong contrasts of colour – like the golden lustre of vermeil against turquoise in this pin – are an eye-catching feature of many Fred A. Block designs.

Cat pin of vermeil sterling silver with turquoise glass beads and clear crystal rhinestone eyes. *1940s*

10cm (4in) long

£200–265

BY

Geoff Roberts

Contemporary British jewellery designer Geoff Roberts is based in North Scotland. His quirky and distinctive pieces are bold in form, vibrant in colour, and spiked with humour. Roberts incorporates printed acrylics and mixed media in his work, much of which is made of flamboyant multicoloured foils laminated over acrylic sheeting.

"Fishwife" pin and earrings composed of polychrome metallic foils laminated over acrylic sheeting. *Late 1990s*

P: 14cm (5½in) wide; E: 7cm (2½in) wide

£40–60

PC

Stylized floral motif earrings of metallic foils laminated over acrylic sheeting. *Late 1990s*

6.5cm (2½in) long

£20–25　　PC

"Broken Heart" pin and earrings in red and gold metallic foils laminated over acrylic sheeting. *Late 1990s*

P: 8.25cm (3¼in) long; E: 5cm (2in) long

£40–50　　PC

Fish earrings of polychrome metallic foils laminated over acrylic sheeting. *Late 1990s*

8.25cm (3¼in) long

£20–30　　PC

Giorgio Armani

Celebrated Italian fashion designer Giorgio Armani established his own label in 1974. His jewellery complements the simple lines, understated elegance, and neutral colours of his fashion designs. Large rings, chokers, and bracelets are bold and vibrant, using an eclectic mix of silver, gemstones, and wood, often with global cultural references.

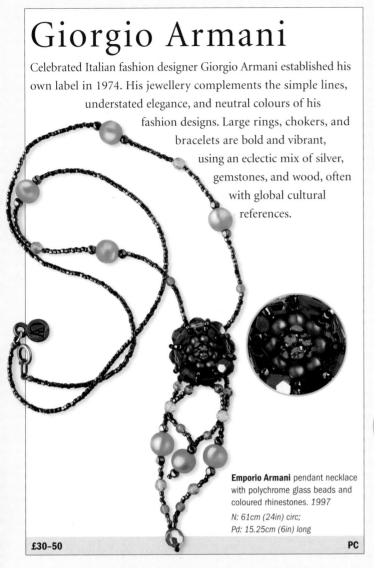

Emporio Armani pendant necklace with polychrome glass beads and coloured rhinestones. *1997*
N: 61cm (24in) circ;
Pd: 15.25cm (6in) long

£30–50   PC

Givenchy

The House of Givenchy, which opened in Paris in 1952, was influential throughout the 1950s and 60s, its simple, elegant style best epitomized by Audrey Hepburn. Givenchy's jewellery features classic designs on a large scale, with much use of gold plating, Lucite, and other plastics.

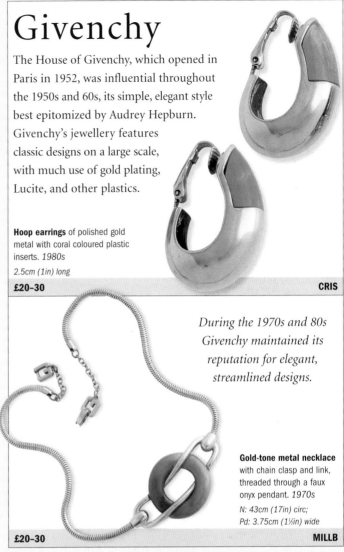

Hoop earrings of polished gold metal with coral coloured plastic inserts. *1980s*
2.5cm (1in) long

£20–30   CRIS

During the 1970s and 80s Givenchy maintained its reputation for elegant, streamlined designs.

Gold-tone metal necklace with chain clasp and link, threaded through a faux onyx pendant. *1970s*
N: 43cm (17in) circ;
Pd: 3.75cm (1½in) wide

£20–30   MILLB

Gorham & Co.

Founded in 1813, the Gorham Manufacturing Company was the largest 19th-century silversmiths in the United States. The chief designer William Codman produced a "martelé" (hand-hammered) line of silverware, which combined the free-flowing lines of Art Nouveau with the craftsmanship of the Arts and Crafts movement.

Native American motif belt buckle of sterling silver with selected gold plating and a marbled turquoise cabochon. *c.1900*
5cm (2in) long

£330–365   CGPC

Twin fish pin of goldwashed sterling silver with green enamelling and a central amethyst glass cabochon. *c.1900*
5.75cm (2¼in) wide

£530–600   CGPC

Rare, irregular-shaped pin of 14-carat gold with a miniature enamelled romantic bacchanalian portrait. *1906*
2.5cm (1in) wide

£800–860   CGPC

Har

Other than the fact it was made in New York in the 1950s, the history of Har jewellery is shrouded in mystery. If anything, this has only enhanced the desirability of a limited but exceptionally distinctive range of exotic, fantastical designs. Har's signature subjects are genies, oriental men, and, especially, sinuous snakes and dragons. The latter, of green-enamelled gold-tone metal encrusted with fantasy stones, are the most sought after of all.

Hinged dragon bangle of gold-tone metal with green enamelling and *aurora borealis* rhinestones. *1950s*

18cm (7in) circ

£450–500   **CRIS**

Oriental head pendant bracelet with silver-tone chain and faux ivory head with glass cabochons and *aurora borealis* rhinestones. *1950s*

B: 18cm (7in) circ; Pd: 3cm (1⅛in) long

£100–120   **CRIS**

Dragon pin and earrings of gold-tone metal with green enamelling and ruby, turquoise, and *aurora borealis* rhinestones. *1950s*

P: 7cm (2¾in) wide; E: 3cm (1⅛in) wide

£650–750   **SUM**

Swirling wheat-sheafs pin of brushed gold-tone base metal. Its simple decoration is uncharacteristic of most Har pieces. *1950s*

5.75cm (2¼in) wide

£20–25   **MILLB**

Exotic pendant necklace with silver-tone metal chain, fantasy coloured stones, and *aurora borealis* rhinestones. *1950s*

Pd: 10cm (4in) wide

£275–300   **SUM**

Fortune-telling male genie pin of gilt base metal with round-cut clear and star-cut sapphire blue rhinestones. *1950s*

6.25cm (2½in) long

£550–650   **SUM**

Rare cobra necklace, pin, bracelet, and earrings parure of gold-tone base metal with green enamelling and fantasy coloured glass stones, including navette-cut *aurora borealis* rhinestones. *1950s*

N: 38cm (15in) circ; P: 7cm (2¾in) wide; B: 18cm (7in) circ; E: 3cm (1⅛in) long

£2,000–2,500   **SUM**

Henry Schreiner

The New York jeweller Henry Schreiner opened his own company in 1951, after designing some early pieces for Christian Dior in the late 1940s and early 50s (*see pp60–65*). Schreiner's creative and exuberant costume jewellery, worn by stars such as Marilyn Monroe, is characterized by its unconventional combinations of colours and paste stones, inverted-set rhinestones, and its use of high-quality diamanté and crystal. Full parures by Schreiner are rare and therefore highly collectable.

Necklace and earrings of gilt metal with aquamarine, jonquil, and *aurora borealis* crystal rhinestones. *1950s*

N: 44.5cm (17½in) circ; E: 3cm (⅛in) long

£700–800   CRIS

Necklace and pendant earrings of silver gilt metal with clear crystal rhinestones and prong-set, pear-cut, ruby red glass drops. *1950s*

N: 38cm (15in) circ; E: 5cm (2in) long

£450–500   CRIS

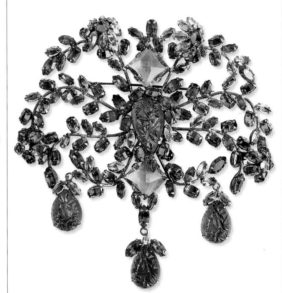

Bush pin of gilt wire backing with prong-set ruby, emerald, and clear crystal rhinestones, square-cut aquamarine pastes, and carved pear-cut, emerald glass drops. *1950s*

11cm (4⅜in) wide

£1,200–1,300   SUM

Necklace and earrings of gilt metal with prong-set rhinestones and drops of coloured glass. *1950s*

N: 5cm (2in) wide; E: 4cm (1½in) long

£750–850   SUM

Prong-set faux moonstone pin with a cluster of inverted amber-coloured rhinestones. *1950s*

7cm (2¾in) wide

£90–100   CRIS

Jonquil keystone crystal pin with a prong-set matrix-cut jonquil glass cabochon. *1950s*

7.5cm (3in) wide

£350–400   CRIS

Floral motif pin and earrings of gunmetal plating with crystal rhinestones and cabochons. *1950s*

P: 6.25cm (2½in) wide; E: 3.75cm (1½in) wide

£200–250   CRIS

Hermès

Thierry Hermès founded his saddlery company in 1837 and gradually introduced the production of boots, jewellery, items for the home, scarves, and bags. Today Hermés is mainly famous for its silk scarves, ties, and exclusive bags and luggage. Everything produced by Hermès is characterized by stylish designs, quality materials, and high standards of craftsmanship.

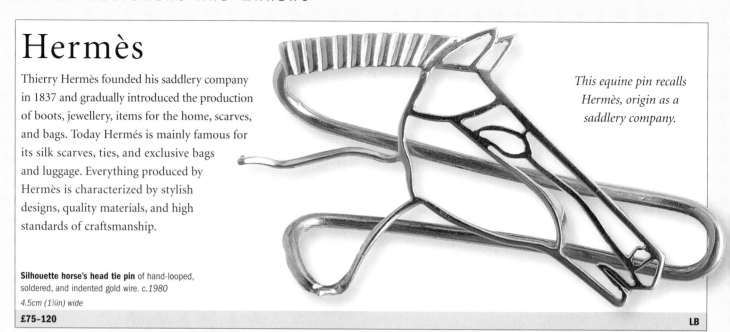

This equine pin recalls Hermès, origin as a saddlery company.

Silhouette horse's head tie pin of hand-looped, soldered, and indented gold wire. *c.1980*

4.5cm (1¾in) wide

£75–120   **LB**

Hervé van der Straeten

Also known for his furniture designs, Paris-based Hervé van der Straeten began making limited-edition costume jewellery in the 1990s. Rare and increasingly collectable, many of his bold compositions are hand-finished in gold-plated brass, and set with pearls or semi-precious stones.

Annealing, planishing, and pleating are characteristic of van der Straeten's metalwork.

Stylized flower pin with matching earrings of hand-beaten gold-plated metal with prong-set faux pearl centres. *Late 1990s*

P: 7cm (2¾in) wide;
E: 4.5cm (1¾in) long

£100–150   **CRIS**

Bow pin with matching earrings of hand-beaten and looped gold-plated metal. *Late 1990s*

P: 10cm (4in) long; E: 4.5cm (1¾in) long

£100–150   **CRIS**

Link necklace of gold-plated metal alternated with ovals of gold-toned Lucite. *Late 1990s*

48cm (19in) circ

£150–200   **CRIS**

Pendant necklace and matching earrings of gold-toned Lucite, the necklace with links of gold-plated metal and a pear-shaped drop. *Late 1990s*

N: 51cm (20in) circ;
E: 5cm (2in) long

£150–200   **CRIS**

Hollycraft

Hollycraft was founded in 1938 as the Hollywood Jewelry Manufacturing Company, but adopted the "Hollycraft" trademark in 1948 and continued in business until the mid 1970s. It is best known for its 1950s costume jewellery and Christmas Tree pins. Intricate and Victorian in style, its pieces have antiqued gold-tone settings with rhinestones, beads, and enamelling adding a characteristic dazzle of rainbow colours. Hollycraft jewellery is highly collectable because, unusually, it is always signed.

Butterfly pin of gilt and silver-gilt metal with black and white enamel. *c.1970*
5.75cm (2¼in) wide

£30–35   JJ

Gilt metal necklace set with rhinestones of diverse shapes, cuts, and colours, including turquoise, aquamarine, pink, orange, and clear. *1950s*
37cm (15⅛in) circ

£95–105   MG

Floral motif necklace with gilt metal chain and castings, the latter set with pink and clear crystal rhinestones. *1960s*
38cm (15in) circ

£185–215   JJ

Floral and foliate pin with faux coral, dark amethyst, and blue *aurora borealis* navettes and channel-set clear rhinestones. *1950s*
7.5cm (3in) long

£60–65   MG

Gilt metal bracelet and earrings with prong-set blue *aurora borealis* rhinestones, and diverse polychrome and *aurora borealis* foil-backed glass cabochons. *1950s*
B: 20.25cm (8in) circ; E: 3.75cm (1½in) long

£160–175   MG

Howard & Co.

Established in Providence, Rhode Island in 1878, Howard & Co. changed its name to the Howard Sterling Company in 1891. It ceased trading in about 1902. The plated and sterling silver jewellery it produced for a quarter of a century – notably buckles, brooches, buttons, and cuffs – is now very collectable. Its mark includes an ornamental lower case "h" and a four-leaf clover.

Belt buckle of sterling silver with applied sterling silver floral imagery. *c.1887*

8.25cm (3¼in) long

£115–120   CGPC

Circular buckle of goldwashed textured sterling silver with ruby and amethyst glass stones and blister pearl centre. *c.1901*

3.75cm (1½in) wide

£225–240   CGPC

Ian St. Gielar

Florida-based jewellery designer Ian St. Gielar was the chief designer for Stanley Hagler until Hagler's death in 1996 (*see pp.112–117*). St. Gielar then set up on his own, designing both under his own name and as Stanley Hagler NYC.

Superbly crafted, St. Gielar's pieces have delicate filigree backings embellished with fine materials such as Murano glass, mother-of-pearl, glass pearls, Limoges porcelain, and antique ivory. All pieces are in limited editions and are signed on a tag.

Bib necklace with pale blue and clear glass drops cascading from a "woven" collar of clear crystal rhinestones. *Late 1990s*

32cm (12½in) circ

£200–250   CRIS

Tasseled scarf of mauve, cranberry, red, and pale green glass beads. *Late 1990s*

112cm (44in) long

£300–350   CRIS

Flower pin with iridescent shell petals and an amber-red glass centre encircled by topaz crystal rhinestones. *Late 1990s*

9cm (3½in) wide

£150–185   CRIS

Iradj Moini

Although originally trained as an architect, Iranian-born Iradj Moini's career really took off after he began designing catwalk jewellery for Oscar de la Renta in the late 1980s. A string of prestigious clients and retail outlets (*see below*) have confirmed his reputation as one of the most imaginative of contemporary designers. His handmade pieces are invariably large, exquisitely detailed, and three-dimensional. Other characteristics include diverse figural and floral imagery, and unusual combinations of materials such as brass, bone, wood, and brightly coloured European crystal and oriental gemstones.

Frog pin with 1950s jade green baroque pastes, clear rhinestones, and ruby red glass cabochon eyes set in a brass wire frame. *Early 1990s*
9.5cm (3¾in) wide

£400–500   **CRIS**

HIGH PROFILE

In addition to being the *couture* jeweller for Oscar de la Renta, New York-based Iradj Moini has also produced pieces for Bill Blass, Carolina Herrera, and Arnold Scaasi. Not surprisingly, working for such influential fashion designers has led to numerous private commissions from fashion cognescenti on both sides of the Atlantic. Considerable demand has also resulted in his jewellery being retailed through Saks Fifth Avenue and other up-market boutiques in New York City and Beverly Hills. The actress Drew Barrymore, for example, purchased a Moini Austrian crystal, gold-plated bracelet from a Los Angeles boutique to wear to the 1999 Academy Awards.

Apple pin with ruby red and emerald green glass stones and clear rhinestones in a brass wire frame.
Early 1990s
11cm (4⅜in) long

£400–500   **CRIS**

***En tremblant* flower pin** with prong-set clear and emerald green rhinestones set in a brass wire frame. *Mid 1990s*
16cm (6¼in) long

£850–950   **CRIS**

***En tremblant* rose motif pin** with prong-set, round-cut clear rhinestones on a ruthenium-plated frame. *Mid 1990s*
13cm (5⅛in) long

£850–950   **CRIS**

Flower pin with mother-of-pearl petals and clear rhinestones on a ruthenium-plated frame. *Late 1990s*
14cm (5½in) long

£600–700   **CRIS**

Bouquet of flowers pin and earrings with French glass petals, carved jade leaves, and clear rhinestone highlights.
Early 1990s
P: 10cm (4in) long; E: 2.5cm (1in) long

£650–750   **CRIS**

Jewelerama

Made primarily in the 1960s, Jewelerama jewellery is unique. An offshoot of the Edmund Scientific Co. of Barrington, New Jersey, its novelty pins – mostly figural and floral, but also subjects such as musical instruments – incorporate machine-polished, circular convex metal discs that produce shimmering refractions of light.

Jewelerama's "Refraction Jewels" have become an interesting and affordable collecting field.

Turbanned genie pin of antiqued gold-tone casting, and magic lamp with gold-tone refractive disc. *1960s*

5cm (2in) long

£15–20 JJ

Floral pin of antiqued white metal casting and a pewter-tone refractive disc centre. *1960s*

6.25cm (2½in) long

£15–20 JJ

Banjo pin and earrings of antiqued gold-tone metal castings with gold-tone refractive disc centres. *1960s*

P: 6.25cm (2½in) long; E: 2cm (¾in) wide

£20–25 JJ

J.J.

The Jonette Jewelry Company, known as J.J., was founded in 1935 in East Providence, Rhode Island. Following its early success with ballerina and mother-of-pearl figural pins, J.J. became renowned for its Christmas Tree pins and novelty pins, featuring animals, charms, and Art Deco motifs with rhinestone details.

Flower pin and earrings of gold-tone metal castings set with clear and sapphire blue rhinestones. *1950s*

P: 6.25cm (2½in) long; E: 2cm (¾in) wide

£35–40 MILLB

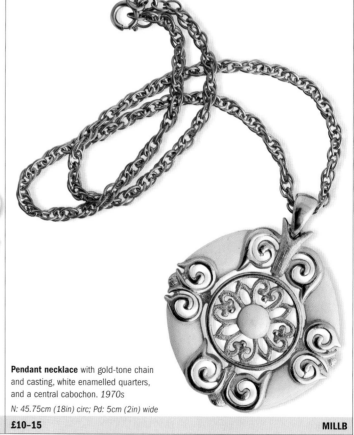

Pendant necklace with gold-tone chain and casting, white enamelled quarters, and a central cabochon. *1970s*

N: 45.75cm (18in) circ; Pd: 5cm (2in) wide

£10–15 MILLB

Puppy and mirror pin in gold-tone base
metal and semi-opaque mirror glass.
c.1990

5cm (2in) wide

£25–30   **ABIJ**

Fish pendant of gold-tone casting with black
rhinestone eye and red painted belly set with
polychrome plastic cabochons. *1970s*

7.5cm (3in) long

£25–35   **JJ**

Cat and goldfish bowl pin of
pewter-coloured base metal casting
and greytone glass. *c.1990*

6.5cm (2½in) wide

£25–30   **ABIJ**

Inside of pin

Safe pin of bronze and gold-tone base metal casting
with hinged door revealing a bag of dollars. *c.1980*

3.75cm (1½in) wide

£15–20   **JJ**

Sleigh pin of pewter-
tone base metal
casting inscribed
with an arrow motif,
and a gold-tone
base metal chain.
1990s

5.75cm (2¼in) long

£10–15   **MILLB**

Cow pin of brown-tone metal casting with three
faux pearl drop udders. *c.1980*

6.5cm (2½in) wide

£15–20   **JJ**

Fruit pin of antiqued and part
brown-enamelled gilt metal
casting with fruits of gold-red
rhinestones. *1980s*

5cm (2in) long

£10–15   **BB**

Biblical figure and snake pin of
antiqued gold-tone casting with
ruby and *aurora borealis* rhinestone
highlights. *1950s*

9cm (3½in) long

£45–55   **JJ**

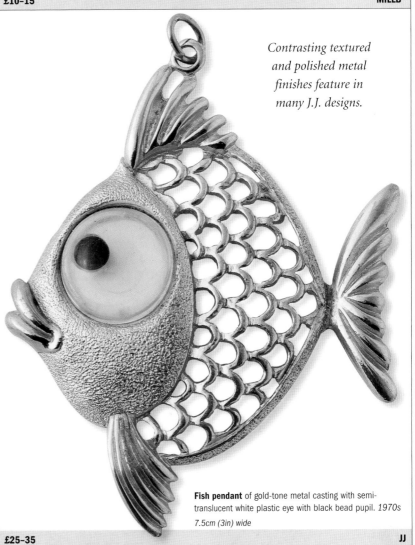

*Contrasting textured
and polished metal
finishes feature in
many J.J. designs.*

Fish pendant of gold-tone metal casting with semi-
translucent white plastic eye with black bead pupil. *1970s*

7.5cm (3in) wide

£25–35   **JJ**

Christmas Tree Pins

Originally a collecting phenomenon in the United States, Christmas Tree pins are now internationally sought after. Seasonal by design, these often exquisite pins have become a hot collecting field all year round.

KICK-STARTED IN CONFLICT

The convention of wearing a festive corsage at Christmas time dates back to the late 19th century. Composed of cloth, ribbon, and various trinkets, these fragile adornments rarely survived more than a few years. In the 1940s, however, more durable metal-frame Christmas jewellery began to appear. Typical pieces included wreaths, bows, santas, snowmen, sleighs, reindeer, and, most notably, Christmas Tree pins. The popularity of the latter really took off during Christmas 1950, when mothers and wives of American servicemen started wearing them and sending them to sons and husbands fighting overseas in the Korean

War. The fashion stuck, and ever since jewellery manufacturers have annually introduced new, limited-edition and instantly collectable Christmas Tree pin designs.

In keeping with the traditional colours of Christmas, most trees are of silver- or gold-tone metal and many feature red and green beads, stones, or enamelling. Most pins exhibit exquisite standards of craftsmanship, and many of the costume jewellery designers featured in this book have produced Christmas Tree pins. However, there are also numerous unsigned but desirable pieces. Prices start at under £30, but can exceed £300 for rare examples by prestigious names.

Frosted white enamel

Eisenberg Ice pin with frosted white enamel, gilt metal, and ruby and emerald rhinestones. *1980s. 6cm (2⅜in) long* **£30–40 CRIS**

Stanley Hagler Christmas Tree pin with hand-wired red and green Murano glass beads and yellow Murano glass fruit drops. *c.1970. 7cm (2¾in) long* **£90–100 CRIS**

Stanley Hagler Christmas Tree pin with hand-wired red and green Murano glass beads and gilt wire stars. *c.1970. 5.5cm (2¼in) long* **£90–100 CRIS**

Trifari pin with jade glass and ruby rhinestones. *1960s. 5cm (2in) long* **£50–80 ROX**

Mylu pin with carved stones and rhinestones. *1950s. 7cm (2¾in) long* **£105–120 ROX**

Trifari pin of brushed gold with faceted beads. *1950s 5cm (2in) long* **£65–70 CRIS**

172

Stanley Hagler Christmas Tree pin with mother-of-pearl petals, red rose montée centres, and jade rhinestones. *1960s 8.5cm (3⅜in) long* **£150–170 CRIS**

Eisenberg Ice pin with polychrome rhinestones on pierced gilt metal casting. *1980s. 5cm (2in) long* **£20–25 CRIS**

Cristobal pin with 1950s Swarovski crystals and peridot and emerald glass. *1990s 7.5cm (3in) long* **£30–35 CRIS**

Hollycraft Christmas Tree pin of textured gilt metal with polychrome rhinestones. *1950s 5cm (2in) long* **£45–50 CRIS**

Semi-matte Russian gold plating

Sphinx Christmas Tree pin with green enamel and clear and ruby rhinestones. *1960s. 7cm (2¾in) long* **£35–40 CRIS**

Cadora cherubs Christmas Tree pin of gilt metal with faux pearls. *1950s 7cm (2¾in) long* **£80–85 ROX**

Stanley Hagler pin with coloured glass beads and *aurora borealis* angel. *1980s. 6cm (2⅜in) long* **£80–90 CRIS**

Art pin with green enamelling and polychrome rhinestones. *1950s 6cm (2⅜in) long* **£40–45 CRIS**

173

Cristobal pin with prong-set red, emerald green, and clear crystal rhinestones. *1990s. 7cm (2¾in) long*
£25–30 CRIS

Eisenberg Ice pin with clear, ruby, and emerald rhinestones (some prong-set), and ruby and emerald navettes. *1980s 6cm (2¾in) long* **£45–50 CRIS**

Larry Vrba pin with prong-set dark blue teardrop cabochons, and ruby and clear rhinestones. *1990s. 11.5cm (4½in) long*
£120–130 CRIS

Unsigned French potted pin of gilt metal with green enamelling, and polychrome and clear rhinestones. *1980s. 5cm (2in) long*
£35–40 CRIS

Sphinx pin of gilt metal with green enamelled leaves and ruby red and clear rhinestones. *1960s. 5cm (2in) long*
£30–35 CRIS

Stanley Hagler pin with textured gilt basket, ruby baguette rhinestones, and emerald glass beads. *c.1970. 5.75cm (2¼in) long*
£80–100 CRIS

Larry Vrba pin with large *aurora borealis* and round-cut clear rhinestones and square-cut Montana blue rhinestones. *1990s 11.5cm (4½in) long* **£80–120 CRIS**

Trifari partridge in a pear tree pin of gilt metal with green, red, and blue enamelling. *1950s. 5cm (2in) long* **£80–85 ROX**

Eisenberg Ice pin, gold-plated with clear and ruby rhinestones and emerald navettes. *1980s. 5.5cm (2⅛in) long* **£25–30 CRIS**

Cristobal pin with pavé-set clear and emerald baguette rhinestones, and ruby glass cabochons. *1990s* 11cm (4¼in) long **£95–100 CRIS**

Clear crystal rhinestones

Art pin of textured gilt metal with clear, red, green, and blue beads and rhinestones. *1950s* 6cm (2⅜in) long **£40–50 CRIS**

Atwood & Sawyer pin with bow base, gold-plated with ruby and emerald rhinestones. *Late 1990s* 5cm (2in) long **£35–40 CRIS**

Unsigned Austrian pin with ruby, amethyst, emerald, and clear rhinestones and clear rhinestone candles. *1950s. 7.5cm (3in) long* **£45–50 CRIS**

Unsigned French pin with matte gold-tone metal basket, large ruby, emerald, and amber glass navettes, carved clear glass flowers, and clear, ruby, and aquamarine rhinestones. *1980s* 7cm (2¾in) long **£35–40 CRIS**

Matte gold-tone metal

Judy Lee

Judy Lee jewellery was sold at parties in people's homes from the 1950s to the 1970s. The 1950s pieces are mostly of floral design and are Victorian in style, using glittering rhinestones and faux pearls set on gold- or silver-tone filigree backings. Later pieces display other historical influences and use various stones set in antiqued metalwork.

Floral burst pin and matching earrings of gold-tone filigree backing with navette- and round-cut clear, topaz, ruby, and grey-green rhinestones. *c.1970*

P: 7cm (2¾in) wide; E: 3.75cm (1½) long

£35–45	ABIJ

Antiqued gold-tone metal bracelet with metallic polychrome glass cabochons. *1970s*

17.75cm (7in) circ

£35–45	ABIJ

Bracelet and earrings of antiqued silver-tone metal set with ruby, sapphire, aquamarine, and *aurora borealis* rhinestones. *Late 1970s*

17.75cm (7in) circ

£50–55	ABIJ

Karl Lagerfeld

German fashion designer Karl Lagerfeld worked for various Paris designers before joining Chanel in 1983 and launching his own-name label. The costume jewellery he created in the 1980s was bold and distinctive. He took well-known motifs, such as coins, pearls, and Chanel's "CC" motif and made them larger and more flashy. These pieces are now very collectable.

Stylized plant form earrings in goldwashed metal, each set with a faux pearl. *c.1990*

2.5cm (1in) long

£30–35	MILLB

"Louis XIV-style" bergère armchair earrings in goldwashed metal with clear crystal beads at the sides. *1980s*

3cm (1⅛in) long

£40–45	JJ

Kerr & Co.

Founded in New Jersey, in 1855, and originally known as Kerr and Thierry, the firm of William B. Kerr & Co. started by making tableware and gold and silver jewellery. From 1892 to 1900, however, the company made Art Nouveau costume jewellery. It produced large quantities of hollow-backed jewellery stamped with imitation repoussé work. Most of the jewellery was heavily influenced by French Art Nouveau designs and was marked with a fleur-de-lys.

Extremely rare two-part cherub belt clasp of silver-plated metal which, when joined, shows the male and female cherubs dancing. *c.1900*

7cm (2¾in) wide

£430–500

Belt clasp undone (above) and joined (right)

CGPC

Art Nouveau floral motif pin of goldwash over sterling silver with three faux moonstone cabochons. *c.1900*

6.25cm (2½in) wide

£230–265   CGPC

Art Nouveau double peacock motif belt buckle of goldwash over sterling silver set with ruby glass cabochons. *c.1900*

9cm (3½in) wide

£300–365   CGPC

Goldwash over sterling silver necklace comprising floral swags intertwined with cherubs. *c.1900*

38cm (15in) circ

£465–535   CGPC

Rare belt buckle comprising coiled cobras of silver-plated metal with a central red crystal rhinestone. *c.1900*

12.75cm (5in) wide

£335–400   CGPC

Kramer

Kramer Jewelry Creations was founded in New York in 1943 and continued production until the late 1970s. Kramer's exuberant and artistic jewellery features high-quality sparkling Austrian rhinestones, both clear and coloured. In the early 1950s, Kramer manufactured pieces for Christian Dior. Kramer's more extravagant styles, especially when in intact parures, are much sought after.

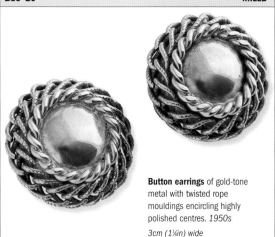

Leopard pin with articulated tail of gilt metal with black enamel spots, emerald rhinestone eyes, and a saddle of pavé-set clear rhinestones. *1950s*

5cm (2in) long

£40–50   **ABIJ**

Circular pin of antiqued, brushed gilt metal with a large faceted "watermelon" glass centre. *1950s*

5.75cm (2¼in) wide

£40–45   **ABIJ**

Leaf motif pin and earrings of antiqued, brushed, and pierced gilt metal with crystal rhinestones. *1970s*

P: 8.25cm (3¼in) long;
E: 3.75cm (1½in) long

£35–40   **ABIJ**

Bracelet and earrings with gilt metal clasp and links, and clear and textured white glass beads. *c.1960*

B: 17.75cm (7in) circ; E: 3.75cm (1½in) long

£30–35   **MILLB**

Stylized leaf motif earrings of gilt metal with black enamelling and faux pearl cabochons. *1950s*

3cm (1⅛in) long

£15–20   **MILLB**

Geometric motifs and bright colours were extremely fashionable in the 1950s.

Button earrings of gold-tone metal with twisted rope mouldings encircling highly polished centres. *1950s*

3cm (1⅛in) wide

£10–15   **MILLB**

Choker necklace of gold-tone metal links and castings, the latter with turquoise glass crosses. *1950s*

39.5cm (15½in) circ

£25–30   **MILLB**

La Pierre

The La Pierre Manufacturing Company was founded in 1885 in New York City, but relocated its factory to Newark in 1893. Until 1929, in addition to silverware it produced good-quality jewellery – notably bangles, belt buckles, and pins, also in silver but sometimes made with "novelty" materials such as celluloid.

Belt buckle with frame and applied scrolling leaves of sterling silver, and two romantic-historical celluloid minatures. *c.1904*

10cm (4in) wide

£465–535 CGPC

Art Nouveau sterling silver bangle with plant form motifs. *c.1902*

7.5cm (3in) circ

£100–115 CGPC

Lanvin

The House of Lanvin, established by Jeanne Lanvin in 1889, is the oldest of the Paris fashion houses and creates stylish, elegant jewellery to complement its collections. After a makeover in the late 1960s, Lanvin produced a series of carved Op Art plastic pendants on chains, which have become highly collectable.

Hinged bangle of gilt metal casting with classic key motif border against red enamelling. *1970s*

21cm (8in) circ

£75–95 LB

Couture **belt** of black velvet with a stylized leaf motif buckle of black glass beads with clear rhinestone highlights around a large pear-cut clear paste stone. *c.1970*

87.5cm (34in) circ

£250–300 SUM

Space Age necklace with gilt metal wire hoop and a circular pendant of black plastic set with a large red plastic cabochon. *1960s*

Pd: 8cm (3in) wide

£120–150 LB

Larry Vrba

From a lowly role at Miriam Haskell (*see pp.98–107*) in 1969, Nebraska-born Larry Vrba enjoyed a remarkably rapid rise to prominence. On leaving Haskell after only nine months of employment, he worked briefly for Castlecliff and then William DeLillo before, just a year later aged 22, returning as Haskell's chief designer. For seven years he designed over a thousand different lines for Haskell – traditional in style, but with a contemporary, often exotic twist. After two years with Les Bernard in the early 1980s, Vrba embarked on a highly imaginative solo career unfettered by corporate restraints. His pieces – large, ornate, and often outrageous – are particularly sought after in the theatrical and transvestite communities (*see box below*).

Larry Vrba's unique designs are visually arresting in their sheer size and profusion of colour. Equally engaging in their imaginative compositions and finely worked detail, they never fail to make a powerful statement.

Large flower pin of gun-metal frame with abalone shell, faux pearls, glass beads, and clear crystal rhinestones. *Late 1990s*

20cm (8in) long

£180–200　　　　CRIS

Knotted bow pin with rope-moulding motif, oxidized gun-metal wire frame, set with fuchsia and rose pink pastes and rhinestones. *1990s*

13cm (5⅛in) wide

£160–180　　　　CRIS

Basket of flowers pin with carved orange and yellow glass, and jade, coral, and yellow glass beads, on a gun-metal frame. *Late 1990s*

11.5cm (4½in) long

£125–150　　　　CRIS

Vase of flowers pin with white mother-of-pearl flowers, carved jade leaves, coral bead berries, and poured glass vase. *Late 1990s*

12cm (4¾in) long

£150–200　　　　CRIS

THEATRICAL GESTURES

It isn't at all surprising that Larry Vrba's bold conceptions have appeared in numerous stage productions. Theatre designers have long appreciated that rather like stage make-up, costume accessories have to be larger-than-life in order to "read" up in the circle or down in the stalls. For similar reasons, Vrba has also received numerous commissions from transvestites requesting ever-more dramatic pieces to go with equally innovative and extravagant costumes – mostly for New York's annual charity drag balls. His big, colourful designs are fully in the spirit of dressing up outrageously, and they also serve the purpose of making larger bodies look more petite.

Heart-shaped vase of flowers pin of gold-plated base metal with mother-of-pearl, glass beads, and rose pink rhinestones. *Late 1990s*

11.5cm (4½in) long

£150–200　　　　CRIS

Liberty

Arthur L. Liberty opened his first shop in London in 1875. From 1894 onwards, he commissioned designs from talented jewellers, such as Archibald Knox, a leading figure of the Arts and Crafts Celtic Revival movement, and Jessie King. Liberty pieces are often made of hammered silver to create a handcrafted effect. The swirling, interlaced metal designs are decorated with peacock blue and green enamelling and semi-precious stones.

The Celtic influence in Liberty pieces is unmistakeable, as are the Arts and Crafts standards of workmanship.

Floral motif necklace of gilt metal set with blue, green, and turquoise *plique-à-jour* enamels. *c.1903*

38cm (14¼in) circ

£3,000–3,500   **NBLM**

Necklace detail

Pendant necklace (unsigned) with gilt metal chain and floral motif castings with enamelling and faux pearl cabochons. *c.1905*

42cm (16½in) circ

£800–900   **RG**

Necklace detail

Pendant necklace (unsigned) with silvered metal chain and clover motif castings, enamelling, and faux pearl cabochons and drop. *c.1910*

42cm (16½in) circ

£1,000–1,200   **RG**

Marvella

Weinrich Bros. Co., founded in 1911, used the name "Marvella" as its trademark and only changed its name to Marvella Inc. in 1965. The Weinrich brothers specialized in imitation jewellery and faux pearls. Necklaces are made of several strands of faceted crystal beads, and faux pearls are combined with rhinestones. The jewellery is marked with different trademarks, many of which include Marvell or Marvella in a longer name, such as "Marvellesque". The company was bought by Trifari in 1982.

Triple-strand necklace, bracelet, and earrings parure with oval and round, variegated green and yellow glass beads, and six oval jonquil glass beads, with filigree gilt metal findings. *1950*
N: 44.5cm (17½in) circ; B: 20.25cm (8in) circ; E: 2.5cm (1in) wide

£50–65   MILLB

Triple-chain necklace of gold-tone metal with faux pearls and three cartouches with large navette-cut clear rhinestones. *1970s*
35.5cm (14in) circ

£20–25   ABIJ

Single earring with faux pearls, amethyst, emerald, and aquamarine glass stones, and gilt metal findings. *1970s*
5.75cm (2¼in) long

£15–20   ABIJ

Drop earrings with faux pearls linked by silver-tone metal chains set with small clear crystal rhinestones. *1950s*
5cm (2in) long

£10–15   MILLB

Leaf and buds pin of gold-tone and silver-tone metal, faux pearls, and pavé-set clear crystal rhinestones. *1960s*
4.5cm (1¾in) long

£30–40   ABIJ

Stylized floral cluster earrings in gold-tone base metal.
1950s
2.5cm (1in) wide

£10–15   MILLB

Monet

Founded by Jay and Michael Chernow in 1929, and known as Monocraft until 1937, Monet became one of the leading costume jewellers during the 1940s. Its simple, classic designs in silver and gold tones, sometimes accented with Austrian crystal highlighters, appealed to the working women of the postwar era. It also pioneered comfortable clip-on earrings, which became very popular. Monet produced jewellery for Yves Saint Laurent during the 1980s and, by constantly adapting to changing fashions, has remained successful right up until today.

Over the years, Monet has continually adapted its jewellery designs to reflect the social scene of the time.

Cross pin of gold-plated casting set with pear-shaped faux pearls and navette-, baguette-, and round-cut clear crystal rhinestones. *1980s*

5cm (2in) diam

£20–25   **ABIJ**

£30–35   **MILLB**

Gold-plated necklace with chain links and oval ornament, the latter with rope moulding border and a glass cabochon. *1980s*

45.75cm (18in) circ

Flower pin with borders of gold-plated metal; the petal surfaces are strands of base metal with white enamelling. *c.1970*

5cm (2in) long

£15–25   **MILLB**

Starfish pins of textured gold-plated metal with pavé-set clear crystal rhinestones. *1980s*

Large: 2.5cm (1in) wide; Small: 2cm (¾in) wide

£25–30   **ABIJ**

Snail pin of gilt metal with clear rhinestone eyes and a shell set with ruby and emerald glass cabochons. *c.1980*

5cm (2in) long

£20–25   **JJ**

Gold-plated necklace with stylized floral design pendant of scrolling, interlaced forms. *1970s*

N: 58.5cm (23in) circ; Pd: 5cm (2in) wide

£10–15   **MILLB**

Moschino

Italian fashion designer Franco Moschino launched his own label in 1983, after working as an illustrator for Gianni Versace. He started with jeans and casual wear, which were soon followed by shoes, lingerie, innovative evening wear, and jewellery. Provocative and iconoclastic, Moschino approached fashion and accessories with a touch of irony and a strong sense of humour. His jewellery is stamped with the mark "Moschino Bijoux".

Antiqued gold-tone metal earrings, the clips with central faux pearl cabochons encircled by a stamped "Moschino Bijoux" mark, and chained to peace symbol pendants. *1980s*

7.5cm (3in) long

£15–20   **MILLB**

Antiqued gold-tone metal earrings, the clips with faux pearl cabochons and the hoop pendants with lattice-work pattern. *1980s*

9.5cm (3¾in) long

£20–25   **MILLB**

FRANCO MOSCHINO

1950 Born near Milan, Italy

1971 After studying at the Fine Arts Academy in Milan, he began his career working as an illustrator for Giorgio Armani, with whom he continued working for 11 years

1983 The Moschino label is launched

1994 Franco Moschino dies and Rossella Jardini, who worked with the designer for many years, becomes Creative Director of Moschino

Murrle Bennet & Co.

From 1884 to 1914, this Anglo-German agency marketed inexpensive jewellery similar to Liberty's. Often designed by Theodor Fahrner (*see pp.72–73*) in Germany, the pieces were usually made of silver or low-carat gold, set with green and blue enamelwork, semi-precious stones, mother-of-pearl, or glass. Fahrner's work was abstract or semi-organic in form, often based on stylized plants or birds. Most pieces bear a mark, either "MB" or "MB & Co.". Those attributed to a particular designer are the most valuable.

Arts and Crafts pendant of silver casting with a raised central lozenge of mottled blue and green enamelling, with indented slivers of turquoise enamelling. *c.1905*

4.5cm (1¾in) long

£300–350   **RBRG**

Art Nouveau pin of goldwashed sterling silver with a central mottled green and brown semi-precious stone cabochon. *c.1905*

4.5cm (1¾in) wide

£250–300   **LYNTT**

Arts and Crafts pendant necklace with Celtic Revival motifs. The chain and pendant of silver set with blue enamel. *c.1905*

41.5cm (16½in) circ;
Pd: 4.5cm (1¾in) long

£650–750   **RG**

Napier

Founded in 1875, Napier originally made silverware, but shifted emphasis to modern jewellery after World War I and stayed in business until 1999. Its early designs are highly collectable, as are its Egyptian-style pieces of the 1920s and 30s. During the 1950s and 60s, Napier produced a wide variety of chunky gilt metal charm bracelets, which became very popular. Coins, antique seals, and oriental motifs are much sought after. Another favourite line is its simple gilt mesh and silver-toned jewellery.

Pendant necklace, bracelet, and pendant earrings parure of filigree gold-plated metal with highlights, and single- and double-tiered drops of clear crystal rhinestones. *Mid 1950s*

N: 41cm (16in) circ; B: 19cm (7½in) circ; E: 7cm (2¾in) long

£100–125 CRIS

Grapes and leaves pin, the leaves of textured, matte-finish gilt metal; the bunch of grapes and wire spiral of polished gilt metal. *1950s*

12.75cm (5in) long

£65–75 CRIS

Elephant pin of gold-plated casting with a sapphire paste stone capped with filigree metal, and a faux ruby and pearls. *Mid 1950s*

3.75cm (1½in) high

£50–55 CRIS

Turtle pin of engraved gilt metal casting with a large jade green glass cabochon with rope moulding border. *1980s*

5cm (2in) long

£25–30 JJ

Gold-plated charm bracelet of various motifs, with faux emerald, turquoise, ruby, amethyst, and pearl stones and beads. *Mid 1950s*

B: 18cm (7in) circ; Longest charm: 5cm (2in) long

£100–125 CRIS

Unusual bracelet with "carved" twin fruit pendants and chain of silver-tone metal. *Late 1950s*

B: 20.25cm (8in) circ; Fruits: 3.75cm (1½in) long

£75–95 CRIS

Ethnic-style necklace, bracelet, and earrings parure with gold findings and diverse polychrome beads and stones of various cuts. *1960s*

N: 152.5cm (60in) circ; B: 17.75cm (7in) circ; E: 3.75cm (1½in) long

£80–95 ABIJ

Coro Duettes

The first major American manufacturer of costume jewelley to make double clips, Coro soon became famous for its animal and floral "Duettes". Much sought after, they have now become a collecting field in their own right.

FAMED FOR THEIR VERSATILITY

Clips were a mainstay of 1920s jewellery, worn on furs or dresses to highlight an attractive feature, such as a lapel or plunging neckline. In 1927, the French fine jeweller Louis Cartier patented the double clip, an ingenious mechanism (*see below right*) that allowed two identical or similar clips to be fastened together and worn as one pin, or detached and worn separately – for example, on both sides of a neckline, or on a lapel and a hat or scarf. The versatility of the double-clip made it a huge success.

Quick to follow suit, Coro created its own version of the double clip, the Coro Duette, in 1931. The initial designs were often Art Deco in style and decorated with pavé-set clear rhinestones. Coro's greatest success, however,

came with the creation of its figural Duettes, featuring flowers, birds and other animals, and characters such as cherubs. Mostly made of vermeil sterling silver, these were decorated with colourful enamelling and crystal rhinestones. Each Duette had a name and was sometimes sold with matching earrings.

Coro Duettes were popular throughout the 1940s, but were waning in popularity by the early 50s, although they were still being marketed in smaller, lighter versions. They are now avidly collected, particularly the unusual and complex pieces such as the "Quivering Camellias" Duette, featuring delicate trembler flowers mounted on springs.

Yellow metal parrots with green, blue, and pink enamelling and pavé-set clear crystal rhinestones. *1940s 6.25cm (2½in) long* **£100–135 ABIJ**

Vermeil sterling silver fish with Lucite bellies, pink and sapphire cabochons, and clear crystal rhinestones. *1940s 4.5cm (1¾in) long* **£375–425 CRIS**

Sterling silver owls with blue enamel and aquamarine and pavé-set clear crystal rhinestones. *1940s 3.75cm (1½in) long* **£150–170 CRIS**

Silver leaves in rhodium-plated metal with clear crystal rhinestones. *c.1940. 6.25cm (2½in) wide* **£100–150 CRIS**

DOUBLE CLIP MECHANISM

Duettes were sold on a metal frame fitted with a brooch pin. When clipped onto the frame, the two individual pieces looked like a single pin. The mechanism varied in styling for each design, but the way in which the pieces locked together remained much the same.

Double clip

Back of double clip

Single clip

Back of clip

Detachable brooch frame

Flowers Duette *c.1950s 6.25cm (2½in) wide* **£100–150 CRIS**

Hearth and mantel motifs of white metal with clear crystal rhinestones and ruby glass "fires". *c.1940 7.5cm (3in) long* **£100–135 MILLB**

Vermeil sterling silver cherubs with ruby and emerald crystal rhinestones and faux pearls. *1940s. 3.5cm (1⅜in) high* **£200–250 CRIS**

Bouquets of flowers in enamelled silver with glass beads and crystal rhinestones. *1930s. 7cm (2¾in) long* **£165–200 ROX**

Dutch couple pin in vermeil sterling silver with ruby, aquamarine, and clear crystal rhinestones. *1940s. 5cm (2in) long* **£360–400 CRIS**

Clear crystal rhinestones

Enamelling over vermeil

Horse heads of vermeil sterling silver with ruby and aquamarine crystal navettes. *1940s 5.75cm (2¼in) long* **£140–180 CRIS**

Owls on branches of vermeil sterling silver with topaz and clear crystal rhinestones. *1940s. 3.75cm (1½in) long* **£155–175 JJ**

"Brave and squaw" in vermeil sterling silver with red and green enamel and ruby and clear crystal rhinestones. *1940s. 4.5cm (1¾in) long* **£650–700 CRIS**

187

Nettie Rosenstein

From the 1930s to the 1960s, fashion designer Nettie Rosenstein designed costume jewellery in addition to clothes. She is best known for her colourful rhinestone pins and earrings, and her unusual silver and enamel pieces of the 1930s Art Deco period. Favourite imagery includes animals, butterflies, flowers, and heraldric motifs.

Crab fur clip of vermeil sterling silver with green, brown, yellow, and red enamelling. *1940s*

4.5cm (1¾in) wide

£100–120   RG

Minstrel pin of vermeil sterling silver with turquoise glass cabochons and clear crystal rhinestones. *1940s*

7cm (2¾in) long

£160–175   ROX

Butterfly fur clip of vermeil sterling silver with dark and pale green, pink, and red enamelling, and faux seed pearls. *1940s*

9cm (3½in) wide

£250–350   RG

Crowned heart motif bangle of vermeil and antiqued vermeil sterling silver with glass cabochons encircling a large red paste cabochon. *Late 1930s*

Motif: 7cm (2¾in) long

£285–315   MG

Panetta

After working for Trifari and Pennino, Italian-born Benedetto Panetta set up his own company in New York City, in 1945. Working with platinum-coloured metal, he crafted replicas of fine jewellery, from enamelled and floral pins to Art Deco-style rhinestone pieces, all of which are now highly collectable.

Snake bangle with two matching rings of gilt metal with black enamel and black and clear crystal rhinestones. *1960s*

B: 7cm (2¾in) wide; R: 7cm (2¾in) circ

£185–215   MG

Platinum-coloured metal ring set with bands and navette-shaped cups of pale amethyst crystal rhinestones. *1960s*

2cm (¾in) wide

£50–55   BBG

Small floral motif pin of gold-tone metal set with turquoise coloured glass beads. *1970s*

3cm (1⅛in) wide

£15–25   BB

Floral motif pin of antiqued gilt metal, the centre and petals with pavé-set clear crystal rhinestones. *1950s*

4.5cm (1¾in) long

£145–155   BBG

Pennino Bros

The New York-based Pennino Bros, founded by Frank and Oreste Pennino, produced fine-quality costume jewellery from around 1926 to 1961. Mostly made by skilled Italian *émigrés*, such as Adrian Scannavino and Beneditto Panetta, its pieces are characterized by intricate workmanship, the use of best-quality Austrian rhinestones, and vermeil sterling silver. Favourite – and highly collectable – forms and features include flowers, bows, scrolls, drapery effects, and abstract designs.

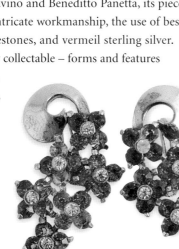

Flower pin and earrings
of vermeil sterling silver with crystal rhinestones. *c.1940*
P: 7cm (2¾in) long;
E: 3.5cm (1⅜in) long

£250–350 · SUM

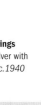

Bouquet of flowers pin and earrings of rose gold vermeil sterling silver with rose pink and clear crystal rhinestones. Mid 1940s
P: 7cm (2¾in) long; E: 2cm (¾in) wide

£400–450 · CRIS

Bow pin of vermeil sterling silver with aquamarine and rose pink crystal rhinestones. *Mid 1940s*
9.5cm (3¾in) long

£200–230 · CRIS

High-quality Austrian rhinestones are a fine feature of Pennino jewellery.

Bow and flowers pin of vermeil sterling silver with aquamarine and small rose pink crystal rhinestones. *Mid 1940s*
6cm (2¾in) long

£200–250 · CRIS

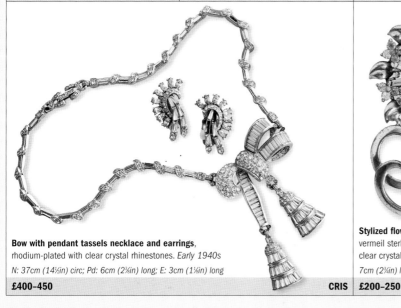

Bow with pendant tassels necklace and earrings, rhodium-plated with clear crystal rhinestones. *Early 1940s*
N: 37cm (14½in) circ; Pd: 6cm (2¾in) long; E: 3cm (1⅛in) long

£400–450 · CRIS

Stylized flower pin with trailing tendrils of vermeil sterling silver and aquamarine and clear crystal rhinestones. *Mid 1940s*
7cm (2¾in) long

£200–250 · CRIS

Stylized flower pin with trailing trendrils of vermeil sterling silver and rose pink and clear crystal rhinestones. *Mid 1940s*
7cm (2¾in) long

£200–250 · CRIS

Pop Art Jewellery

Pop Art was a vibrant expression of the youth movement of the 1960s and early 70s, which created art to reflect popular culture. Pop Art costume jewellery reflects influences ranging from the Space Age to "flower power", and includes pastiches of traditional or classic forms. Bold, often highly colourful designs in plastics and metals, these pieces are rarely signed.

"Flower power" earrings with semi-translucent petals and opaque, deep purple centres. Unsigned. *Late 1960s*

3.75cm (1½in) wide

£10–15   **MILLB**

Large papier mâché hoop earrings painted to look like traditional stone, bone, or leather Native American earrings. Unsigned. *1960s*

9.5cm (3¾in) long

£30–35   **MILLB**

Large straw boater pendant earrings in candy striped plastic and gold-tone base metal. Unsigned. *Early 1970s*

9cm (3½in) long

£10–15   **MILLB**

Gold-tone metal link belt with candy coloured plastic and a long disc pendant. *Early 1970s*

101.5cm (40in) long incl. pd

£10–15   **MILLB**

Plastic necklace comprising elastic-strung crimson, tangerine, banana, and white plastic beads. *Early 1970s*

50cm (19⅝in) circ

£10–15   **MILLB**

Large pendant choker made from gold-tone wire, the spiral pendants a pastiche of Ancient Roman forms. *Early 1970s*

N: 43cm (17in) circ; Pd: 20.5cm (8in) long

£50–65   **MILLB**

Open bangle of gold-tone metal set with citrine rhinestones and smokey quartz. *Early 1970s*

19cm (7½in) circ

£30–35   **MILLB**

Open bangle of gold-tone metal with a shield ornament. Stylistically a pastiche of Classical Greco-Roman forms. *Early 1970s*

21.5cm (8½in) circ

£20–25   **MILLB**

Classical form earrings comprising pendants of gold-tone metal coins. *c.1970*

10cm (4in) long

£10–15   **MILLB**

Open collar necklace with a large pendant in gold-tone metal with two black plastic beads. *1970s*

N: 30.5cm (12in) circ;
Pd: 15.25cm (6in) long

£35–50   **MILLB**

Rebajes

Jeweller and sculptor Francisco Rebajes was born in Spain in 1906. In 1934 he opened a studio shop in New York City, selling jewellery and *objets d'art*. He ran his business until 1967, then returned to Spain where he made jewellery until his death in 1990. Rebajes was a star of the Modernist jewellery movement. His bold, dramatic pieces, with their characteristic soft finish, were carefully handcrafted and drew their inspiration from sources as diverse as ethnic masks and Surrealism.

A master of copper jewellery, Rebajes created distinctive pieces with a soft patina.

Stylized "African head" copper pin with copper wire necklace and earrings. *Late 1940s*

8cm (3in) long

£200–240   **CRIS**

Cast copper hoop earrings in the form of flying wings or flames. *c.1950*

3cm (1⅛in) long

£15–20   **BB**

Copper chain pendant necklace with three scrolled feather or leaf motifs. *1950s*

N: 48cm (19in) long; Pd: 5.75cm (2¼in) wide

£65–100   **MILLB**

Regency

Little is known about the history of Regency costume jewellery, other than that it was made from the 1950s to 70s by the Polowitz family-owned Regina Novelty Company, based in New York City. Such scant provenance has, however, in no way detracted from its desirability to collectors. Regency's signature piece is the butterfly, which was made in various colourways and slightly differing forms. Like the mostly floral and foliate motif pieces also made under the Regency brand, much of their attraction resides in the consistently high quality of the rhinestones employed. Usually prong-set in sumptuous complementary or contrasting colours, they are invariably a feast for the eye.

Gold-plated necklace and earrings with prong-set *aurora borealis* and emerald green round and teardrop cabochons. *1950s*

N: 44cm (17¼in) circ; E: 2.5cm (1in) long

£150–180   **CRIS**

Flower and leaf motif necklace and earrings, silver-plated with navette- and round-cut *aurora borealis* and clear rhinestones. *Late 1950s*

N: 39cm (15¼in) circ; E: 3.5cm (1⅜in) long

£150–175   **CRIS**

Floral motif pin, gun-metal-plated with ruby red rhinestones and cabochons with *aurora borealis* centres. *1960s*

5cm (2in) wide

£60–70   **CRIS**

Necklace, bracelet, and earrings, gold-plated with navette- and round-cut aquamarine and lime green rhinestones. *1950s*

N: 39cm (15¼in) circ; B: 18.5cm (7¼in) circ; E: 4cm (1½in) long

£200–250   **CRIS**

Bracelet and earrings with round- and navette-cut aquamarine, lime green, and amethyst rhinestones. *1950s*

B: 16.5cm (6½in) circ; E: 3cm (1⅛in) long

£140–160   **CRIS**

Leaf motif pin and earrings, gold-plated with round- and navette-cut *aurora borealis* and lime green rhinestones. *Mid 1950s*

P: 5.5cm (2⅛in) long; E: 3cm (1⅛in) long

£100–125   **CRIS**

Scrolling leaf pin and earrings, gold-plated with round- and navette-cut, prong-set aquamarine and amethyst rhinestones. *1950s*

P: 5cm (2in) long; E: 2.5cm (1in) long

£75–85   **CRIS**

Butterfly pin, gold-plated with prong-set, navette and round orange-red glass cabochons and jonquil, *aurora borealis*, and amber rhinestones. *Mid 1950s*

5.5cm (2⅛in) wide

£85–90   **CRIS**

Butterfly pin, gold-plated with prong-set round- and navette-cut *aurora borealis*, aquamarine, and jade rhinestones. *Mid 1950s*

4.5cm (1¾in) wide

£85–90   **CRIS**

Réja

Founded by Sol Finkelstein in 1939, the Déja Costume Jewelry Inc. of New York changed its name to the Réja Jewelry Co. in 1941. Up until production ceased in 1952, it created many pieces of exceptional design and craftsmanship. Although best-known for its dramatic figural pins (including human, animal, fish, bird, and insect designs), Reja also made exquisite floral pieces. Most were produced in vermeil sterling silver, the thickness and warm tones of which impart a feeling of quality and substance. Other characteristic materials include enamel, faux pearls, rhinestones, and large, coloured glass stones of American origin.

Flower pin of vermeil sterling silver with green, pink, and white enamelling, aquamarine pastes, and clear rhinestones. *c.1939*
8.5cm (3⅜in) long

£250–400   **ROX**

Stylized jellyfish pin of sterling silver with faux pearls, small faux sapphires, and clear rhinestones. *1940s*
9cm (3½in) long

£150–200   **RG**

Bacchanalian mask design of vermeil sterling silver with rose-gold-plated grapes and green enamelled leaves. *Mid 1940s*
P: 7.5cm (3in) long; E: 3.5cm (1¾in) long

£600–700   **CRIS**

Blackamoor head pin and earrings of vermeil and black-enamelled sterling silver with clear rhinestones. *1940s*
P: 6cm (2¾in) long; E: 3cm (1¼in) long

£400–600   **ROX**

Stork pin of vermeil sterling silver with clear rhinestones and a large faux aquamarine. *1940s*
7cm (2¾in) long

£80–110   **RG**

Leaping stag pin of vermeil sterling silver with clear rhinestones and a large faux aquamarine. *1940s*
7.5cm (3in) wide

£120–140   **RG**

Turtle pin of vermeil sterling silver with clear and pavé-set green rhinestones. *1940s*
5cm (2in) wide

£120–150   **RG**

Bracelet, pin, and earrings of vermeil sterling silver with opaque pinkish-red cabochons and clear rhinestones. *1947*
B: 19cm (7½in) circ; P: 9cm (3½in) wide; E: 3.75cm (1½in) long

£250–300   **RG**

Renoir – Matisse

Founded in Los Angeles in 1946 by Jerry Fels, Renoir of California specialized in solid copper jewellery. Although produced in the spirit of the late 19th- and early 20th-century Arts and Crafts movement – for which hand-worked copper was a favourite medium – most of its pieces display the geometric or abstract forms and patterns characteristic of mid-20th-century art and design. In 1952, Fels established a subsidiary company, Matisse Ltd., which specialized in copper jewellery with colourful enamel decoration. Many pieces, especially the pins, employ more naturalistic imagery, notably artists' palettes and different types of leaf. Production at both companies ceased in 1964, leaving a very distinctive legacy: once seen, Renoir and Matisse jewellery becomes instantly recognizable thereafter.

Matisse copper twin-leaf pin with white and gun-metal grey enamelled highlights. *Mid 1950s*

8cm (3⅛in) long

£45–50   CRIS

Renoir copper bangle with raised, round, geometric motifs, most commonly described as "Swiss Cheese" decoration. *Late 1940s*

4cm (1½in) wide

£75–100   CRIS

Renoir copper bangle with rope moulding edges and hooped wire decoration. *Mid 1950s*

2.5cm (1in) wide

£75–90   CRIS

Matisse artists' palette and brushes pin with blue, yellow, brown, and red enamelling on copper. *Mid 1950s*

7cm (2¾in) long

£65–80   CRIS

Matisse maple leaf pin and earrings with blue and blue-black enamelling on copper and copper berry highlights. *Mid 1950s*

P: 6.5cm (2½in) long; E: 3cm (1⅛in) long

£95–100   CRIS

Mastisse maple leaf pin and earrings with white and yellow ochre enamelling on copper. *Mid 1950s*

P: 6.5cm (2½in) long; E: 3cm (1⅛in) long

£95–100   CRIS

Richelieu

The Richelieu mark was first used in 1911 by Joseph H. Meyer Bros., which was established in Brooklyn, New York in the early 1900s. The company, which merged with Lisner in the late 1970s (*see pp.88–89*), produced costume jewellery for both women and men, embracing many styles fashionable during the 20th century. It is, however, best-known for its use of faux pearls. The majority of Richelieu pieces that collectors will come across today date from the 1960s to the 1980s. Relatively inexpensive, they typically combine polished gold-tone metals with faux pearls, crystal rhinestones, or colourful cabochons, although antiqued metal pieces in various historical-revival styles can also be found, usually at slightly higher prices.

Antiqued gold-tone metals, usually combined with colourful pastes, are characteristic of Richelieu's historical-revival pieces.

Art Nouveau Revival cartouche pin with scrolled leaf decoration and pendants, in antiqued gold-tone metal with a faux cornelian cabochon.
1960s
7.5cm (3in) wide

£40–45   ABIJ

Geometric form earrings of highly polished gold-tone metal and hinged pendants with three sections of pavé-set, round-cut, clear crystal rhinestones. *1980s*
3cm (1⅛in) long

£15–20   MILLB

Oval faux pearl earrings of champagne colour with a highly lustrous finish.
1970s
2cm (¾in) long

£10–15   MILLB

Drop earrings of highly polished gold-tone metal and navette-shaped faux coral inserts. *1980s*
5.75cm (2¼in) long

£15–20   MILLB

Plastic Jewellery

First made in the mid 19th century, plastic jewellery gained popularity from the 1920s onwards. Quick to produce and reasonably priced, it was readily available and appealed to customers from all income brackets.

A TRULY MODERN MATERIAL

Celluloid, one of the first plastics, was invented by Alexander Parkes in 1855. It had the colour and texture of ivory, but could be dyed to look like tortoiseshell or horn. Celluloid jewellery, popular during the late 1890s, was gradually eclipsed first by Galalith and later by Bakelite, more stable and less inflammable plastics. Lucite, a solid, clear plastic, was first introduced in 1937 and was soon used for costume jewellery. By the 1950s it had more or less replaced Bakelite, which was more expensive to produce.

Plastics are both malleable and versatile, qualities that have appealed to many jewellery designers. They can be moulded, carved, tinted, laminated, and attached to other materials, allowing a designer greater creative freedom than traditional materials, such as metal or glass. Plastics are also quick and easy to produce. Inevitably, much plastic jewellery was mass-produced, but interesting and well-preserved pieces from the 1920s, 30s, 40s, and 50s are much sought after by collectors.

Art Deco pieces are worth looking out for, as are intricate floral pins, some of which are decorated with rhinestones, and novelty period pieces. Trifari's Jelly Belly figurals (*see p.127*) with a central Lucite "stone" are also highly collectable.

Bathing belles pin in red, black, yellow, and flesh-coloured celluloid. *Late 1920s* 4.5cm (1¾in) long **£25–35 JJ**

Art Deco stylized horse pin in blue acrylic with clear acrylic eyes. *1930s. 10.75cm (4¼in) long* **£20–30 JBC**

Floral motif necklace with clear Lucite links and drops, and clusters of crystal rhinestones. *1950s. 82cm (32in) long* **£400–500 CSAY**

Hinged bracelet and pendant hoop earrings in turquoise plastic. *1950s. B: 18cm (7in) circ; E: 5cm (2in) long* **£20–30 ECLEC**

Parrot pin in shades of red, black, yellow, and brown Lucite. *c.1940 9cm (3½in) long* **£95–105 TR**

American courting couple pin with revolving umbrella in coloured plastic. *Late 1920s. 5.75cm (2¼in) long* **£45–60 JJ**

Basket of flowers pin with green and coral Lucite and clear crystal rhinestones. *Late 1930s. 5.5cm (2⅛in) long* **£80–100 CRIS**

American flower pin in yellow and green Lucite on a silver filigree backing. *Late 1950s 12.5cm (5in) wide* **£125–150 CRIS**

American flower pin in yellow, amber, and cream Lucite on a silver backing. *Late 1950s 14cm (5½in) wide* **£125–150 CRIS**

Italian flower pin with pale green-brown Lucite petals and faux jet lucite beads. *1980s. 6.5cm (2½in) wide* **£50–70 CRIS**

American elasticated "Mah Jong" bracelets of faux ivory and ebony plastic. *Late 1950s 17.75cm (7in) circ* **£125–150 CRIS**

Scotty dog head pins in black and yellow Lucite with chromed steel eyes. *Late 1930s 3cm (1⅛in) wide* **£165–235 ROX**

Bush pin and earrings with carved Lucite and prong-set *aurora borealis* rhinestones on gold-tone backs. *Late 1950s. P: 7cm (2¾in) long; E: 3.5cm (1⅜in) long* **£60–80 CRIS**

American flower pin with petals and leaves of green, yellow, amber, and black Lucite on a silver filigree backing. *Late 1950s. 12cm (4¾in) wide* **£125–150 CRIS**

197

Robert

Robert is the trademark of the Fashioncraft Jewelry Company, founded in New York in 1942, which changed its name to Robert Originals, Inc. in 1960. Many Robert pieces use natural motifs reminiscent of Art Nouveau jewellery, with faux pearls, coloured glass, and crystal rhinestones set into gilded filigree metalwork. The pieces are usually marked, although the trademarks vary. "Original by Robert" was used from 1942 to 1979, when the company ceased trading.

Floral motif pin of antiqued filigree gilt metal with prong-set pear-, round-, and oval-cut clear crystal rhinestones. *1950s*

5.5cm (2¼in) long

| £95–105 | MAC |

Butterfly pin of gilt metal with black poured glass body and blue and green enamel wings. *1960s*

4.5cm (1¾in) wide

Art Nouveau pin with sapphire, ruby, pink, and clear crystal rhinestones, clear Lucite cabochons, and a black enamel crescent set in filigree gilt metal. *1950s*

7.5cm (3in) long

| £635–665 | TR |
| £35–45 | JJ |

Figural pin of an oriental man with gilt metal casting and bands of red and blue enamel. *1950s*

5cm (2in) long

| £145–155 | JJ |

Bird and umbrella pin of gilt metal casting with red, brown, pink, and green enamelling. *1950s*

6.25cm (2½in) long

| £35–40 | JJ |

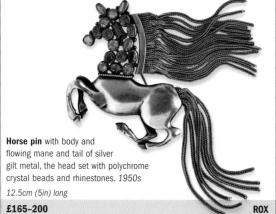

Horse pin with body and flowing mane and tail of silver gilt metal, the head set with polychrome crystal beads and rhinestones. *1950s*

12.5cm (5in) long

| £165–200 | ROX |

Floral motif earrings with gilt wired clusters of faux pearls and faceted clear crystal beads. *1950s*

3.75cm (1½in) long

| £30–35 | JJ |

Floral motif necklace with chain links of gilt metal set with clear crystal beads and rhinestones. *c.1960*

N: 51cm (20in) circ; Floral motif: 7cm (2¾in) wide

| £165–180 | MAC |

Robert DeMario

The Robert DeMario Company was founded in New York in 1945 and continued trading until the early 1960s. DeMario pieces are distinctive for their bold designs, featuring clusters of colourful rhinestones and glass beads. Produced on a small scale, DeMario jewellery is rarer than most marked vintage costume jewellery.

Floral motif pin of gilt metal with large faceted emerald green crystal stones and small clear crystal rhinestone highlights. *1950s*

5.75cm (2¼in) wide

£80–85   **ROX**

Pin and earrings with pale blue crystal cabochons and rhinestones set in silver gilt metal. *Late 1950s*

P: 6.5cm (2½in) wide; E: 3.5cm (1⅜in) wide

£100–150   **CRIS**

Robert Goossens

Born in Paris, Robert Goossens was the chief jewellery designer for Coco Chanel from 1960 until her death in 1971, and worked with her to produce many hallmark pieces, such as her Byzantine crosses and "barbaric" jewels. Goossens's workshops have since created fabulous jewellery for many other couturiers, drawing much inspiration from the art of ancient civilizations.

"I take a pinch of Byzantine, a hint of Etruscan, a sprinkling of Celtic or Egyptian. And I make a Goossens cocktail."
Robert Goossens

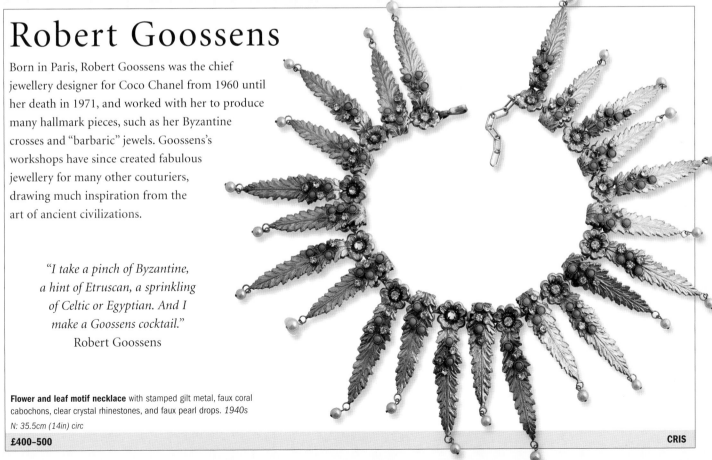

Flower and leaf motif necklace with stamped gilt metal, faux coral cabochons, clear crystal rhinestones, and faux pearl drops. *1940s*

N: 35.5cm (14in) circ

£400–500   **CRIS**

Sandor

Sandor was a small costume jewellery company founded by Sandor Goldberger in 1938. Innovative in approach, its signature pieces are delicate floral designs in sterling silver, beautifully decorated with enamelling and rhinestones. It also produced attractive figural pieces that are much sought after today. The company ceased operations in 1972.

Sandor jewellery is renowned for its artistry and craftmanship. The fact that it is also rare makes it highly collectable. Most pieces are marked "Sandor", but those produced in 1939 and 1940 are marked "Sandor Goldberger".

Floral bouquets are characteristic of Sandor's jewellery. The sensitive blend of enamelwork and rhinestones shows fine attention to detail.

Floral bouquet pin of vermeil sterling silver with pale blue, pink, olivine, and peach enamelling, and round-cut, prong-set rose pink crystal rhinestones. *Late 1930s*
9cm (3½in) long

£635–765   TR

Floral sprig pin of vermeil sterling silver with olivine and blue enamelling, and aquamarine, blue, and clear crystal rhinestones. *Late 1930s*
10.75cm (4¼in) long

£635–765   TR

Flower pin of sterling silver with selected vermeil, clay coloured enamelling, amethyst pastes, and crystal rhinestones. *Late 1930s*
10cm (4in) long

£735–800   TR

Pendant pin of filigree vermeil sterling silver with amber glass cabochons and jade green and clear crystal rhinestones. *Late 1930s*
9cm (3½in) long

£865–935   TR

Floral sprig pin of vermeil sterling silver with green and white enamelling and citrine and clear crystal rhinestones. *Late 1930s*
8.25cm (3¼in) long

£300–335   TR

S & B Lederer & Co.

Founded in Providence, Rhode Island in 1878, and later also operating out of offices on Fifth Avenue in New York City, S & B Lederer Company remained on company listings until 1931. Its gold-plated and silver jewellery – the silver sometimes textured and contrasted with gilt or copper highlights – is of very good quality and of unusual design. These increasingly valuable pieces bear a variety of company marks, including "S. B. & L.", sometimes accompanied by an inverted triangle and sometimes with a star.

Medal pin with an heraldic motif, of hand-beaten and textured sterling silver with copper and gold-plated dragon, and antiqued gold soldier's face. *c.1900*

3.75cm (1½in) wide

£935–1,065　　　　　　　　　　　　　**CGPC**

Sarah Coventry

From 1949 to 1984, Sarah Coventry was a successful company selling costume jewellery through parties in people's homes. The company did not design or make its own jewellery but purchased designs that were then manufactured by other jewellers. The pieces made in the 1950s and 60s were modestly priced but very attractive and beautifully executed. The better pieces and limited production hostess sets are now especially prized.

Leaves and berries medallion pin of antiqued brushed gold-tone metal with *aurora borealis* rhinestones. *1960s*

6.25cm (2½in) wide

£30–35　　　　　　　　　　　**ABIJ**

Floral motif earrings of latticework silver-tone metal with faceted silver-tone metal cabochon centres. *c.1980*

5.75cm (2¼in) wide

£15–25　　　　　　　　　　　**MILLB**

Cross pin of goldwashed base metal with embossed bead motif borders, red and white oval glass cabochons, and a central dark blue round glass cabochon. *1970s*

6.25cm (2½in) wide

£30–35　　　　　　　　**JJ**

Bunny pin of polished and embossed gold-tone metal with one ruby glass cabochon eye and a garnet glass cabochon nose. *1960s*

5cm (2in) high

£15–25　　　　　　　　**ABIJ**

Gold-tone metal pin with faux pearl highlights and an enamelled "miniature" of the *Mona Lisa*. *1970s*

3.75cm (1½in) long

£15–25　　　　　　　　**JJ**

Selro

Little is known about the Selro Corporation, owned by Paul Selinger, which was based in New York City, and produced a distinctive range of colourful costume jewellery during the 1950s and 60s. Pieces by Selro are much prized by collectors for their dramatic designs. The company is best known for the brightly coloured moulded plastic faces, particularly devils' faces, which it incorporated in necklaces and earrings. However, Selro also produced many delicate and very feminine pieces.

Necklace and earrings of gilt metal with prong-set red and emerald green glass stones, white beads, and *aurora borealis* rhinestones. *Early 1950s*
N: 43cm (17in) circ; E: 3.75cm (1½in) long

£235–265   **JJ**

Devils' heads pendant necklace and earrings with silver-plated chain and castings, moulded and incised red Lucite devils' heads, and round and oval black glass cabochons. *Late 1950s*
Large pd: 4.5cm (1¾in) long;
E: 2.5cm (1in) long

£125–150   **CRIS**

Necklace, bracelet, and earrings of white metal chain and castings set with blue glass cabochons and aquamarine crystal rhinestones. *Early 1950s*
N: 43cm (17in) circ;
B: 17.75cm (7in) circ; E: 3.75cm (1½in) long

£165–185   **JJ**

Shiebler

George W. Shiebler & Co was a silver manufacturer based in New York City during the late 19th and early 20th centuries. Known for his creativity and high-quality craftsmanship, Shiebler was an Aesthetic Movement designer. His work featured beautiful and highly detailed naturalistic motifs, such as insects, animals, leaves, and flowers. Shiebler silver is now in very high demand.

Sterling silver belt pin with a frog, snakes, and wings encircling a gilded neoclassical-style bust of a female. *c.1903*
12.75cm (5in) wide

£1,200–1,460   **CGPC**

Twin leaf pin of engraved sterling silver with applied insects – one in sterling silver, the other in a matte-finish copper alloy. *c.1903*
7cm (2¾in) long

£400–500   **CGPC**

Cross pin of asymmetrical shape with a sterling silver casting and a large faceted sapphire blue crystal cabochon. *c.1903*
5.75cm (2¼in) wide

£500–600   **CGPC**

Open cuff bangle of sterling silver with applied, highly naturalistic floral and foliate imagery. *c.1903*
6.25cm (2½in) wide

£1,260–1,400   **CGPC**

Swarovski

The world's leading supplier of crystal stones to jewellery manufacturers since 1892, Swarovski launched its first line of fashion jewellery in 1985, featuring its clear crystal rhinestones. This high-quality jewellery is manufactured in limited editions and is only available initially through a collector's club.

Lyre pin in gilt metal with pavé-set Swarovski clear crystal rhinestones and faux pearl highlights. *1990s*
5.75cm (2¼in) long

£75–95	RITZ

CRYSTAL RHINESTONES

Born in 1862 in Bohemia, Daniel Swarovski became a gem cutter in his father's business. After experimenting with cutting glass stones, he managed to produce small, very high-quality, brilliant-cut crystal rhinestones. These were soon in such demand with jewellery manufacturers that Swarovski invented a mechanical stone-cutter that could shape and facet large quantities of equally perfect stones. Swarovski maintains its reputation for producing crystal rhinestones of unrivalled quality to this day.

Violin and bow pin (from a set of 7 instruments) in gilt metal with pavé-set Swarovski clear crystal rhinestones and faux pearl highlights. *1990s*
6.25cm (2½in) long

Sun motif pin and earrings with gilt metal castings and pavé-set clear Swarovski crystal rhinestones. *1990s*
P: 7cm (2¾in) wide; E: 5cm (2in) wide

£100–140	RITZ

£75–95	RITZ

Swoboda

Founded in Los Angeles in 1956, Swoboda, Inc. produced fine pieces of semi-precious stones and cultured pearls in gold-plated settings. Pins were the most popular line, with motifs ranging from flowers to insects, animals, and crowns. None of its jewellery was marked before 1966, when the trademark "Swoboda" was first used.

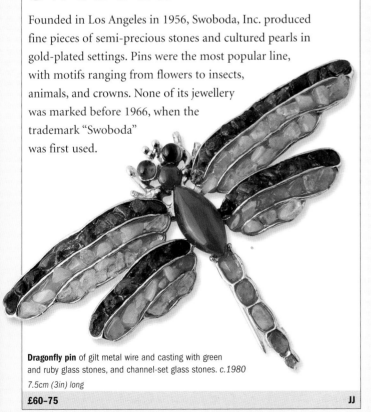

Dragonfly pin of gilt metal wire and casting with green and ruby glass stones, and channel-set glass stones. *c.1980*
7.5cm (3in) long

£60–75	JJ

Tortolani

Italian-born Francisco Tortolani founded Tortolani Jewelry and, from 1950 to 1976, created an award-winning line of fine costume jewellery. Each piece was hand-cast in pewter, polished by hand, then finished in gold or silver plate and signed on the back. Original pieces of Tortolani jewellery are highly prized.

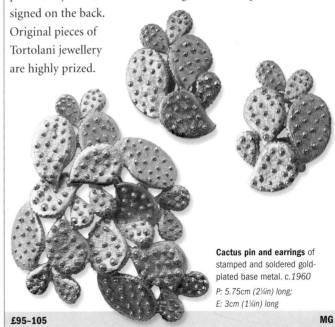

Cactus pin and earrings of stamped and soldered gold-plated base metal. *c.1960*
P: 5.75cm (2¼in) long;
E: 3cm (1¼in) long

£95–105	MG

Unger Bros

In business from 1872 to 1914, Unger Bros produced fine silverware. From about 1890, the company made an impressive range of Art Nouveau sterling silver jewellery, mostly designed by Emma L. Dickinson, as well as dresser and desk sets, flatware, and smoking accessories. Unger pieces are often heavily chased with floral or foliate motifs. Cherubs and animals are also featured. The most collectable pieces are those with unusual shapes, or those featuring female or Native American images.

Goldwash over sterling silver bracelet
comprising filigree scrolling leaf form cartouches with twin floral motif centres. c.1900

19cm (7½in) circ

£265–300   CGPC

Eagle head cufflinks with goldwash over sterling silver castings and ruby red glass cabochon eyes. c.1905

2cm (¾in) long

£435–500   CGPC

Owl's head cufflinks of sterling silver with amber and brown glass cabochon eyes. c.1905

1.5cm (⅝in) wide

£435–500   CGPC

Bonneted lady's head belt pin in sterling silver with highly naturalistic detail and in exceptional condition. c.1905

7.5cm (3in) long

£535–735   CGPC

Classic Art Nouveau motif belt pin of a girl with flowing hair. In sterling silver with selected matte finish gold plating. c.1905

4.5cm (1¾in) wide

£400–535   CGPC

Belt pin with a goose head bursting out of an egg. In textured sterling silver with eyes of ruby red glass cabochons. c.1905

4.5cm (1¾in) wide

£500–700   CGPC

Vivienne Westwood

Celebrated fashion designer Vivienne Westwood started designing in 1971, using her shop on the King's Road, London, as a showcase for her ideas. Iconoclastic, she is perhaps best known for her association with late 1970s punk rock, bondage, and her witty reinterpretation of traditional British symbols. Most of her pieces are made of silver or gold-plated pewter decorated with clear Swarovski crystals and large faux pearls.

Bows, hearts, and emblems of royalty, such as crowns and orbs, are recurring motifs in Westwood's witty jewellery designs.

Royal crown with velvet lining, fake fur trim, and gold-tone metal frame. The latter with fleur-de-lys, royal orb, and finial set with faux pearls, clear pastes, and crystal rhinestones. *1980s*

16cm (6¼in) long

£500–550 REL

Royal orb necklace with gold-tone metal chain, faux pearls, and clear rhinestone highlights. *1980s*

N: 78cm (30½in) circ; Pd: 5.75cm (2¼in) long

£85–95 REL

Gold-tone metal royal orb earrings with round faux pearls and pendants, and clear rhinestone highlights. *1980s*

7.5cm (3in) long

£100–110 REL

Triple-strand faux pearl choker with a royal orb and clasp of silver-tone metal – the orb and cross finial studded with pavé-set clear crystal rhinestones. *1980s*

N: 34.25cm (13½in) circ

£85–90 REL

Chain choker with four chains of gilt metal, three strands of faux pearls, and a gilt metal clasp with a royal orb motif. *1980s*

32cm (12½in) circ

£110–120 REL

Bow and heart pendant earrings of silver-tone metal with black and pavé-set clear rhinestones. *1980s*

3.75cm (1½in) long

£65–70 REL

Scottish Agate Jewellery

During the second half of the 19th century, Queen Victoria's pride in her Scottish ancestry and the popularity of Sir Walter Scott's romantic novels made all things Scottish – including jewellery – highly fashionable.

HIGHLAND COLOURS

Now highly sought after, Scottish pebble jewellery – silver jewellery set with inlays of agate, granite, and other local stones – first became popular when Queen Victoria bought Balmoral Castle in 1848. The designs of the jewellery were based on those of traditional Celtic pieces, but were more elaborate and were often commissioned to suit individual tastes.

Agate, a banded and variegated form of chalcedony, has been used in jewellery since Roman times and is usually cut *en cabochon*, as ovals or other shapes. The rich, earthy colours of the different forms of agate – mossy greens, rusty reds, and ochres – combined with the grey of granite, were symbolic of the Scottish landscape and the tartans worn by different clans.

Scottish agate jewellery borrowed the forms of Celtic jewellery, such as the dirk or dagger pin, and the circular brooch with a long hinged pin known as a penannular. It also incorporated Scottish motifs such as the thistle, the harp, the Celtic cross, and heraldic coats of arms, by setting shaped pieces of polished agate into elaborate engraved silver.

Most of the jewellery is unmarked, but some of the pieces are signed by makers such as Sangster of Aberdeen or J.P. Hutton, which increases their value. Otherwise the value of a piece depends on its age – the earliest pieces date back to the late 18th century – or the sophistication of the motif or decoration.

Crowned paisley motif brooch inlaid with red, yellow, brown, black, and blue agate. *1850s. 7cm (2¾in) long* **£NPA LYNH**

Silver garter brooch with montrose blue agate and a topaz. *1880s 6.5cm (2½in) long* **£500–800 LYNH**

Buckled bracelet with silver links and mounts set with various agates. *1880s. 22cm (8½in) long* **£900–1,250 LYNH**

Shield motif brooch in silver with citrine stones and red and black agate. *1880s 7cm (2¾in) wide* **£750–1,500 LYNH**

Silver penannular brooch with Montrose blue agate and citrine and topaz stones. *1860. 7cm (2¾in) wide* **£550–650 JHB**

Silver shield brooch with a large citrine paste, inlaid with red, black, and blue agate. *1880s 5.5cm (2⅛in) wide* **£650–950 LYNH**

Engraved silver brooch with thistle motif and four panels of blue agate. *c.1870 5cm (2in) wide* **£500–550 RBRG**

Butterfly brooch by J.P. Hutton, with red and Montrose blue agate set in a silver frame. *1880s. 7.5cm (3in) wide* **£700–1,100 LYNH**

Kilt brooch in the form of a dirk in blue agate and glass with gilded metal highlights. *1880s. 7.5cm (3in) long* **£420–460 GS**

Silver buckle brooch with a central four-leaf clover motif in grey-green granite. *1860s 5.75cm (2¼in) wide* **£450–700 LYNH**

Sun brooch with silver-set calibre-cut agates and a yellow agate cabochon centre. *1890s 6.25cm (2½in) wide* **£650–900 LYNH**

Silver brooch with C-scroll and crescent forms, agate highlights, and a faceted paste. *1860s. 5.75cm (2¼in) wide* **£280–320 GS**

Silver brooch with blue, brown, and black agate and carved green glass flowers. *1890s. 6.5cm (2½in) wide* **£100–120 GS**

Silver brooch by Ellen Dunnet with engraved scrolling acanthus, red and moss agate, and topaz and amethyst pastes. *1870 7cm (2¾in) long* **£650–1,000 LYNH**

Silver harp motif brooch with engraved flowers and red and black agates. *1880s 5.75cm (2¼in) wide* **£800–1,000 LYNH**

Pendant brooch in gold with scrolling leaf and shell motifs and scalloped and bell-shaped panels of moss agate. *c.1900 6.5cm (2½in) long* **£550–850 JHB**

Silver brooch with scrolling leaf and crescent moon motifs, faceted topaz centre, and agate highlights. *c.1860s. 5.75cm (2¼in) wide* **£350–450 GS**

Agate bar pin by Sangster of Aberdeen. *1880s 8.25cm (3¼in) long* **£450–700 LYNH**

Interlaced knot brooch of silver-set Montrose blue agate. *1880s. 7.5cm (3in) wide* **£700–1,000 LYNH**

Engraved gold pendant-fob with a spinning disc mounted with agate. *c.1900 3.75cm (1½in) wide* **£100–150 JHB**

Silver link bracelet with geometric and heart-shaped mounts set with various agates. *c.1865. 20.25cm (8in) long* **£550–650 JHB**

Montrose blue agate bracelet with gold-capped links and a single pearl highlight. *1890s 24cm (9½in) long* **£400–450 CRIS**

Fleur-de-lys brooch with three Montrose blue agate feathers set in silver. *1880s 6.25cm (2½in) wide* **£700–1,000 LYNH**

Rosette brooch with carved and polished agate petals on a slate back. *1880s 5cm (2in) wide* **£350–450 LYNH**

Knot motif brooch with interlaced bands of red, black, pink, and grey agate set in a silver mount. *1880s. 6.5cm (2½in) wide* **£600–800 LYNH**

Engraved silver crescent brooch set with panels of agate. *1880s. 6.5cm (2½in) wide* **£220–250 GS**

Cross brooch with a silver lattice pattern inlaid with red and black agate, set in a silver mount. *1870s. 6.25cm (2½in) long* **£350–550 LYNH**

Kilt pin in the form of a dirk in engraved silver with Montrose blue agate and three ruby red paste cabochons. *1880s 10.5cm (4in) long* **£150–180 LYNH**

Leaf motif brooch with panels of red, black, lavender, and moss agate set in a silver mount. *1880s. 6cm (2⅜in) long* **£400–700 LYNH**

Love knot brooch with interlaced bands of engraved silver-mounted Montrose blue agate. *1880s. 6.25cm (2½in) long* **£400–800 LYNH**

Vogue (Les Bernard)

Trading from the mid 1930s to the early 1970s (*see box right*), Vogue is best known for its fine-quality, 1950s Austrian crystal bead rope necklaces, and for its 1940s patriotic flag and figural pins. The latter are now relatively scarce and highly desirable. Effectively an offshoot of Vogue, Les Bernard Inc. has been making innovative and distinctive jewellery since the early 1960s, utilizing materials as diverse as marcasite, Austrian crystals, enamel, chromed steel, and various plastics and fabrics.

Vogue blackamoor pin and earrings of vermeil sterling silver with black enamel, glass cabochons, and a crystal rhinestone. *1940s*
P: 7cm (2¾) long; E: 2.5cm (1in) long

£200–250　　　　　**RG**

HISTORY

1915 Vogue trademark first used by the Park Importing Company of New York City on its faux pearl and beaded costume jewellery
1936 Vogue company founded by Harold Shapiro, Jack Gilbert, and George Grant
1940s Produces highly successful patriotic and figural pins
1950s Becomes renowned for its bead rope necklaces
1962 The Shapiro family sells its interest in Vogue, which continues to trade until 1973
1963 onwards Harold Shapiro's son Bernard and craftsman Lester Joy combine their names and found Les Bernard Inc. Known especially for elaborate pieces with intricate combinations of marcasite and rhinestones.

Les Bernard interlaced scroll pendant earrings of marcasite and clear and pale green rectangular and pear-cut rhinestones. *1980s*
8.25cm (3¼in) long

£95–105　　　　　**JJ**

Les Bernard butterfly necklace with gold-tone metal chain and butterfly casting, and red enamelled butterfly wings. *1970s*
Butterfly: 7.5cm (3in) wide

£15–20　　　　　**MILLB**

Les Bernard necklace with heart-shaped, relief-moulded pendant of gold-tone metal hung from black cotton cord. *1980s*
N: 45.75cm (18in) circ;
Pd: 6.25cm (2½in) long

£15–20　　　　　**MILLB**

Les Bernard clown with umbrella pin of gold-tone metal casting with red, black, and white enamelling. *c.1970*
5cm (2in) long

£20–25　　　　　**JJ**

Les Bernard necklace with a pendant of clay-enamelled, gold-tone metal with glass beads, hung from strands of shell beads. *1970s*
N: 51cm (20in) circ; Pd: 9.5cm (3¾in) long

£45–55　　　　　**JJ**

Les Bernard bangles of black enamelled plastic with round-cut, foil-backed clear rhinestones. *1970s*
20.5cm (8in) circ

£65–80　　　　　**JJ**

Volupté

From its foundation in 1926 in Elizabeth, New Jersey, until it ceased trading in the late 1950s, Volupté was best known for its elegant powder compacts, purses, and cigarette cases. However, it also produced a limited quantity of costume jewellery. Most pieces were intricate designs of oriental, Islamic, or Art Deco influence, usually worked in gold- or silver-tone metal and sometimes embellished with crystal rhinestones. Many have a soldered tag stamped "Volupté".

Intricately crafted designs of fine quality and exceptional beauty are a hallmark of all Volupté pieces. Their scarcity makes them all the more attractive to current collectors.

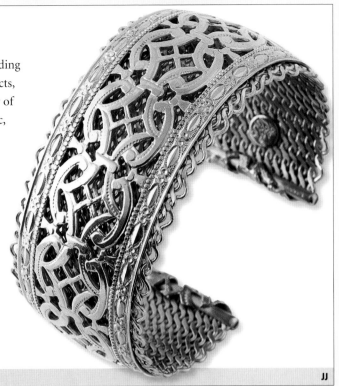

Open bangle of gold-tone metal, the inner band of wire mesh and the outer band pierced and chased with arabesque patterns. *1950s*
16.5cm (6½in) circ

£45–55 | JJ

Warner

Founded by Joseph Warner in 1953, the Warner company produced costume jewellery under his direction until 1971. Usually executed in gold-tone or japanned metal, and often embellished with polychromatic crystal rhinestones, its pieces are mostly of floral or insect design, although novelty subjects, notably umbrella pins, were also produced. The most sought after, however, are its intricately crafted open-and-shut mechanicals. Comparatively rare, they have been steadily increasing in price.

Open pin

Closed pin

Umbrella pin with open-and-shut mechanism, of gold-tone metal set with floral motifs of coloured and clear rhinestones. *c.1960*
7cm (2¾in) long

£30–35 | JJ

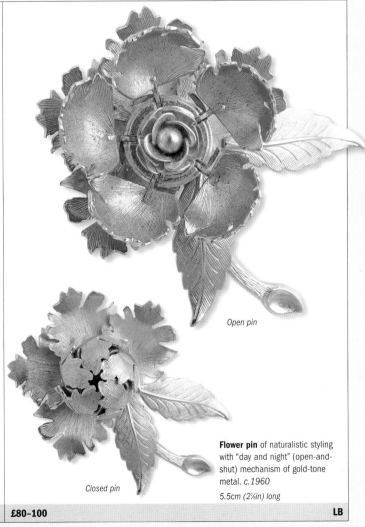

Open pin

Closed pin

Flower pin of naturalistic styling with "day and night" (open-and-shut) mechanism of gold-tone metal. *c.1960*
5.5cm (2⅛in) long

£80–100 | LB

Whiting & Davis

Founded in Massachusetts in 1876, Whiting & Davis is primarily known for its beautiful, finely woven gold and silver mesh evening bags. In 1907, however, the company started creating a distinctive line of jewellery, using its expertise at making mesh to create silver and silver-plated metalwork as a basis for its pieces. Its jewellery ranges from delicate mesh chokers to dramatic bracelets and chunky earrings, many of which display Victorian or Art Nouveau influences. Its mesh spiral snake bracelets in particular are considered highly collectable.

Necktie earrings of gold-plated metal and mesh, the knot set with clear crystal rhinestones. *1970s*

7cm (2¾in) long

£35–35   ABIJ

Pendant snake head earrings of silver-plated, punched, and engraved metal. *1960s*

4.5cm (1¾in) long

£15–20   ABIJ

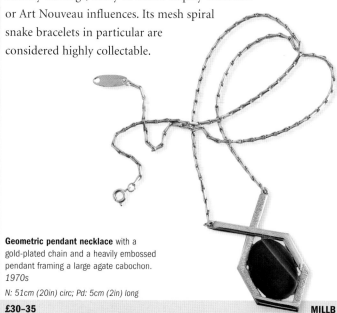

Geometric pendant necklace with a gold-plated chain and a heavily embossed pendant framing a large agate cabochon. *1970s*

N: 51cm (20in) circ; Pd: 5cm (2in) long

£30–35   MILLB

Gold-plated link bracelet with safety chain and ruby red glass cabochons. *Early 1960s*

19cm (7½in) circ

£35–45   ABIJ

Silver-plated coiled snake bangle with expandable mesh wrist band, and solid punched and engraved head. *1960s*

30.5cm (12in) circ

£30–35   JJ

Necklace and matching bracelet with gold-plated chains, tassels, and mountings, and oval and round black glass cabochons. *1950s*

N: 51cm (20in) circ; B: 20.25cm (8in) circ

£35–50   ABIJ

Antiqued gold-plated bracelet with safety chain, with section of engraved cross-hatching, and with applied stylized floral and foliate motifs. *1970s*

17.75cm (7in) circ

£30–35   MILLB

YSL

Christian Dior protégé Yves Saint Laurent established his own fashion house in 1961 and launched the first YSL collection the following year. His style has ranged from beatnic chic to the exotic and refined. His jewellery, introduced in the 1970s, is theatrical, colourful, and displays the same clarity of form inherent in his clothing.

Asymmetrical earrings with coloured crystal rhinestones prong-set in gold-plated castings with turquoise and red enamelling. *Late 1980s*

5cm (2in) long

£60–80   **CRIS**

Geometric motif necklace with gilt metal and twin strands of white faux pearls. *1980s*

45.5cm (18in) circ

£30–40   **MILLB**

Gold-plated earrings of oval form with suspended lozenge-shaped centres set with faceted sapphire blue glass stones. *c.1980*

3.75cm (1½in) long

£20–45   **LB**

Bar pin of gold-tone metal set with square- and rectangular-cut fuchsia and pale amber glass stones. *Late 1970s*

6.25cm (2½in) long

£45–55   **MILLB**

Zandra Rhodes

London fashion designer Zhandra Rhodes launched her first eccentric fashion collection in 1969. Her costume jewellery, handcrafted by innovative designers such as Andrew Logan (*see p.138*) and Mick Milligan, displays a similar individualism increasingly sought after by collectors.

Bold, stylized, and unique, Zandra Rhodes's pieces are now hot property.

Stylized figural pin by Mick Milligan, of stamped, pierced, corrugated, and spiralling gold-tone metal with a small cluster of clear rhinestones. *1970s*

15cm (6in) long

£NPA   **LB**

Stylized female head pin of skin-coloured plastic with black and lipstick rouge highlights. *1970s*

7.5cm (3in) wide

£NPA   **LB**

Gallery of unsigned pieces

Collectable designs from around the world

Most costume jewellery is unsigned and these pieces constitute a veritable Aladdin's cave of treasures, with prices to suit all pockets. Because unsigned pieces have no marks to enhance their value, they cost less, yet often share the same quality of design, materials, and craftsmanship as signed designer pieces. Without provenance, the best investment is in quality materials, such as sterling silver, vermeil, and Austrian crystal rhinestones, in sophisticated and innovative settings, and, above all, in pieces that are in excellent condition.

You may choose to collect pieces from a particular period that interests you, or themed pieces, featuring animals, bows, or flower baskets, for example. With a little background research, you may even be able to recognize an unsigned piece from a well-known maker.

Necklaces

There are necklaces to suit every taste, ranging in style from the long sautoirs of the 1920s flapper to the fantasy coloured necklaces of the 1950s and the plastic pendant necklaces of the 1960s. As with all costume jewellery, seek out interesting and attractive pieces, made from good-quality materials. Innovative stone cuts and unusual colour combinations are worth looking out for, along with interesting period details. Always try necklaces on to make sure that they suit you and sit well on the neck, and check whether any stones are missing and that clasps fasten properly.

The streamlined geometric forms of the 1920s and 30s Art Deco style are now perennial favourites with collectors.

Gilt metal link necklace with hollow-centre shield motifs of mottled red glass and a gilt metal clasp. *1920s*

39cm (15¼in) circ

£50–80   ECLEC

Snake necklace of gilt metal, the head with a faceted amethyst glass stone and sapphire crystal rhinestone eyes. *1920s*

32.5cm (13in) circ

£225–240   BY

Art Deco pendant necklace with yellow and black diamond motifs and a gilt metal chain. *1930s*

N: 45.75cm (18in) circ; Pd: 5.75cm (2¼in) long

£95–105   BB

Faux coral necklace with links and balls, the larger ball flanked by two rings of clear crystal rhinestones. *1920s*

42cm (16½in) circ

£135–200   BY

Crystal bead necklace of textured clear beads with white inclusions, and filigree silver and gilt metal floral motifs. *1920s*

49cm (19in) circ

£100–165   BY

Pendant necklace with red plastic neckband and graduated, articulated discs of polished steel. *c.1970*

Pd: 16cm (6¼in) long

£1,000–1,500　　　　　　LB

French necklace of gold-plated metal, green and clear glass beads, and clear crystal rhinestones. *c.1930*

42cm (16½in) circ

£200–265　　　　　　BY

Murano glass necklace with green glass leaves and yellow and orange-red glass bead fruits. *c.1960*

41cm (16in) circ

£75–120　　　　　　LB

Silver link necklace set with clear crystal rhinestones and faceted ruby glass shield motifs. *c.1930*

36cm (14in) circ

£70–100　　　　　　ECLEC

Silver link necklace with hemispheres, roundels, and baguettes of clear glass. *1930s*

35cm (13¾in) circ

£60–100　　　　　　ECLEC

Fruit and berry motif necklace of yellow and green frosted glass interspersed with faux pearls and clear and aqua rhinestones. *1950s*

58cm (22½in) circ

£80–100　　　　　　CRIS

French Art Deco necklace of matte-finish, gold-plated metal with triangular sections of black enamelling. *1930s*

43cm (17in) circ

£340–380　　　　　　CRIS

Bunches of grapes necklace of ruby red glass beads alternated with hoops of clear glass. *1920s*

42cm (16½in) circ

£60–100   ECLEC

French necklace of gilt metal with faux pearls, ruby glass cabochons, and aquamarine and pink glass drops. *1920s*

43cm (17in) circ

£600–735   TR

Triple-strand faux pearl necklace with a pendant of gilt metal, clear crystal rhinestones, and faux pearl drops. *1950s*

N: 36cm (14in) circ; Pd: 8cm (3in) long

£140–160   CRIS

Glass necklace of faceted clear crystal stones and three emerald green poured glass stones. *1930s*

39cm (15¼in) circ

£100–135   BY

French necklace with gilt metal chain, faux pearls, and polychrome glass stones and beads. *1920s*

45.75cm (18in) circ

£600–735   TR

French necklace with silver links, clear crystal rhinestones, and red, blue, green, and black carved glass stones. *1920s*

35.5cm (14in) circ

£120–150   RG

Twin-strand necklace of faceted grey glass beads and a floral motif of gilt metal, pink glass, and faux pearls. *1960s*

44cm (17in) circ

£170–200   **CRIS**

Gilt metal link necklace with oval hoops of mottled amber-coloured glass. *c.1930s*

39cm (15¼in) circ

£40–70   **ECLEC**

Rosette necklace of gilt metal with bead moulding encircling turquoise glass cabochons. *1960s*

47cm (18¼in) circ

£65–75   **CRIS**

Attribution, albeit unsigned, to the prestigious French maker Rousselet enhances the value of this attractive necklace.

Floral motif necklace with silvered metal links and round- and navette-cut *aurora borealis* rhinestones. *1950s*

40cm (15½in) circ

£30–50   **ECLEC**

Pendant necklace, attributed to Rousselet, with cranberry coloured glass beads and clusters of small and larger faux pearls. *1930s*

N: 51cm (20in) circ; Pd: 7.5cm (3in) long

£335–400   **BY**

Necklace Sets

It is often assumed that necklaces were originally sold with other pieces in parures or demi-parures, but this was not always the case. One of the great pleasures of collecting costume jewellery, however, lies in tracking down the various components of a matching set. By acquiring a whole set, the collector not only adds to the interest of a necklace, but often increases its value as well.

Parures and demi-parures are highly desirable when they are of an attractive design and all the stones are intact.

Japanned metal link necklace and earrings with sapphire blue crystal stones in round, pear, and navette cuts. Made in West Germany. *Late 1940s*

N: 39.5cm (15½in) circ; E: 2.5cm (1in) wide

£435–500   **ROX**

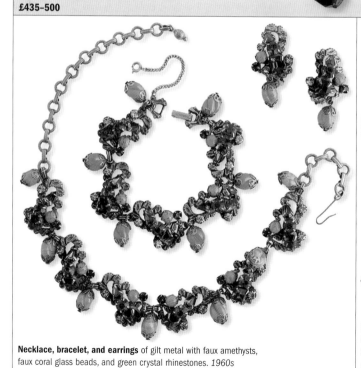

Necklace, bracelet, and earrings of gilt metal with faux amethysts, faux coral glass beads, and green crystal rhinestones. *1960s*

N: 43cm (17in) circ; B: 21cm (8in) circ; E: 3.75cm (1½in) long

£155–180   **BY**

Choker, pin, and earrings of solid, woven, and filigree gilt metal set with pink, green, moonstone, and clear rhinestones. *1930s*

Choker: 31.75cm (12½in) circ;
P: 9cm (3½in) wide; E: 2.5cm (1in) wide

£540–1,000   **ROX**

Floral motif necklace and earrings of vermeil sterling silver set with faux pearls. *1940s*

N: 36cm (14in) circ; E: 4cm (1½in) long

£55–65   **RG**

Murano glass fruits and leaves necklace and bracelet with aquamarine cabochons, orange and red fruits, and unusual opaque green leaves. *1950s*

N: 42cm (16½in) circ;
B: 16.5cm (6½in) circ

£200–235 BY

Four-strand necklace and floral motif pendant earrings with carved frosted citrine, olivine, and gold glass beads, and a bow and hoops strung from tiny coral coloured beads. *1950s*

N: 44cm (17in) circ; E: 5cm (2in) long

£150–175 CRIS

Necklace and bracelet with strands of faux pearls and orange glass beads, *aurora borealis* rhinestone highlights, and green enamelled leaves. *1950s*

N: 35.5cm (14in) circ; B: 15.25cm (6in) circ

£140–160 CRIS

Necklace and bracelet of gilt metal with peridot green rhinestones and glass cabochons and drops. *Mid 1950s*

N: 38cm (15in) circ; B:16.5cm (6½in) circ

£90–100 CRIS

Necklace and pendant earrings with faceted rock crystal beads and drops and small rock crystal spacers. *1930s*

N: 41cm (16in) circ; E: 5cm (2in) long

£95–105 BY

Necklace and bracelet with cream celluloid chain links and tan-coloured celluloid discs. *1930s*

N: 40cm (15½in) circ; B: 17.75cm (7in) circ

£235–300 MAC

Pendant necklace and earrings of gold-plated metal with mottled green glass cabochons. *c.1970*

N: 38cm (15in) circ;
Pd: 9cm (3½in) long;
E: 3cm (1¼in) wide

£40–60 ECLEC

Bangles

A popular fashion accessory from the 1920s to the early 1940s, bangles are often made from unusual materials and have interesting features. Stylish Bakelite bangles are highly sought after – particularly when handcarved or decorated with polka dots or zigzags – as are early Lucite bangles in desirable period colours.

Squirrel bangle of gold-tone metal with ruby crystal rhinestone eyes, probably made by Sphinx for Saks of Fifth Avenue. *1980s*

17.5cm (6¾in) circ

£25–30   **CRIS**

Elasticated bangle with raised and chamfered squares of onyx and amber Bakelite. *1940s*

3cm (1¼in) wide

£20–40   **ECLEC**

Tasseled bangle, possibly by Miriam Haskell, of gold-plated metal with white glass beads. *c.1940*

16.5cm (6½in) circ

£40–45   **JJ**

Open copper bangle with motif commemorating the 1939 New York World's Fair. *1939*

6.25cm (2½in) wide

£25–35   **AIS**

Wooden bangle with copper clasp and carved wooden horse's head set on a disc of caned leather. *1940s*

Disc: 5cm (2in) wide

£80–100   **CRIS**

Plastic bangle with carved floral and foliate motifs in white, cream, grey, black, and shades of green. *1930s*

23cm (9in) circ

£10–20   ECLEC

Cast phenolic hinged bangle in mottled green and yellow with two applied Scottie dogs. *Late 1930s*

7cm (2¾in) wide

£165–235   BY

Lucite bangle in "apple juice" colour with reverse carved and coloured flowers and foliage.
Late 1930s

7cm (2¾in) wide

£335–400   BY

Expandable bangle of gold-tone metal with emerald green, ruby red, and clear crystal rhinestones. *1950s*

17cm (6½in) circ

£75–85   CRIS

Cast phenolic bangle with laminated stripes in brown, red, and yellow.
Late 1930s

7.5cm (3in) wide

£165–235   BY

Cast phenolic bangle with laminated stripes in yellow, mottled yellow-brown, and green.
Late 1930s

8.25cm (3¼in) wide

£165–200   BY

Open copper bangle and cast phenolic scarab with selective gold painting and steel cabochons. *1920s*

5cm (2in) wide

£135–200   BY

Bracelets

Bracelets are an interesting collecting field in their own right, reflecting the changing styles of costume jewellery during the 20th century. A key Art Deco accessory, they were more popular than pins up until the 1940s. Look out for good-quality, 1940s, vermeil, retro style bracelets and showy decorative pieces from the 1950s, resplendent with fantasy pastes in unexpected colour combinations.

Rhodium-plated link bracelet with peridot green glass bead berry motifs. *1930s*

17cm (6¾in) circ

£150–175   **CRIS**

Stamped antiqued gold-tone metal bracelet set with green and gold glass cabochons and blue rhinestones. *1950s*

19cm (7½in) circ

£30–40   **ECLEC**

Faux amethyst bracelet of gilt metal, translucent plastic, crystal rhinestones, and faceted amethyst glass. *c.1930*

6.5cm (2½in) wide

£665–1,000   **BY**

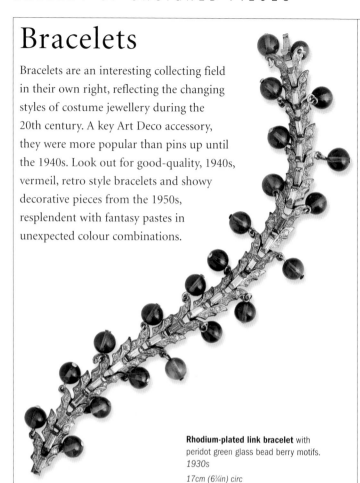

Textured gold-tone metal link bracelet with alternating links of pavé-set clear crystal rhinestones. *Late 1950s*

19cm (7½in) long

£65–75   **CRIS**

French silver Art Deco bracelet with clear crystal rhinestones, emerald glass cabochons, and "fruit salad" stones. *1930s*

18.5cm (7¼in) circ

£1,000–1,200   **TR**

Wristwatch bracelet in gold-plated metal; the watch-face encircled by clear crystal rhinestones. *1940s*

Face: 3.5cm (1⅜in) wide

£100–125 CRIS

Gold-plated metal bracelet with prong-set aquamarine blue, *aurora borealis*, and sapphire crystal rhinestones. *1950s*

17cm (6¾in) circ

£40–45 BY

Gilt metal bracelet with "butterfly wing" glass cabochons showing a tropical shoreline. *1950s*

18cm (7in) circ

£40–60 ECLEC

Gilt metal bracelet with red and green fruit salad glass stones, green baguettes, and clear crystal rhinestones. *1940s*

17cm (6¾in) circ

£215–250 BY

Solid silver bracelet with interlaced diamond motif of square-cut sapphire blue crystal rhinestones. *1950s*

17.75cm (7in) circ

£240–280 CRIS

Cocktail bracelet in vermeil sterling silver with scenes from *The Marriage of Figaro* in polychrome crystal rhinestones. *1940s*

20.25cm (8in) circ

£700–800 CRIS

Rose bracelet with gold-plated clasp and links, and round-cut rose pink crystal rhinestones. *1950s*

19cm (7½in) circ

£70–80 CRIS

Wristwatch bracelet of gilt metal set with polychrome glass beads, faux pearls, and round- and baguette-cut rhinestones. *1950s*

17cm (6¾in) long

£95–120 CRIS

225

Flower, Fruit, and Leaf Pins

The most common and traditional subject matters for pins, flowers, fruit, and leaves have always provided a wealth of inspiration for jewellery designers. The most valuable pieces are those that display complex and innovative designs, high-quality pastes in rich colours, and exquisite craftsmanship. Baskets or vases of flowers and fruit pins constitute worthwhile collecting fields in their own right.

Large rhinestones in flamboyant fantasy colours were popular features of flower pins during the 1950s and 60s.

Floral pin with lime green navettes and round aquamarine, emerald, clear, and *aurora borealis* rhinestones. Made in Canada in the style of the Regency company. *1960s*

7.5cm (3in) wide

£45–55   CRIS

Palm tree pin of sterling silver with channel-set emerald and clear crystal rhinestones. *1920s*

5cm (2in) long

£375–425   CRIS

Retro style floral pin of sterling silver with sapphire glass cabochons and clear crystal rhinestones. *1940s*

6.25cm (2½in) long

£60–90   RG

Flower pin with open-and-shut mechanism, of gilt metal with blue enamelling and clear crystal rhinestones. *1950s*

9cm (3½in) long

£165–235   BY

Bouquet of flowers pin with prong-set faux amethysts, polychrome enamelled highlights, and clear crystal rhinestones. *1940s*

10cm (4in) long

£100–135   BYA

Vase of flowers pin of vermeil sterling silver with faceted ruby, emerald, and apple green glass stones, and clear crystal rhinestones. *1940s*

8.25cm (3¼in) long

£215–250　　　　　　　　　　　　　　　　BY

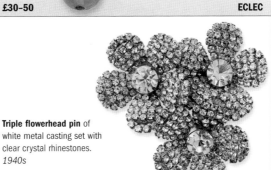

Leaf and berry pin with faux pearl berries, emerald green glass leaves, and a mottled jade green glass drop. *1950s*

5cm (2in) long

£30–50　　　　　　　　　ECLEC

Triple flowerhead pin of white metal casting set with clear crystal rhinestones. *1940s*

5cm (2in) wide

£60–80　　　　　　　　　JJ

Byzantine-style floral pin of gilt metal casting set with clear crystal rhinestones and faux pearls. *1960s*

10cm (4in) long

£45–55　　　　　　　　　CRIS

Floral pin, possibly by Schreiner, with prong-set ruby red and clear crystal rhinestones on a gilt metal back. *1950s*

5cm (2in) wide

£95–120　　　　　　　CRIS

Floral motif pin with gold-tone metal back and clusters of prong-set *aurora borealis* rhinestones. *1950s*

6.25cm (2½in) wide

£20–25　　　　　　　　　PC

Flower and leaf pin made in Canada with green navettes and carved blue glass stones in gold-plated settings. *c.1970*

7.5cm (3in) wide

£55–65　　　　　　　　　CRIS

Floral pin, possibly by Schreiner, with clear, lime green, and diamond-cut white crystal rhinestones, and a lime green glass cabochon. *1950s*

8.25cm (3¼in) long

£120–145　　　　　　　　CRIS

Creature Pins

Creature pins have become an extremely popular collecting field, and many collectors specialize in a particular species. From bird pins, with their romantic associations with departure, to butterfly brooches, to quirky pins featuring colourful creatures such as lobsters, there is a wealth of imagery to choose from. Both naturalistic and highly stylized designs are collectable, as are the much rarer and sometimes very expensive articulated creature pins.

Regardless of size, highly stylized creature pins create a far more dramatic visual impact than their more naturalistic or whimsical counterparts.

Stylized hummingbird pin of gold-plated metal casting with turquoise Lucite rings and aquamarine crystal rhinestone eyes. *1960s*

8.25cm (3¼in) long

£35–40   **CRIS**

Peacock pin of gilt metal casting with black enamelling and polychrome and clear crystal rhinestones. *1950s*

6.5cm (2½in) long

£25–30   **CRIS**

Bird-of-paradise pin in silver set with marcasite. *1920s*

9cm (3½in) long

£300–350   **CRIS**

Hummingbird pin of gilt metal casting set with clear and ruby rhinestones and pavé-set turquoise crystal cabochons. *1950s*

6.25cm (2½in) long

£15–20   **CRIS**

Flamingo pin of vermeil sterling silver with faceted yellow glass body and pavé-set clear crystal rhinestones. *1940s*

9cm (3½in) long

£215–250   **BY**

Crested bird pin of gold-tone metal with black enamelling and clear crystal rhinestones. *1950s*

7.5cm (3in) long

£10–15   **CRIS**

Toucan pin of gilt metal casting with blue, green, and red enamelling and ruby glass cabochon eyes. *1950s*

5.75cm (2¼in) long

£10–15   **CRIS**

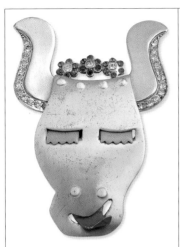

Bull pin of sterling and vermeil sterling silver with red enamelling and sapphire, ruby, emerald, and clear crystal rhinestones. *1930s*

9cm (3½in) long

£350–400   **CRIS**

Violin-playing cricket pin of gold-plated metal with enamelling and pavé-set clear crystal rhinestones. *1930s*

6cm (2⅜in) long

£85–115   **BY**

Poodle pin of gold-tone metal casting set with faux pearls.
1950s

4.5cm (1¾in) wide

£10–15   **ECLEC**

Banjo-playing frog pin with articulated strumming arm, of green carved cast phenolic with painted banjo. Extremely rare. *1930s*

7cm (2¾in) long

£1,335–1,665   **BY**

Rare "catwalk" butterfly pin of French jet, pale blue glass beads, and variegated agate stones. *1990s*

19cm (7½in) wide

£270–300   **CRIS**

Butterfly pin with gilt wire frame set with pink, mauve, ruby red, and green rhinestones.
1950s

5.75cm (2¼in) wide

£75–85   **CRIS**

Elephant watch pin in vermeil sterling silver with faux sapphire body and clear crystal rhinestones. *1940s*

7cm (2¾in) wide

£95–105   **BY**

Lobster pin with *en tremblant* claws, of base metal with red and black enamelling. *1930s*

8.25cm (3¼in) long

£45–55   **TR**

Tropical fishes pin, possibly by Mazer Bros., of gilt metal casting with black and ivory enamelling, clear crystal rhinestones, and "metallic" faux pearls. *1940s*

7cm (2¾in) wide

£140–160   **CRIS**

Miscellaneous Pins

This diverse category embraces pins of wide-ranging imagery, including abstract and geometric pieces. Favourite motifs are crosses, shields, masks, flowing fabric subjects such as bows and drapery, and the eye – a jewellery motif that extends right back to ancient times. Look out for bold and original designs, good-quality materials, and pins that are characteristic of a particular period.

Maltese Cross pin with scrolling forms of filigree gold wire set with faux baroque pearls and clear rhinestones. *1960s*

6.5cm (2½in) wide

£30–35	CRIS

Art Deco African mask pin of black and red Bakelite with chromed steel eyebrows and mouth. *1920s*

6.5cm (2½in) long

£160–190	RITZ

Pendant cross pin of vermeil sterling silver with polychrome rhinestones, faux pearls, and mottled turquoise glass cabochons. *1940s*

7.5cm (3in) long

£100–120	RG

Musical clef pin of vermeil sterling silver with a large aquamarine paste, and emerald, sapphire, ruby, and aquamarine crystal rhinestones. *1940s*

10cm (4in) long

£75–85	CRIS

Retro bow pin in sterling silver with clear crystal rhinestones and a large aquamarine glass stone. *1940s*

7cm (2¾in) wide

£90–100   CRIS

Eye pin of vermeil sterling silver with clear and sapphire crystal rhinestones, a black glass cabochon, and faux pearl drops. *1940*

5cm (2in) wide

£225–240   BY

Shield pin of sterling silver with faceted and baguette clear crystal rhinestones, and ruby, sapphire, and emerald glass stones. *1920s*

5cm (2in) long

£135–165   BY

Moorish-style pin of antiqued gilt metal with a large faux amethyst, turquoise and blue glass cabochons, and white, red, turquoise, and black enamel. *1920s*

6cm (2⅜in) wide

£120–145   BY

Zebra pin-pendant of vermeil sterling silver with black enamelling, clear crystal rhinestones, and an emerald glass cabochon. *1940s*

5cm (2in) long

£100–120   ABIJ

Entwined snakes pin in brass with a large jade green plastic stone and four jade green drops. *c.1917*

6.25cm (2½in) long

£120–145   CGPC

Organic shape pin in gilt metal with a turquoise and gold ceramic cabochon and three similar ceramic drops. *c.1910*

3cm (1⅛in) wide

£80–95   CGPC

Bow pin, possibly by Coro, of rhodium-plated casting with round, baguette, and pavé-set clear crystal rhinestones. *1930s*

8.25cm (3¼in) long

£90–100   CRIS

Human Figurals

Human subjects lend themselves to whimsical designs and have provided the motifs for a witty, creative style of costume jewellery, especially during lean times, such as World War II. Pastiches of jazz musicians, clowns, ballerinas, and scarecrows abound, as do exaggerated portrayals of human faces. Articulated figures with moveable arms and legs are particularly worth collecting.

African mask fur clip of cold enamelled base metal with clear and ruby red crystal rhinestones. *1930s*

4.5cm (1¾in) wide

£50–60 PC

Novelty porter and suitcase pin in black, red, and blue Bakelite with plaited bow, chain, and highlights of gilt metal. *1930s*

8.25cm (3¼in) long

£300–335 TM

Ballroom dancer pin in vermeil sterling silver with black enamelling and faux sapphires, ruby baguettes, and emeralds. *1940s*

9cm (3½in) long

£215–250 BY

Green cast phenolic pin of a seated Asian man in profile playing a pipe. *1930s*

5.75cm (2¼in) long

£100–135 BB

Caliph pin of gold-tone metal with black enamelling, aquamarine and turquoise glass cabochons, clear rhinestones, and a faux pearl. *1960s*

7cm (2¾in) long

£45–60 CRIS

Caliph pin of vermeil sterling silver with black glass face, faux sapphire cabochons, and clear crystal rhinestones. *1940s*

5cm (2in) long

£60–80 RG

£165–200 BY

Naturalistic detail with an extravagant sense of movement is invariably eye-catching.

Woman's torso and head pin of vermeil sterling silver with pavé-set clear crystal rhinestones. *1940s*

7cm (2¾in) long

BY

Pins and Earrings

A pair of earrings, especially with a matching pin, has been the starting point of many a costume jewellery collection. As ever, well-crafted pieces made from high-quality materials command the highest prices. Most costume jewellery earrings are clips, so it is best to try them on before buying to check that they don't pinch.

Scrolling bow pin and earrings of rose-vermeil sterling silver with large aquamarine glass stones. *1940s*

P: 9cm (3½in) long;
E: 3.5cm (1¼in) long

£145–165 — CRIS

Ballerina pin and earrings in vermeil sterling silver with faceted aquamarine and sapphire glass stones and clear crystal rhinestones. *1940s*

P: 9cm (3½in) long; E: 2.5cm (1in) long

£215–250 — BY

Stylized leaf form pin and earrings in sterling silver set with round- and baguette-cut clear crystal rhinestones. *1940s*

P: 7cm (2¾in) long; E: 3cm (1⅛in) long

£70–100 — RG

Cat and goldfish pin and earrings of vermeil sterling silver with crystal rhinestones and Lucite bowls with carved goldfish. *1940s*

P: 5.75cm (2¼in) long; E: 2cm (¾in) long

£1,000–£1,335 — BY

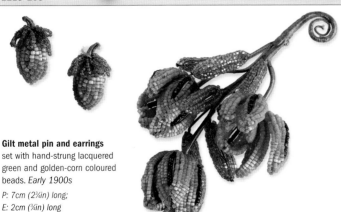

Gilt metal pin and earrings set with hand-strung lacquered green and golden-corn coloured beads. *Early 1900s*

P: 7cm (2¾in) long;
E: 2cm (¾in) long

£200–335 — ROX

Floral motif pin and earrings with aquamarine crystal rhinestones and dark blue glass cabochons prong-set in gilt wire backs. *1950s*

P: 7cm (2¾in) long; E: 3.5cm (1⅜in) long

£75–85 — CRIS

Fantasy coloured stones, especially iridescent aurora borealis stones, have been popular with collectors since the mid 1950s.

Gilt metal earrings with prong-set topaz glass cabochons and *aurora borealis* rhinestones. *1950s*

4cm (1½in) long

£35–45   CRIS

Gilt wire frame earrings with prong-set topaz, olivine, clear, and *aurora borealis* rhinestones. *1950s*

3.75cm (1½in) long

£30–35   CRIS

French earrings in gold-tone metal with green and white enamelling, clear crystal rhinestones, and French jet cabochons. *1960s*

3.25cm (1¼in) long

£25–30   CRIS

Silvered metal earrings with emerald green, turquoise, and coral glass cabochons, and faux baroque pearls. *1960s*

3.25cm (1¼in) wide

£25–30   CRIS

Faux precious earrings with citrine glass ovals and triangles, and clear crystal rhinestones. *1950s*

3.25cm (1¼in) wide

£30–35   CRIS

Oval earrings in textured gold-tone metal with a trellis pattern and turquoise glass cabochon centres. *1950s*

2.5cm (1in) long

£20–25   CRIS

Handbag earrings with gold-tone metal castings and patterned white enamelling. *c.1970*

3.75cm (1½in) long

£85–100   LB

Ruthenium-plated bow and pendant hoop earrings with round- and baguette-cut clear crystal rhinestones. *1930s*

6.5cm (2½in) long

£150–200   CRIS

Oval earrings with filigree gilt metal castings and faux turquoise centres. *1960s*

2.5cm (1in) long

£15–20   CRIS

Shield-shape earrings with faceted citrine and ruby red glass prong-set in white metal. *1960s*

2.5cm (1in) long

£35–45   ROX

Floral motif earrings with textured gilt metal castings, rings of faux pearls, and larger faux pearl centres. *1950s*

2.5cm (1in) wide

£30–35   CRIS

Austrian earrings of antiqued filigree gilt metal with amethyst coloured glass cabochon centres. *1930s*

2.5cm (1in) long

£25–35   JJ

Bow and pendant wreath earrings in silver with clear crystal rhinestones and faux sapphire pendant centres.
1920s

5.5cm (2⅛in) long

£1,665–2,600   **TR**

Wing motif earrings of vermeil sterling silver set with clear crystal rhinestones.
1940s

5cm (2in) long

£120–150   **RG**

Art Deco multiple-pendant earrings of japanned metal with green glass cabochons and drops.
1930s

7cm (2¾in) long

£60–100   **ECLEC**

Pendant earrings in silver and marcasite with faux coral glass drops.
Early 1900s

6.25cm (2½in) long

£80–120   **RG**

Pendant earrings with prong-set amber and blue *aurora borealis* cabochons.
Mid 1950s

4cm (1½in) long

£30–35   **CRIS**

Cluster earrings with prong-set aquamarine crystal rhinestones and prong-set amber and red glass cabochons. *1940s*

3.25cm (1¼in) long

£80–100   **PC**

Star motif earrings in silver set with bands of round-cut aquamarine crystal rhinestones.
1950s

3.25cm (1¼in) wide

£35–40   **CRIS**

"Jewels of India" earrings of silver-tone metal set with faux lapis and faux coral cabochons, and clear crystal rhinestones. *1960s*

7.5cm (3in) long

£45–55   **CRIS**

Appendices and index

Further information and resources for collectors

This section of the book contains a wealth of essential, practical information for avid costume jewellery collectors. An extensive glossary of materials and techniques explains all the specialist terms used in the book, and this is followed by a comprehensive guide to designers' and makers' marks. There is also a key to the specialist dealers' codes used in the price guides. The directory of other dealers, auction houses, and museums provides not only the addresses of useful specialists who may be able to help you in your search for particular pieces, but also lists the museums that have good collections of costume jewellery, an invaluable source of further background information.

Glossary

Acrylics A type of plastic, which may be transparent or opaque and can be in varied colours. Lucite and Plexiglas are common acrylics.

Agate A common stone used in jewellery. It is found in a wide range of colours, including black, grey, brown, red, green, pink, blue, and yellow.

Alloy A metallic material that is a combination of two or more different metals.

Amber A semi-precious gemstone formed from the hardened resin of trees. Transparent or translucent, it is usually golden-orange, but can also be dark red.

Apple juice Golden-yellow plastic that is the colour of apple juice.

Aquamarine A transparent, semi-precious gemstone that is light blue or pale sea-green in colour.

Art Deco A style that originated in Paris and was popular from the mid 1920s until the late 1930s. Art Deco pieces are characterized by geometric lines and angles, with very few curves.

Articulated Connected with flexible joints or segments. The term is often used to describe pieces of jewellery that have moving parts.

Art Nouveau A style popular from the 1890s until World War I. Art Nouveau pieces are characterized by flowing, free-form imagery based on organic forms.

Arts and Crafts A late 19th-century movement that advocated simple craftsmanship, using the natural beauty and quality of materials to artistic effect.

Aurora Borealis Rhinestones named after the Northern Lights, which have an iridescent fantasy finish, created with a polychrome metallic coating.

Baguette-cut A cut that makes a gemstone or paste into a long, rectangular shape.

Bakelite A robust and attractive plastic, often in strong colours, which was much used in costume jewellery from the 1920s to 40s.

Bangle A stiff bracelet. Some bangles have a hinge; others are solid and have to be slipped over the hand.

Baroque pearl A bumpy, irregular-shaped pearl. Baroque pearls can be either natural or artificial.

Bar pin A rectangular pin usually worn horizontally.

Base metal A non-precious metal, sometimes also called pot metal. Brass, pinchbeck, and white metal are all base metals.

Berlin ironwork A style of cast iron jewellery, much suited to mourning wear, first made by the Royal Berlin Foundry in the first half of the 19th century.

Bib necklace A necklace with flowing pendants or chains at the front that form a bib look.

Brilliant-cut A popular cut for gemstones. The standard brilliant has 57 facets, or 58 if the gem is cut with a flat face at the base.

Bristows (Bristol stones) Rock crystal stones found in a seam of rock near Bristol, which were brilliant-cut to imitate diamonds.

Bugle bead A long, thin, tube-shaped glass bead.

Cabochon A stone that has a rounded, domed surface with no facets, or a paste with a flat back.

Cairngorm A yellowish-brown type of smoky quartz often used in traditional Celtic jewellery.

Calibré-cut Individually cut to follow the exact outline of an irregular-shaped design.

Cameo A stone or shell with a design cut into it in relief, often in a naturally contrasting colour.

Casting A process in which metal is shaped by melting it and pouring it into a mould.

Celluloid An early, highly flammable plastic introduced in 1869. It was used in costume jewellery and hair accessories until approximately the 1920s.

Chain mail Mesh of tiny plates or rings of metal woven together to form a metal fabric.

Chalcedony A decorative stone, part of the quartz family. Agate, cornelian, chrysoprase, and onyx are all forms of chalcedony.

Channel-set Setting in which stones or pastes are held in place in a metal channel by a slight rim around the edges of it.

Chasing A method of embossing or engraving metal, especially silver, using a hammer and a punch to create the desired effect.

Châtelaine A term used to describe a decorative pair of brooches connected by a chain.

Charm bracelet A bracelet hung with small ornaments known as charms, originally thought to bring the wearer good luck.

Choker A short necklace worn high on the neck.

Citrine A yellow or golden form of quartz. Natural citrine is pale yellow but it is extremely rare.

Clasp A fastener that can open and close to attach two parts of a piece of jewellery together.

Cloisonné A method of applying enamel to metal. Metal wire is used to make a frame, which is then filled with enamel.

Cluster setting A setting in which small stones or pearls are set around a larger stone.

Coral A rock-like substance formed from skeletons of marine invertebrates. It can be pink, red, orange, white, or blue

Cornelian A type of quartz that is usually translucent red in colour.

Crystal Highest quality, very clear glass that contains at least 10 per cent lead oxide and looks like natural or rock crystal.

Cuff bracelet A stiff, wide bracelet.

Cultured pearls Pearls produced in controlled conditions to make them a regular size and shape.

Cut steel Tiny, faceted steel studs used in early costume jewellery.

Damascening The inlaying of a soft metal into a hard metal.

Demi-parure A partial matching set of two or three pieces of jewellery.

Diamanté Faceted, highly reflective crystal or glass stones cut to resemble gemstones. See *Rhinestone.*

Double clip See *Duette.*

Drop A small suspended stone or ornament.

Duette A pin or brooch that can be worn as two separate pins or clipped together as one.

Embossed A type of surface decoration in which a design is raised slightly above the surface.

Emerald A precious gemstone that is rich green in colour. A variety of beryl, the finest gems are transparent and flawless.

Enamel A glassy substance that is fused to metal, porcelain, or other surfaces, using heat.

Engraving A type of decoration in which a design is etched into the surface with a sharp tool.

En tremblant A piece of jewellery with a motif that is mounted on a tiny spring so that it trembles when the wearer moves.

Essence d'orient A fish-scale coating that is used on glass or plastic beads to create faux pearls.

Faceting The cutting and polishing of the surface of a stone, which make it reflect light.

Faience Glazed coloured earthenware that can be used to make beads.

Fantasy pastes Man-made, unusual-coloured crystal stones that look deliberately false.

Faux False. A faux gem is an imitation of a real one.

Figural jewellery Commonly used to describe designs modelled on human, animal, bird, fish, or insect forms.

Filigree Intricate metal decoration created by twisting gold or silver wire into lacy patterns and soldering them into place. Imitation filigree is made of stamped metal.

Findings The functional parts of jewellery, such as clasps, hooks, links, and settings.

Foil back A reflective sheet of metal or foil placed behind a gem or paste to enhance its colour and make it reflect more light.

Foliate Like a leaf.

French jet Shiny cut black glass designed to imitate real jet. It was frequently carved.

Fruit salads Costume jewellery set with red, green, and blue moulded glass or plastic stones.

Fur clip A large decorative pin with a spring clasp designed to hold a fur stole in place around the wearer's shoulders or neck.

Galalith An early form of plastic used in some European costume jewellery up until the 1920s.

Gilding A process by which a base metal is plated with a very thin layer of gold.

Graduated strand A necklace of beads or pearls that increase in size from the back of the neck towards the centre front.

Granulation A method of soldering tiny beads of metal to the surface of metal to form a pattern.

Hairwork jewellery Jewellery containing or made of locks of hair. It was popular in the mid 1800s as a way of remembering loved ones who had died.

Hallmark An official mark made in metal that indicates the fineness of the metal and the name or inprimatur of the manufacturer.

Hammered A term describing metal that has been shaped or decorated with a hammer.

Inlay Any material that is embedded in another contrasting material, so that their surfaces are level or flush.

Intaglio A design cut into a gem, a piece of glass, or plastic. Signet rings often have an intaglio.

Invisible setting Technique in which real or faux stones are fastened from the back, so it looks as if there is no metal mount.

Iridescent Term used to describe something that reflects many rainbow-like, changing colours.

Japanned A process that colours metal a dull black colour.

Jelly Belly An animal pin that has a clear Lucite or glass stone in the centre for the "belly".

Jet A fine-grained rock formed from fossilized wood. Black and opaque, it has a velvety lustre and was popular for mourning jewellery during the 19th century.

Jonquil A pale yellow-coloured rhinestone, named after the spring flower of the same colour.

Lapiz lazuli An opaque dark blue rock. It is usually cut as cabochons or beads and polished.

Lariat A style of long necklace popular in the 1920s and 50s that has no clasp and is knotted, looped, or held together by a ring.

Locket A pendant that can open up. Lockets can hold a charm, a photo, a lock of hair, or another precious keepsake.

Love token A piece of jewellery given as a gift to a loved one. It may be inscribed with a message or a name, or have a motif symbolizing love and affection.

Lucite A clear, strong plastic (acrylic resin) that was patented by the DuPont company in 1937.

Machine stamping A process in which sheet metal is cut and shaped by machine rather than by hand. Many medallions and jewellery findings are made in this way.

Maltese Cross A cross whose four arms of equal length increase in width the further they get from the centre.

Marcasite Iron pyrites cut to look like diamonds used extensively in the 1920s and 30s. They are often confused with cut steel.

Marquise-cut An oval-shaped gemstone or rhinestone that is pointed at both ends. (The same as a navette-cut).

Millefiori A glassmaking technique (meaning "a thousand flowers" in Italian) in which canes of different coloured glass are fused together in bundles so that the cross section creates a pattern when sliced. Millefiori glass can also be made into beads.

Modernism A 20th-century design movement that promoted simple, angular, geometric forms and repudiated excessive ornamentation.

Moonstone A semi-translucent, semi-precious stone that is milky blue with a white sheen, like moonshine. Some varieties are grey, yellow, pink, or green in colour.

Mother-of-pearl The iridescent coating on the inside of oyster shells. Mother-of-pearl is often used to make buttons as well as jewellery.

Mourning jewellery Jewellery worn when people are in mourning for a deceased loved one. It is often made of jet or contains a memento of the deceased, such as a lock of hair or a portrait.

Murano glass Glass from the glass factories of Murano, near Venice in Italy, which have been making glass since the 14th century.

Nacre Another term (derived from French) for mother-of-pearl. Also used to describe the outer pearlized shell of a faux pearl.

Navette-cut An oval-shaped gemstone or rhinestone that is pointed at both ends. The same as a marquise-cut.

New Look A look created by Christian Dior in 1947, characterized by an exaggeratedly feminine hourglass silhouette and full skirts.

Niello A method of ornamenting metal by engraving and filling up the lines with a black compound. Can also be used to describe the compound used in niello-work.

Opalescence A milky blue-white type of iridescence, similar in colour to opals.

Papier-mâché A material made from paper pulp or sheets of paper pasted together, which is painted and varnished so it resembles wood.

Parure A complete matching set of four or five pieces of jewellery, usually containing a necklace, earrings, a brooch or pin, and a bracelet (or two bracelets). See *Demi-parure*.

Paste Crystal or ordinary glass with a high lead content, which has been cut and faceted to look like a gemstone. Also known as diamanté and rhinestone.

Pâte-de-verre (also known as poured glass). A paste of crushed glass that has been coloured with metal oxides, then moulded and fired.

Patina A subtle sheen or change in colour that some metals acquire when they are exposed to the air over a period of time. Patina can be an aid to dating jewellery.

Pavé-set Setting in which stones are set so close together (literally "paved") that the backing is not visible and the effect is one of a continuous jewelled surface.

Pear-cut A teardrop-shaped cut for stones.

Pectoral An ornament worn on the chest.

Pendant An ornament hanging from a necklace, pins, or earrings.

Perspex A colourless and transparent form of plastic much used in 1960s jewellery.

Pewter A blueish-grey metal alloy that is composed mostly of tin combined with lead, antimony, bismuth, copper, or silver.

Pin An ornament that can be pinned to a garment (also called a brooch).

Pinchbeck An alloy of copper (also known as "false gold") that looks like gold, invented by the British watchmaker Christopher Pinchbeck in the early 18th century.

Plating A process in which one metal is coated with another. In costume jewellery, inexpensive base metals are often plated with more expensive ones, such as gold.

Plique-à-jour Translucent enamel with no backing in a wire framework, which creates an effect like that of stained glass.

Pop art An art movement of the 1960s that drew its inspiration from popular culture and everyday materials.

Porcelain Fine, white earthenware (china) that is thin and semi-transparent. Most commonly used for fine tableware, porcelain is also made into beads.

Pot metal A greyish base metal, made from an alloy of tin and lead, which was widely used in early 20th-century costume jewellery.

Poured glass See *Pâte de verre*.

Prong-set A setting in which stones are held in position by claw-like metal prongs.

Repoussé A metal design formed in relief. Special punches are used to form the designs on the surface of the metal.

Resin A substance obtained from the sap of certain trees, or its synthetic counterpart, used in the production of plastics.

Retro jewellery A bold, chunky style of jewellery popular in the late 1930s and 40s, influenced by Art Deco machine-age forms. Retro costume jewellery was often made in vermeil and featured geometric shapes.

Rhinestones Faceted, highly reflective crystal or glass stones cut to resemble gemstones. The original rhinestones were quartz stones (rock crystal) dug out of the River Rhine. See *Diamanté*

Rhodium A silvery grey metal in the platinum family that is often mistaken for silver. It is used for plating in costume jewellery because it is unusually hard and resistant to rust.

Rock crystal A naturally occurring colourless, transparent form of quartz from which brilliants were frequently cut at one time, as imitation diamonds.

Rondelle A small disc that is used as a spacer between beads in necklaces or bracelets.

Rope of pearls A string of pearls that is over 1m (40in) long.

Rose montée A faceted, flat-backed rhinestone, often mounted in a pierced metal cup, so that it can be wired onto clothes or jewellery. Rose montée was not used much in jewellery, but was frequently used in embroidery for *haute couture* clothes.

Ruby One of the most prized gemstones, the classic ruby is rich red in colour.

Russian gold plating A coppery gold matte finish first used on costume jewellery in films in the 1940s because it reduced the glare produced by studio lights.

Rutheniam A metal in the platinum group that is used for plating in costume jewellery.

Safety catch A secondary fastening on a fine chain or necklace that is used as a back-up, to make sure that the piece is not lost if the primary clasp opens.

Sapphire A precious gemstone that ranges in colour from light to deep blue. Sapphires can also be yellow, green, pink, or colourless.

Scatter pins Small pins or brooches, popular in the 1950s, that are worn in a group.

Seed pearls Tiny pearls, either real or artificial, that are less than 2mm (⅟₁₆in) in diameter and weigh less than one quarter of a gram.

Setting The method of securing a stone in a piece of jewellery. There are many different types of setting, such as prong-setting and pavé-setting. Some settings are closed, meaning that there is metal behind the stone. Open settings have no metal behind the stone, allowing light to shine through the stone.

Spacer A decorative bead that is used between larger beads or pearls in a necklace, to separate them and set them off.

SS An abbreviation for sterling silver.

Star-setting A setting in which a stone is set within an engraved star. The stone is held in place by a small grain of metal soldered to the base of each ray of the star.

Step-cut A rectangular or square-shaped gemstone cut with several facets parallel to the edges of the stone.

Sterling silver An alloy that is 925 parts pure silver and 75 parts base metal, such as copper, which increases the silver's hardness.

Surrealism An early 20th-century movement in art and literature that sought to obscure the boundaries between dream and reality by portraying things that didn't make sense in a hyper-realistic manner.

Swarovski crystals Top-quality, brilliant-cut crystal rhinestones produced by the Swarovski company and much used by costume jewellery designers and couturiers.

Teardrop-cut A gemstone cut that is the shape of a teardrop.

Topaz A semi-precious, transparent gemstone that ranges in colour from deep golden yellow and pink to blue and green.

Tortoiseshell A mottled brown and yellow horn-like material originally made from the shell of the rare Hawksbill turtle, now a protected species. The tortoiseshell used in jewellery nowadays is made from plastic.

Translucent A term used to describe stones that allow some diffused (scattered) light to pass through them.

Transparent A term used to describe materials that allow light to pass straight through them.

Trembler A piece of jewellery that has a motif or parts of it set on a spring or springs; these parts appear to tremble whenever the wearer of the jewellery moves.

Trifanium A very shiny metal alloy patented by the Trifari company, which looked just like real gold but did not tarnish.

Turquoise An opaque semi-precious stone that varies in colour from an intense blue-green to bright blue. It is usually cut and polished into rounded beads or cabochons.

Vauxhall glass Named after early mirror glass made at a glassworks in London, Vauxhall glass was workable shiny glass, often black or a deep Burgundy red, that was popular for use in trinkets and other jewellery in the late 18th and 19th centuries.

Vermeil Sterling silver plated with gold. Also called silver gilt or gold wash. During the 1940s, most American costume jewellery was made of vermeil sterling silver.

Designers' and Makers' Marks

Identification marks and signatures are commonly found on the clasp of necklaces, bracelets and earrings, and on the back of pins. They can stamped directly onto the piece, or onto a small tag which is then soldered to the jewellery. Examine pieces closely as marks are sometimes in unexpected locations or are only clearly visible through a jeweller's eyeglass. The following is a selection of some of the stamps and copyright marks of the designers and makers featured in this book.

Alice Caviness
1945–present

CHANEL
Chanel
1920s–present

Art
1940s–late 1960s

Christian Dior
c.1947–present

Avon
1871–present

CINER
Ciner
c.1931–present

BEAUJEWELS
Beaujewels
Late 1940s–early 1970s

Coppola e Toppo
Late 1940s–1986

B.S.K.©
B.S.K.
c.1950–early 1980s

Coro
Coro
1919–1979

Corocraft
1933–1979

FLORENZA©

Florenza
Late 1940s–1981

DeRosa
1935–c.1970

FREDA. BLOCK

Fred A. Block
1930s–1950s

De Nicola
Late 1950s–1973

Carnegie

Hattie Carnegie
1918–1980s

EISENBERG
ICE©

Eisenberg
1940s–present

Henry Schreiner
1951–1970s

Eisenberg
ORIGINAL

Eisenberg
c.1930–1945

Hobé

Hobé
1920s–present

Fahrner
1855–1979

HOLLYCRAFT
COPR. 1953

Hollycraft
1948–mid 1970s

JJ
c.1935–present

©BOUCHER **Marcel Boucher**
1937–1972

JOMAZ **Jomaz**
1946–1981

MARVELLA **Marvella**
1911–1982

 Joseff
1930s–present

 Matisse
1952–1964

©KJL **Kenneth Jay Lane**
1963–present

MAZER BROS. **Mazer Brothers**
1927–1981

KRAMER **Kramer**
1943–late 1970s

 Miriam Haskell
1926–present

©LISNER **Lisner**
c.1938–1979

©PANETTA **Panetta**
1945–early 1980s

REBAJES

Rebajes
1934–1967

SANDOR

Sandor
1938–1972

REGENCY

Regency
1950s–1970s

©SARAH COV.

Sarah Coventry
1949–1984

Réja

Réja
1941–1952

Schiaparelli

Schiaparelli
1920s–late 1950s

Renoir

Renoir
1946–1964

TRIFARI©

Trifari
1918–present

Robert
1942–1979

©VENDOME

Vendome
1944–1979

Robert DeMario
1945–early 1960s

WEISS

Weiss
1942–1971

Key to Dealer Codes

Each piece of jewellery shown in this book has an accompanying letter code which identifies the dealer or auction house that is either selling or has sold it. The following list is the key to these codes. It should be noted that inclusion in this book in no way constitutes or implies a contract or a binding offer on the part of any contributing dealer or auction house to supply or sell the pieces illustrated, or similar items, at the prices stated. It should also be noted that the code PC, and any code ending in PC, denotes the piece comes from an anonymous or named private collection.

ABAA
Abacus Antiques
Grays Antiques Market
58 Davies Street
London W1Y 2LP
Tel: 020 7629 9681

ABOIJ
Aurora Bijoux
Jenny Stephens
E-mail: aurora@aurorabijoux.com
www.aurorabijoux.com

AIS
Arthur Ivan Spike
South Street Antiques Center
615 South 6th Street
Philadelphia
PA 19147–2128
USA
Tel: 001 215 592 0256

ANA
Ancient Art
85 The Vale, Southgate
London N14 6AT
Tel: 020 8882 1509
Fax: 020 8886 5235

BB
Barbara Blau
South Street Antiques Center
615 South 6th Street
Philadelphia
PA 19147-2128
USA
Tel: 001 215 592 0256

BBG
Baubles
Bunny Brooks Goldberger
South Street Antiques Center
615 South 6th Street
Philadelphia
PA 19147-2128
USA
Tel: 001 215 487 0207

BONBAY
Bonhams, Bayswater
10 Salem Road
London W2 4DL
Tel: 020 7313 2727
Fax: 020 7313 2701
www.bonhams.com

BY
Bonny Yankauer
bonnyy@aol.com

CAA
Contemporary Applied Arts
2 Percy Street
London W1T 1DD
Tel: 020 7436 2344
Fax: 020 7436 2446

CBU
Chéz Burnette
South Street Antiques Center
615 South 6th Street
Philadelphia
PA 19147-2128
USA
Tel: 001 215 592 0256

EC
Chris & Eddie's Collectibles
South Street Antiques Center
615 South 6th Street
Philadelphia
PA 19147–2128
USA
Tel: 001 215 592 0256

CGPC
Cheryl Grandfield Private Collection

CRIS
Cristobal
26 Church Street
London NW8 8EP
Tel/Fax: 020 7724 7230
E-mail: steven@cristobal.co.uk
www.cristobal.co.uk

CSAY
Charlotte Sayers F.G.A.
Stand 360
Grays Antique Market
58 Davies Street
London W1K 5LP
Tel: 020 7499 5478

CVS
Cad Van Swankster at "The Girl Can't Help It"
Stands G100 & G116
Alfies Antique Market
13-25 Church Street
London NW8 8DT
Tel: 020 7724 8984
Fax: 020 8809 3923

DN
Dreweatt Neate

Donnington Priory Salerooms

Donnington

Newbury

Berkshire RG14 2JE

Tel: 01635 553553

Fax: 01635 553599

E-mail: fineart@dreweatt-neate.co.uk

www.auctions.dreweatt-neate.co.uk

DO
DODO

Liz Farrow

Alfies Antique Market

Stands F071, 072 & 073

13-25 Church Street

London NW8 8DT

Tel: 020 7706 1545

ECLEC
Eclectica

2 Charlton Place

Islington

London N1 8AJ

Tel/Fax: 020 7226 5625

E-mail: eclecticaliz@yahoo.co.uk

EL
Elms Lesters

Painting Rooms

Flitcroft Street

London WC2H 8DH

Tel: 020 7836 6747

Fax: 020 7379 0789

E-mail: gallery@elms-lesters.demon.co.uk

FM
Francesca Martire

Stands 131-137

First Floor

Alfies Antique Market

13-25 Church Street

London NW8 0RH

Tel: 020 7724 4802

www.francesamartire.com

GCA
Griffin & Cooper Antiques

Dale W. Griffin & Joseph P. Cooper

South Street Antiques Center

615 South 6th Street

Philadelphia, PA 19147-2128

USA

Tel: 001 215 582 0418 / 3594

GS
Goodwin's Antiques Ltd

15 & 16 Queensferry Street

Edinburgh EH2 4QW

Tel: 0131 225 4717

Fax: 0131 220 1412

JBC
James Bridges Private Collection

JHB
Joseph H Bonnar

72 Thistle Street

Edinburgh EH2 1EN

Tel: 0131 226 2811

Fax: 0131 225 9438

JJ
The Junkyard Jeweler

E-mail: thejunkyardjeweler@tias.com

www.tias.com/stores/thejunkyardjeweler

L&T
Lyon and Turnbull Ltd.

33 Broughton Place

Edinburgh EH1 3RR

Tel: 0131 557 8844

Fax: 0131 557 8668

E-mail: info@lyonandturnbull.com

www.lyonandturnbull.com

LB
Linda Bee

Grays Antique Market Stands R18-19

1-7 Davies Mews

London W1K 5AB

Tel/Fax: 020 7629 5921

LCG
Lesley Craze Gallery

34 Clerkenwell Green

London EC1R 0DU

Tel: 020 7608 0393

Fax: 020 7251 5655

E-mail: gallery@lesleycraze.demon.co.uk

www.lesleycrazegallery.co.uk

LH
Lucy's Hat

South Street Antiques Center

615 South 6th Street

Philadelphia

PA 19147-2128

USA

Tel: 001 215 592 0256

E-mail: shak06@aol.com

LYNH
Brian & Lynn Holmes

Stands 304-306

Grays Antique Market

58 Davies Street

London W1K 5LP

Tel/Fax: 020 7629 7327

LNXG
Lennox Gallery Ltd

Grays Antique Market

4 Davies Mews

London W1Y 2LP

Tel: 020 7491 0091

Fax: 020 7491 0657

E-mail: lengal4@aol.com

MAC
Mary Ann's Collectibles

South Street Antiques Center

615 South 6th Street

Philadelphia

PA 19147-2128

USA

Tel: 001 215 923 3247

Key to Dealer Codes cont.

MARA
Marie Antiques
Stands G136-138
Alfies Antique Market
13-25 Church Street
London NW8 8DT
Tel: 020 7706 3727
E-mail: marie136@globalnet.co.uk
www.marieantiques.co.uk

MG
Mod-Girl
South Street Antiques Center
615 South 6th Street
Philadelphia
PA 19147-2128
USA
Tel: 001 215 413 0434

MILLB
Million Dollar Babies
Marian Barba
BY APPOINTMENT ONLY
47 Hyde Blvd
Ballston Spa
NY 12020
USA
Tel: 001 518 885 7397

NBLM
N Bloom & Son Ltd
12 Piccadilly Arcade
London SW1Y 6NH
Tel: 020 7629 5060
Fax: 020 7493 2528
www.nbloom.com

RBRG
RBR Group at Grays
Stand 175
Grays Antique Market
58 Davies Street
London W1Y 2LP
Tel/Fax: 020 7629 4769

REL
Relick
8 Golborne Road
London W10 5NW
Tel/Fax: 020 8962 0089

RITZ
Ritzy
Christopher St James
7 The Mall
Camden Passage
Islington
London N1 0PD
Tel: 020 7704 0127

RG
Richard Gibbon
34/34a Islington Green
London N1 8DU
Tel: 020 7354 2852
E-mail: neljeweluk@aol.com

ROX
Roxanne Stuart
E-mail: gemfairy@aol.com

SM
Sparkle Moore at
"The Girl Can't Help It"
Stands G100 & G116
Alfies Antique Market
13-25 Church Street
Marylebone
London NW8 8DT
Tel: 020 7724 8984
Mobile: 07958 515614
Fax: 020 8809 3923
www.sparklemoore.com

SUM
Sue Mautner
Stands A18-19
Antiquarius
135 King's Road
London SW3 4PW
Tel: 07743 546744

TM
Tony Moran
South Street Antiques Center
615 South 6th Street
Philadelphia
PA 19147-2128
USA
Tel: 001 215 592 0256

TR
Terry Rodgers & Melody
30 Manhattan Art and
Antique Center
1050 2nd Avenue
New York
NY 10022
USA
Tel: 001 212 758 3164
Fax: 001 212 935 6365
E-mail: melodyjewelnyc@aol.com

WAIN
William Wain
Stand J6
Antiquarius
135 King's Road
Chelsea
London SW3 4PW
Tel: 020 7351 4905

Directory of Other Dealers, Auction Houses, and Museums

Below is a comprehensive list of additional specialist costume jewellery dealers and leading auction houses, plus a selection of international museums that hold collections of costume jewellery.

UK

Beauty and the Beast
Joel Rothman
Unit Q9, Antiquarius
131–141 King's Road
London SW3 8DT
Tel: 020 7351 5149

Christie's South Kensington
85 Old Brompton Road
London SW7 3LD
Tel: 020 7581 7611
Fax: 020 7321 3321
www.christies.com

Diana Antique Jewellery
Stands G104–105
Alfies Antique Market
13–25 Church Street
London NW8 8DT
Tel: 020 7724 2229
E-mail: dijewellery@aol.com
www.dianaantiques.co.uk

Hallmark Antiques
Stands 319 & 356
Gray's Antique Market
1–7 Davies Street
London W1K 5LP
Tel: 020 7629 8757
Fax: 020 7266 3587

Jezebel
14 Prince Albert Street
Brighton
East Sussex BN1 1HE
Tel 01273 206091
Fax 01273 206091

Ian Lieber
29 Craven Terrace
London W2 3EL
Tel: 020 7262 5505

Steinberg & Tolkein
193 King's Road
London SW3 5EB
Tel: 020 7376 3660
Fax: 020 7376 3630

Stevie Pearce
Stand G144, Alfies Antique Market
13–25 Church Street
London NW8 8D
Tel: 020 7723 2526
E-mail: stevie@steviepearce.co.uk

Sylvie Spectrum
Stand 372, Grays Antiques Market
58 Davies Street
London W1Y 2LB
Tel: 020 7629 3501
Fax: 020 8883 5030

Tadema Gallery
10 Charlton Place, Camden Passage
London N1 8AJ
Tel: 020 7359 1055

The Gilded Lily
Stands 145–146, Grays Antique Market
58 Davies Street
London W1K 5LP
Tel: 020 7499 6260
E-mail: jewellery@gilded-lily.co.uk
www.graysantiques.com

USA AND CANADA

Absolutely Vintage
Joan Vogel Elias
www.absolutelyvintage.net

Agnes Lee at the New Pagoda Speciality Company
International Antique
Center Building
30 West 26th Street
New York, NY 10010 USA
Tel: 001 212 645 1964
Fax: 001 212 732 1452
E-mail: newpagoda@aol.com

Alice's Vintage Costume Jewelry
E-mail: alice@alicejewels.com
www.alicejewels.com

Annie Sherman
P.O. Box 9036
Kailua-Kona 96745
Hawaii USA
E-mail: annie96740@yahoo.com
www.AnnieSherman.com

Antique Designer Costumer Jewelry
Valerie Gedzuin
www.valerieg.com

Antiquing On Line – The Jewelry Box
www.antiquingonline.com

Azillion SPARKLZ
www.sparklz.com

249

Directory of Other Dealers, Auction Houses, and Museums cont.

Bobbie's Baubles

www.bobbiesbaubles.com

Broadwater Rose Jewels

The Blue Crow Antique Mall

32124 Lankford Hwy Route 13

Keller, VA 23401 USA

Tel: 001 757 442 4150

www.broadwaterrosejewels.com

Christie's East

219 East 67th Street

New York NY 10021 USA

Tel: 001 212 606 0400

Fax: 001 212 452 2063

www.christies.com

Collectible Costume Jewelry

Suzanne Smith

www.costumejewelry.com

Deco Jewels

131 Thompson Street

New York NY 10012 USA

Tel: 001 212 253 1222

Doyle New York

Auction House

175 East 87th Street

New York NY 10128 USA

Tel: 001 212 427 2730

Fax: 001 212 369 0892

E-mail: info@DoyleNewYork.com

www.doylenewyork.com

Eclectica Vintage Jewellery and Collectibles

Laurel Ladd Ciotti

P.O. Box 671 McIntosh

FL 32664 USA

www.eclecticala.com

Eleen Chesner

Victorian Silver, New York

BY APPOINTMENT ONLY

Tel: 001 212 254 5564

Fantasy Jewels

P.O. Box 5697

Baltimore

MD 21210 USA

Tel: 001 410 435 5599

E-mail:Bobbi@FantasyJewels.com

www.fantasyjewels.com

For Your Ears Only

Karen & Gary Foggin

Wilmington, DE USA

Tel: 001 302 764 2954

E-mail: foggin@earthlink.net

www.oldjewels.com

Illusion Jewels

E-mail: jewels@illusionjewels.com

www.illusionjewels.com

Ira Scheck

984 S. Kenosha Court

Pueblo West

CO 81007 USA

Tel: 001 719 647 1568

E-mail: irascheck@aol.com

Jewel Diva

Chris and Connie DeNave

www.jeweldiva.com

Joseff of Hollywood

Janice Widdowes

E-mail: Bobana1950@aol.com

www.joseffofhollywood.com

Katie Atikian Antiques

E-mail: katerooa@aol.com

www.kateroo.com

Manhattan Art & Antique Center

1050 Second Ave

New York, NY 10022 USA

Tel: 001 212 355 4400

Fax: 001 212 355 4403

www.the-macc.com

Morning Glory Antiques & Jewelry

Jane H. Clarke

12815 Central NE

Albuquerque

NM 87123 USA

www.morninggloryantiques.com

Past Perfection

Cheryl Kilmer

www.pastperfection.com

Plastic Fantastic

Karima Parry

Pennsylvania USA

E-mail: info@plasticfantastic.com

www.plasticfantastic.com

Rago Modern Auctions

333 North Main Street

Lambertville

NJ 08530 USA

Tel: 001 609 397 9374

Fax: 001 609 397 9377

www.ragoarts.com

Remember When

www.tias.com/stores/rewhen

Sassy Classics

Sassy Classics

P.O. Box 2140, Pine

AZ 85544 USA

Tel: 001 928 476 2112

Sandot's Costume Jewellery

Sandy Butterfield

www.sandot.com

Sotheby's Chicago

215 West Ohio Street

Chicago

Illinois 60610 USA

Tel: 001 312 396 9599

Fax: 001 312 396 9598

www.sothebys.com

Sotheby's New York

1334 York Avenue

New York, NY 10021 USA

Tel: 001 212 606 7000

Fax: 001 212 606 7016

www.sothebys.com

South Texas Trading Company

Bee Gee McBride and John Borgstrom

P.O. Box 857, Port Aransas

TX 78373 USA

Tel: 001 800 484 9293, enter 3474

www.southtexastrading.com

The Glitter Box

Sheila Pamfiloff

PO Box 35, Walnut Creek

CA 94597 USA

Tel: 001 925 937 7554

E-mail: pamfil@glitterbox.com

www.glitterbox.com

The Poet's Wares

E-mail: poetswares@tias.com

www.tias.com/stores/poetswares

This 'n' That

124 West 25th Street

New York, NY 10001 USA

Tel: 001 212 255 0727

Fax: 001 718 338 1887

E-mail: Anita613@aol.com

Three Jacks Vintage Costume Jewelry & Collectibles

1121 W. Sherman Ave

Fort Atkinson

WI 53538 USA

www.tias.com/stores/threejacks

Yesterjewels

Bonni Mancini

www.yesterjewels.bigstop.com

AUSTRALIA

Over The Moon Antiques

Les and Sue Wright

Shop 4 Gays Arcade

Adelaide, Australia

Tel: 00 61 (0)8 8359 2844

Susie M

5A/26 Wellington Street

Collingwood

Victoria 3066, Australia

Tel: 00 61 (0)3 9419 1033

Tel: 00 61 (0)3 9419 1106

E-mail: info@susiem.com.au

The Banana Room

125 Melbourne Street

North Adelaide

SA 5006, Australia

Tel: 00 61 (0)8 239 0755

Fax: 00 61 (0)8 8390 1243

Email:petavanrood@metropolis.net.au

MUSEUMS

Ashmolean Museum

Beaumont Street

Oxford OX1 2PH

Tel: 01865 278000

Fax: 01865 278018

www.ashmol.ox.ac.uk

Cheltenham Art Gallery & Museum

Clarence Street, Cheltenham

Gloucestershire GL50 3JT

Tel: 01242 237 431

Fax: 01242 262 334

E-mail: ArtGallery@cheltenham.gov.uk

www.cheltenhammuseum.org.uk

Egyptian Museum

Midan El Tahrir

Cairo 11557, Egypt

Tel: 00 202 5782448 / 452

Fax: 00 202 579697

www.egyptianmuseum.gov.eg

Il Museo del Bijoux di Casalmaggiore

Via A. Porzio, 9, 26041

Casalmaggiore, Italy

Tel: 00 39 0375 42309

Le Musée de la Mode et du Textile

Union centrale des arts décoratifs

107-111 rue de Rivoli

75001 Paris, France

Tel: 00 33 (0)1 44 55 57 50

www.ucad.fr

Liverpool Museum

William Brown Street

Liverpool L3 8EN

Tel 0151 478 4399

E-mail: themuseum@liverpoolmuseums.org.uk

www.liverpoolmuseums.org.uk

The British Museum

Great Russell Street

London WC1B 3DG

Tel: 020 7323 8000

email: information@thebritishmuseum.ac.uk

www.thebritishmuseum.ac.uk

The Kremlin Museum

The Kremlin

Moscow, Russia

Tel: 007 95 202 4256 / 202 3776

Fax: 007 95 921 6323

www.kreml.ru/

The Metropolitan Museum of Art

1000 Fifth Avenue

New York

NY 10028 USA

Tel: 001 212 535 7710

www.metmuseum.org

Victoria & Albert Museum

Cromwell Road

London SW7 2RL

Tel: 020 7942 2000

www.vam.ac.uk

Index (Page numbers in *italics* refer to illustrations)

Acknowledgements

AUTHORS' ACKNOWLEDGEMENTS

The authors would like to thank the following people for their substantial contibutions to the production of this book:

Photographer Graham Rae for his unflagging humor and consistently wonderful pictures. Also Mike Malloy for additional photography.

All of the dealers, auction houses, and private collectors for kindly allowing us to photograph their jewelry, and for taking the time to provide a wealth of information about it.

The team at DK for all the long hours, dedication, and skill they have committed to the project, including Mandy Earey and Kelly Meyer for tackling a vast array of images and turning them into a visual treat, Paula Regan for her unflagging patience and encouragement, Angela Wilkes and Amber Tokeley for their editorial research and generation of copy, and finally, Julie Oughton and Heather McCarry for expertly overseeing the development of the text and design.

Also special thanks to Mark Hill, Meg Watson, Sara Sturgess, Cara Miller and, especially, Julie Brooke at the Price Guide Company (UK) Ltd for sourcing a wealth of oral, written, and visual information.

And finally, special thanks to Stephen Miners, Yai Thammachote, and Kevin Miners at Cristobal, without whom this project would never have gotten off the ground.

PUBLISHER'S ACKNOWLEDGEMENTS

Dorling Kindersley would like to thank Juliet Duff for picture research, Scott Stickland and Jonathan Brookes for digital image coordination, Philip Gilderdale and Martin Dieguez for design contribution, Caroline Hunt for proofreading, and Dorothy Frame for compiling the index.

PICTURE CREDITS

The publisher would like to thank the following for their kind permission to reproduce their photographs. (Abbreviations key: t=top, b=bottom, r=right, l=left, c=centre).

11: Kobal Collection; 14: Bridgeman Art Library, London/New York/Egyptian National Museum, Cairo, Egypt (t and bcl), Werner Forman Archive/The Egyptian Museum, Cairo (bl); 15: Heritage Image Partnership/The British Museum (cbl, ctl, t); 16: Michael Holford (bl, br, t); 18 Bridgeman Art Library, London/New York/Ashmolean Museum, Oxford (bc), Bridgeman Art Library, London/New York/British Museum, London (t), Bridgeman Art Library, London/NewYork/City of Liverpool Museum, Merseyside (br), Bridgeman Art Library,London/NewYork/Kremlin Museums, Moscow, Russia (bl); 19: Bridgeman Art Library, London/New York/S.J.Philips, London (c); 19: Corbis /Elio Ciol (bl); 19: Michael Holford (br); 55: Corbis; 56: Corbis/Hulton-Deutsch Collection; 57: Bridgeman Art Library, London/New York/Private Collection (b); 57: The Picture Desk/The Art Archive/Dagli Orti (tr); 57: Topham Picturepoint (tl); 60: Corbis (b), Corbis/Bettmann (t); 61 Corbis/Bettmann (b); 61 Vin Mag Archive (t); 69: The Picture Desk/Advertising Archives; 72: Mary Evans Picture Library (br); 74: Corbis (tl), Vin Mag Archive (br); 76: Hulton Archive/Getty Images (br); 78: Corbis/Bettmann (tl), Corbis/Arte & Immagini srl (bc); 79: Ronald Grant Archive (br); 79: Photos 12 (bl); 84: Corbis/Stephanie Colasanti (br); 84:Kenneth Jay Lane (tl); 86: Corbis/Bettmann (br); 90: Corbis/Bettmann (tl); 91:Corbis/Bettmann (tr); 94: The Picture Desk/Advertising Archives (br); 96: The Picture Desk/Advertising Archives (bc). 98: Vin Mag Archive (br); 99: Camera Press (tr); 99: Corbis/Horace Bristol (bl); 108: Hulton Archive/Getty Images (tl); 108: Topham Picturepoint (bl); 109: Mary Evans Picture Library (tr); 109:Corbis/Hulton-Deutsch Collection (bl); 112: Corbis/Bettmann (tl), Corbis/Gail Mooney (br); 113: Corbis (tr), Corbis/Kelly-Mooney Photograhy (bl); 118: The Picture Desk/Advertising Archives (br); 119: Corbis/Bettmann (tr), Corbis/Sygma (br); 130: Vin Mag Archive (br); 135: Hulton Archive/Getty Images; 215: Corbis/Hulton-Deutsch Collection; 237: Corbis/Bettmann.

Scottish Agate Jewellery p.209